My First Love

The Stories that Created the Songs

HARMINME LOVE

authorHOUSE®

AuthorHouse™
1663 Liberty Drive
Bloomington, IN 47403
www.authorhouse.com
Phone: 1 (800) 839-8640

Published by AuthorHouse   04/21/2017

ISBN: 978-1-5246-8888-2 (sc)
ISBN: 978-1-5246-8889-9 (hc)
ISBN: 978-1-5246-8887-5 (e)

Library of Congress Control Number: 2017906044

Print information available on the last page.

*H*ello my name is "Harminme Love" pronounced (HARMONY) and first let me say thank you for choosing to read my book. I started out writing poetry at a young age around 12 and it was when I turned 13 my first song was written. Writing songs was not something I set out to do and was due to my mother's disciplinary actions where it all began. My mother would beat me repeatedly till one day hitting me would no longer break me down and I physically acquired a numbness to her lashes on my flesh.

I can still recall the day when after she finished beating me I looked at her and smile and said are you done. She then waited until my father came home for him to beat me. My father who was a Marine, I had not yet came to mentally master his strikes but that day too had come. Since the beatings had no effect on me my mother found other ways of punishment she would withhold desert, not let me play outside, no talking on the phone to friends, take my toys away, no playing videogames and even no television. Like all things in time I grew angry and mad and lashed out even more, honestly I think it was just the bull in me from being a Taurus and like a bull when I see red I attack, not back down.

I recall most of my childhood life crying then humming myself to sleep. When nights I wasn't crying for some reason it took me longer to fall to sleep. I realized I needed noise for me to fall to sleep faster, and so I turned on the radio and found it soothing to me and fell asleep quickly. As the punishment with my mother went on with taking this and that away I no longer threw a fit and would go to my room with such easement. It didn't take my mother long to catch on that music was my fulfillment and her way to control "the bull". This one method of punishment is what I feared and dreaded the most because without my radio, without music I felt truly alone.

I saw myself as an outsider to my family and when my mother took my radio away hope itself felt lost. I thought my mother had finally won and there is no alternative for me. With complete silence in the room I began to imagine and play out stories in my head, fairy tales as they were. Since I couldn't escape physically I mentally formed a place of acceptance. I created a place where no one yell at me, didn't judge me, and put me down. I rescued myself and right then I realized even though I couldn't escape physically from this room which was a prison; I had the power to free myself mentally.

Sitting in my room I would daydream which freed me from the reality that I was living. I was now a shell and held my emotions inward away from the family I saw as an ambush to my existence, never letting my guard down for it was them against me. For my birthday one year my mother had given me a pink dairy with a heart lock and a key, as a pre-teen this was the best gift ever. Now that I had a dairy I was able to write my emotions down which didn't last long due to my mother breaking into my dairy to see what I was writing. Now that I look back on it, part of me gives her some benefit of the doubt, thinking maybe she was looking for a way in since I tried hard as hell to keep my family at a distance.

I continued to write in my dairy but adding stuff that wasn't true and knew if my mother acted on it or brought it up would end up telling on herself that she was invading my privacy. As time went on I stop writing in my dairy all together but since writing released a lot of tension emotionally that I had I ended starting a notebook with poetry. I actually found it easy to rhyme words and now I was expressing my feelings in a productive way that even got me to open up to my family. Writing poetry was a sense of pride and accomplishment and when I shared it with others found that the feedback was positive.

Now that I found my skill set I wanted to perfect it, share it with others and master it the best way I could. I entered poetry contests and wrote in school sharing with classmates and teachers. I can't recall what the exactly triggered it but it was at the age of 13 when one of the poems I was writing ended up becoming a song. A light in me had lit up brighter than any star in the sky and I knew then creating music was my calling. I went out and purchased a notebook that was strictly for my poems and songs, at first some of the songs I didn't write down but just would sing around the house.

I watched a lot of music videos and listened to music on the radio constantly. My mother who showed great support at the time let me enter into local talent shows. Since I was still getting familiar with my musical creations I would sing my favorite songs by my favorite artist at the time. I won a few talent shows which boosted my self-esteem because I belonged to something and something in returned belonged to me. But as you grow you realize life is not like the fairy tales with happy endings. The family I let my guard down for, once again proven I was across enemy lines.

My mother made a statement to me I would never forget she said there are many talented people in the world, and I shouldn't get my hopes up about making it in the entertainment business. That was very painful to hear and for a while I stopped writing. It was almost a year's time before I ended up writing songs again. My father was stationed at Camp Lejeune and one of my best friends was in an abusive relationship. I was thinking to myself why is she putting up with this and at such a young age. We were in 6th or 7th grade and she would come to school covering her black eye with makeup.

I wasn't sure and didn't ask at the time, what was the reason she put up with it and was it because it was something that was going on in her home. Seeing her already scared and in pain I didn't force anything on her but did go to the school counselor and mentioned I had a friend that was in an abusive relationship and I'm not sure how to help her. I figured it was a part of life a boy hitting a girl, a man beating a woman, a husband punching his wife. I saw this scene myself in and out of school and so as a child felt that was what marriage was, that this was what love was. I remember thinking to myself though the physical wounds healed it still was mental slavery because you felt owned.

My friend would mentioned how he loved her and how she shouldn't have made him angry. She was trapped, and the only way she broke free was when her father's orders were up and they transferred out overseas somewhere. The song I wrote for her deals with a woman in an abusive relationship and how hitting a woman doesn't make you a man. Even now as I write this book I think about her and hope she has found a man to love her and her body and her soul for she is a precious jewel and when a man who truly loves a woman he will treat her like a priceless collection.

Not long after she left my so called family was going through some issues as well. My mother and father were separating and my mother, sister, and I headed back home to North Carolina. Honestly at first I was kind of glad seeing now it was two against one instead of three against one. I remember living in a house with my Aunt and her daughter but eventually we moved into an apartment complex in town. It was seventh or eighth grade and students were drawn to my because of how I talked indicating I had an accent so they knew I wasn't from here. I mentioned my father was a Marine and we travel a lot. In middle school I met a girl who later throughout my high school years became my best friend. She was pretty much everything opposite of me, she was loud, outgoing, adventures, flirtatious, and very social.

My best friend and I "Nicole" were inseparable, when you saw one you saw the other in and outside of school. We often told people we were sisters. Nicole when met, was far from being innocent and inexperienced I was still a virgin at the time we met but being her friend temptation followed like a fog condensing with the morning sun. The day I lost my virginity really wasn't the day I lost my "virginity" though this guy who I had feelings for, for so long the moment only lasted a few minutes before we were interrupted by his mother knocking on the door.

My second encounter with sex Nicole was with me because we were dating brothers at the time; and though I was no longer a virgin I felt as though that was the day my virginity REALLY was taken. I was sore for days and the thought having sex again was nerve wrecking, but leave it to my best friend Nicole to convince me it gets better… sure enough she was right. Needless to say I had problems with Trey, I was dealing with baby mama drama where two girls he was fucking was pregnant at the same time. Trey wanted very much to keep me at his bedside due to feeling like a well fit glove fitted just for him, a rare find.

After months of battling other girls and lies I finally left Trey He tried for weeks to win me back even using my best friend Nicole to lure me in. I will never forget the day I was lured into the playground where I stayed and as soon as I turned the corner and saw him I turned back. He cried out to me not to go and ran towards me begging and pleading for forgiveness. He grabbed me and held me tight saying please just hear me out. I loosen up and walked back while he was still holding my hand, in case I decided to run. He stated he was still fucking his babies mother (both of them) and I never gave him a reason to be unloyal but couldn't turn down pussy. I looked at him like wow did he just really say that shit.

Though I was angry and hurt part of me respected his honesty. I stood there looking at him with tears in my eyes asked him "why I wasn't enough" and he reached in his pocket and pulled out a load of money and said here. I looked at him and asked why are you giving me this. Trey made a comment and still till this day I would NEVER forget, he said "I would rather be broke and happy with you, then rich and unhappy without you" and me being young and dumb those were the words that lead me back into his web. Things were good for a while his baby mamas stop calling and harassing me so I assume he had put them in "their place".

I had figured that the worst to be behind me and then one night me and my friend Nicole was out at the end of the road at the apartment complex I stayed at and along with a few of the pre-teens that lived there as well. Nicole mentioned she had something to tell me and that no matter what she wanted and valued our friendship and we were sisters for life. I always told Nicole nothing would every come between us. I waited tensely for what she needed to tell me and I was sitting on the edge of the road while she stood next to me. She started with remember the day we skipped school and you met me at Trey house; I was like yeah. She went on to say do you remember when you came in and it seemed as though I was crying and you asked me if I was alright, I said… yeah. Nicole went on to say the day before I had got there her and Trey had sex and she was sorry.

5

I stood up and looked at her and asked her to say that again. She cried out it was an accident and it had been eating her up inside and she wanted me to know the truth. I felt like a part of my soul had left my body, I couldn't speak, I could hardly breath. She reached out to me for comfort and I yelled don't you DARE touch me. A few minutes had past and I just looked up at the stars wanting GOD to take this pain away I was feeling wanting him to rip it out my body and forcing it out my throat trying not to cry out feeling the frustration and lost. I said me and Trey had broken up after that time and you helped us get back together knowing you had fucked HIM!!! Why would you do that, she said because it meant nothing it was a mistake.

As if things could not have gotten any worst here comes Trey on his bike heading towards us. He looked at me and then he looked at Nicole and said, you told her. I started running towards home and he dropped his bike running behind me and forced me up against the brick between the buildings. I shut my eyes tightly not wanting to look at him not wanting to see the painful image of him and Nicole fucking in the same bed minutes later he laid me down in. I let him talk but I had no words not even one. After that night I was through with Trey and Nicole and after almost 2 months of wanting to forget this chapter of my life we were best friends again. I could deal with Trey fucking his babies mamas but Nicole was all I had; I loved her and like my own shadow she was what made feel worth existing outside and inside the family I loathe.

To get past Trey, I was on the prowl for "a new comforter". This guy was no thug like Trey and was from a small town about 30 minutes away. Mr. Saint Bates was well educated and seem to have a positive future ahead of him. I really didn't concern myself with Nicole and Mr. Saint because they for some reason did not seem like each other. I asked him one day why he did not like Nicole and he said straight she's a HO; and after what I knew about her and went through with Trey I couldn't rise to her defense because the truth had already risen from the grave.

Nicole was the topic of many our fights and arguments but I wouldn't and couldn't cut her loose no matter what. Things back on the home front was a battle field as well, with my mom, her boyfriend, and sister it felt like a chess game knock one piece off the board just to have another one take its place. At least the new "black knight" waved a sword wanting to be my savior building a wall between the heated fights and favoritism with my sister and me. The "black knight" seemed understanding and concerned with my emotions. We would often talk and he would pass on advice about life, boys, and growing up.

One day I decided I would do like most of the teenage girls in this town who escaped their parents' household and that was to get pregnant. I had told Mr. Bates my plan and surprisingly enough he was all for it. Mr. Bates and I tried repeatedly over and over to get pregnant and after 3 months I went to him and told him I wanted to stop, he asked why; mentally I was saying "because your ass is shooting blanks" but I just told him we can try later when I'm close to graduating and him in the military. But Mr. Bates and I didn't even make through the summer, Nicole hating him just as much as he hated her found out Saint Bates was still involved his baby mother and other girls all spread out in different cities. I don't need to say how she got this information just that even a guy's best friend will rat him out for some pussy and head which Nicole was a champ on the track; bitch earned her title.

After the second failed relationship and me about to start high school, I then turned my focus back to my music, writing and this time had new material to write about. Nicole and I would walk the streets and go to the pool hall where I wanted to take up the game. The owner of the pool hall took me under his wing and taught me how to play pool and he was an older gentleman with lifelong lessons and stories which I had studied like a course wanting to pass in the pool game of life. While at the pool hall I caught the eye of several men and boys going in and out but the pool man Hartford guarded me like a stick in his hand ready to break.

As I was walking back one day across town heading home Nicole and I stopped at the park down the street. Nicole was at the corner of the road talking to some guy and I was on the merry go round turning and thinking what was the purpose of my life and what did the future hold for me. I would often picture myself as a ghost dead or never been born wondering how the family I go home to now would be and if my mother and stepfather would have stayed together having one less battle to fight, and believe me I put up a HELL of a fight. My thoughts were interrupted from Nicole calling my name out. I looked up and there was a guy on a bike with his shirt off passing the park.

Nicole was dropping signals left and right committing on his body and muscles and asked if he had a girl. I could hear their conversation from the merry go round and he laughed at her said "you just get right to the point, don't you". I heard him say, so what's up with your girl she looks like she lost her best friend. Nicole mentioned I had recently broke up with my boyfriend, which was Saint Bates and feeling down. I could feel his eyes on me trying to see through to my soul. I heard him ask Nicole for my name and I knew then I was his interest of pursuit even though he was Nicole's. She walked him over to me and I avoided eye contact just wanting to be left alone; thinking to myself "damn can't a sister get time to grieve before the next heartbreak comes along".

Nicole went back to talking to her friend near the road and left me and the man with the bike and no shirt on talking. I have to admit I really didn't have much to say to him. But I made it very clear I was not interested in getting involved with anyone at the moment. He asked how old I was I said 15 and I asked how old are you he said 21. He replied we can take things slow and just be friends I just want to get to know you. He asked for my phone number but I ended up giving him Nicole's number since I told him me and her are ALWAYS together. He asked where I stayed I mentioned down the road at the apartment complex on the right hand side. He laughed I asked what's so funny he said that's where I stay at, so we're neighbors.

The first couple of weeks he would call Nicole and set up a time where he would call back and talk to me or meet him across town or at the pool hall. Conversations on the phone were long and memorable. We talked about our past, our family, past relationships. I felt so at ease around him as if though I could tell him anything. The school year was quickly approaching and I would soon be in high school with new challenges and pressure but it mostly did not cross my mind because not only did I have

Nicole to go through with me but Devin, the man may have not rode in on a horse but he was my knight and shining armor.

Devin stayed with his mother, sister, and 2 younger brothers in the same apartment complex. His bedroom faced the front where he was able to see me coming and going. I could see him peeping through the blinds and I just smiled. Nicole and I went to the pool hall after school where she ran into what I call the next bed runner, his name was Wayne and he was an older gentleman and being in a same town Wayne knew Devin and we soon all started hanging out together at Wayne's house. It may have been pressure from Devin's friends but I started seeing less of him as days past and was at Wayne's house alone feeling like a third wheel.

Wayne had a nephew who looked like a famous actor at the time and was a smooth talker and I knew his ass won't no good. Coby, Wayne's nephew was good looking and he knew it which made him also arrogant. Coby would try to flirt with me knowing good and well I was Devin's girl. Even though part of me felt abandoned by Devin spending more time with his boys on the other side of town he would call Wayne's house and we talk and too many times with those phones calls he mentioned he was on his way and 9 out of 10 times never showed up. Even as a third wheel being around Nicole and her man, we all still had fun.

There was talk on the street about Devin and his son's baby momma Ivory sleeping together and he was staying with her. Being upfront with each other like we were; I asked him about it and he mentioned she was jealous because we were together and she wanted him. He mentioned he was with me and no one else. I actually ran into Ivory on the street one day. Nicole and I was walking and saw Ivory and she had Devin's little boy in a stroller. Nicole actually knew who she was and spoke to her. While Nicole and her were talking I looked at her, then the baby, and quickly stared off into the distance.

During the conversation between her and Nicole she made it a point to introduce herself to me; I said yes I know who you are. She then did the unthinkable she said don't you think you too young to being dating Devin. I turned my head and said what, I'm old enough to say and do what

I want and if my age doesn't bother Devin it shouldn't bother anyone else; it was then I knew this bitch was going to be a problem. Later on that night Devin and I met up at Wayne's and we walked and talked. I told Devin I saw his son today and Ivory who absolutely felt some kind of way about us being together. Devin mentioned he didn't care what others thought and I made him happy.

Things were good for a few weeks and then came the cycle again of Devin hanging out with his boys on the other side of town. He admitted in previous conversations we had that his boys were somewhat jealous when him and I would hung out together. I asked why I couldn't just hang out with him and them together he said his boys were into a lot of stuff he didn't want me exposed to and I would be safer. He wanted me to keep the innocence I had about me, it was then I felt the protection of his love and wanted him even more. Devin and I had be involved for 3 months and yet we still had not had sex.

On one of our nightly walks I asked him why we had not had sex yet and if he wanted to be with me in that way. Devin stated he did want to be with me sexually but did not feel the need to rush it and wanted the time and place to be perfect; I wasn't just some random chick to fuck and he had feelings beyond the physical domain. I was thinking damn, I'm ready to take it out for a test drive, but admire his discipline. While walking to Wayne's place after school one day Nicole was talking to Devin on the phone when I arrived and the look on her face when she handed me the phone could not prepare me for what Devin was about to say.

When I put the phone to my ear I heard Devin's voice he sounded so sad and hesitate. I asked him what was wrong, he said not to worry but he was locked up. I said locked up where, how, and why; he mentioned it was for child support and will be out in 30 days. While Devin was locked up we wrote letters to each other which brought us even closer together. We were able to write things on paper we feared or didn't know how to say face to face. It was tough going day in and day out with Devin being locked up; Nicole did all she could to get my mind off of him and on Sundays would go down to the jailhouse with me while I visited him.

The visits at the jailhouse were somewhat awkward because his son's mother was also there waiting to see him. If for some reason she got there before me and visited Devin I noticed she waited around after my visit with him. Nicole would talk to Ivory but I had nothing to say to her. My focus was on Devin and no one else. The following weekend I spent at Nicole's house which we spent most of the weekend walking the streets and at Wayne's house. That weekend Wayne brought some alcohol which he knew I wasn't into beer or 40ozs so he brought a new bottle of liquor called "night train".

Night train put me in the mind of drinking a sweet wine and nearly killed the whole bottle by myself. Nicole and Wayne headed in the house upstairs to Wayne's room to have sex and I stayed on the porch outside just thinking about Devin and wishing he was out. Coby Wayne's nephew pulled up with his girlfriend who dropped him off in front of the house. As he made his way up to the stairs he looked at me and laughed looking at the bottle of night train next to the chair he said "girl you drinking that, I know you fucked up". I smiled and said no… I'm fine, Coby sat in the chair next to me on the porch and took my cup and bottle of night train and poured him some in the cup.

He asked where everyone was at, I said Nicole is upstairs with Wayne doing what they do best and I'm down here enjoying the fresh air. Coby replied, damn I heard Devin was locked up, tough break. I could tell by Coby's tone, his ass wasn't sincere because he was smiling when he said "tough break". I took the cup of night train out his hand and poured me some more from the bottle. Coby stood up and grabbed my hand and said come on, I said and where are you taking me, Coby said we going upstairs. I replied I am fine outside and I'm not going upstairs with you so you can try and fuck me. Coby stated "no, Harminme I just want to get you from outside and the wine going to hit you hard if you don't walk around." I wasn't sure what he meant until I stood up and everything around me started spinning.

Coby grabbed me and held me for a minute and looked at me and said now you feeling it. I felt like I wanted to throw up, Coby walked me slowly up to his room where I laid on his bed. My head was throbbing and the room spinning and the next thing I felt was Coby rubbing my leg moving up to my thigh and then unbuttoning and unzipping my pants. I sat up quickly and said no, stop, Coby replied I want you, Harminme, and I know you want me too. I said no I am with Devin, Coby laughed saying Devin's ass is locked up. He whispered in my ear just let it happen, he wasn't rough but we both was determined and forceful till I no longer had the strength or ability to stay fully awake to fight him. I could feel him on top of me and inside of me breathing on my neck.

Though it lasted minutes thoughts of Devin ran through my head, Nicole asked the next day when I sober up how was he, and I said to be honest if it wasn't for the weight of his body on me and the hotness of his breath on my neck I would of have never known he was having sex with me. Nicole busted out laughing in tears and I as well. I said girls are absolutely hung up on his looks because he is definitely not hung anywhere else; luckily for him I wasn't sober because that was nothing but a "ghost dick". As the days after that incident passed I felt such guilt, and shame for betraying Devin this way. The word on the street was Devin was out, which was a surprise to me since I haven't heard from him.

It had been about 3 days but I finally got a call from Devin wanting to see me. We met downtown at the waterfront in a gazebo, I arrived before him and waited and about 10 minutes later he showed up. He started walking towards me and I just stood there unable able to move full of excitement and turmoil at the same time thinking about the night Coby and I had sex. We hugged one another for so long and so tight like my breath went into his body. When we released one another I asked why you didn't you contact me as soon as you got out, he mentioned he had some things to take care of. We sat there in silence for like a minute and I looked at him and said Devin something happen while you were locked that I need to tell you.

Devin one night while drinking over at Wayne's I ended up having sex with Coby. Devin turned his back to me and there was a moment of silence, he then turned around and said I know, I heard. With, the look of confusion and surprise on my face I asked who told you. He said it doesn't matter, I was hurt at first but then I blamed myself for leaving you in an environment I knew was filled with some shady niggas. I didn't know how to adjust after that comment since only 3 people knew about that night and I'm sure Coby wouldn't have been stupid enough to approach Devin with such dishonor. I told Devin I understand if you wanted to end things due to what happened.

Devin replied, no, what we have is special and greater than what happened between you and that nigga; I'm not saying I'm okay with what went down but I can't let you go. As time went on it seemed like all focus was against me and Devin; from my mother to his two babies mommies, and ex-girlfriends that apparently didn't like the fact I had sex with someone else being labeled as Devin's girl and Devin not leave me. Devin had a reputation where if you fucked him over with another man he would leave your ass, no questions asked. I apparently had a soft spot with him and bitches were hella jealous and hella mad. I felt like I had an invisible shield around me, no one could break through.

In a few short months that unbreakable shield started to get some cracks. Ivory made it obviously a mission to locate me and inform Devin was living with her and they were sleep together and to prove it she invited me over to her apartment. I went just to see why this bitch was so confident and sure enough there was Devin's clothes, shoes, and even the letters I wrote him while he was locked up. I kept my cool and told Ivory thank you for the home tour. On the walk back across town a car had pulled up next to me and here comes Devin getting out of the back seat. He asked where I was coming from, I smiled and said, we need to talk. He told his boys to go ahead and he would catch up with them later.

Not wanting to come off as irritate, I calmly asked are you fucking your son's mother, he laughed like what where is this coming from. He replied "no" I said why in the hell is your clothes and letters I wrote you in a dresser in her apartment. He asked is that where you are coming from, I replied "yes". He stated he has clothes everywhere, even at his boys' house, he mentioned his mother and he were constantly at each other throat and sometimes he would crash out at random places, even at his son's mother's place but he stated he slept on the couch and he was not fucking her. He said, can't you see she is just trying to messed with you anyway and anyhow she can, my heart is with you, I love you.

That were the first time I heard those words "I love you" his letters from jail would end with love Devin but never was the words I love you written or said until now. When he spoke them a chill came over me like "damn he meant that shit". I said I love you too. After dodging that bullet another one was waiting in the barrel. There were times Devin would come over to my mom's place late at night and we would have sex down stairs while my mom and her boyfriend, Nick slept upstairs. One night Nick came out the bedroom from upstairs, he went to the bathroom and started making his way down the steps. Devin started to head out the back door but I didn't want him to leave so I told him to hide in the bathroom.

Nick usually goes to the kitchen for a midnight snack or drink which he did, I was on the floor watching a horror movie which Nick was not a fan of horror movies. Nick headed back to the stairs and half way up he stopped and turned around, at this point my heart started racing and I had a look of confusion like "what the fuck is he doing". For some strange reason Nick goes back in the kitchen and head to the downstairs bathroom when he cut the light on, I heard a scream and shuffle. Devin was trying to make it to the backdoor but Nick said "no wait Harminme get your mother".

As I slowly walked up the steps I was thinking, this is my last night as live and breathe. I opened up the bedroom door and called to my mother, she awoken in confusion saying "yes Harminme what do you want" I said Nick wants to see you down stairs it's important. She got up and headed down stairs, I slowly walked behind her thinking if I pushed her down the steps then it would buy me and Devin time; but I didn't. When she walked into the kitchen she saw Devin and Nick sitting at the table. She knew right away what took place. My mother called the police, while waiting for them to arrive Nick and my mother had to get their questions in.

My mother made a comment to Devin, saying you're a grown man, 21 years old, there's no women out there your age to go with. Devin told her, "age did cross my mind at first and at times thought to leave but as

14

I came to know her, saw not a 15 year old girl and she was more mature and smarter than any woman I had been with. I'm sorry but I love her." I stood against the wall in the kitchen with smile on my face like damn this mutherjumper is brave, he just told my mother he loved me. My mother, mentioned, well I hope it's worth going to jail for because she is underage, Devin came back with no, she's not state law says she's legal. My mother said "I doubt that and I will see you in court".

The police came and took Devin away. My mother grounded me for a month the only places I could go were home, school, and work. I felt like a prisoner, my mother and her boyfriend would drive out to both jobs to make sure I was working and to make sure Devin wasn't around. Devin and I stayed low until his court date; we sent messages through Nicole and he would come to my job at night and we would sit in car and talk. The day Devin was scheduled to go to court, all day I couldn't focus. I wanted to be down at the courthouse during the trail and tell the Judge any and everything I could to keep him from being locked up; hell I would of took his spot in jail if I meant getting out my mom's house and releasing me at 18.

I was home when my mother came in from the court hearing, and I wanted to jump out the chair and yell what happened, but from the look on her face and her not rubbing shit in, things obviously did not go HER way. It wasn't until the next day when I was able to use the phone at school and call one of Devin's friends to schedule a time I would call back. When I called later on; I asked him what happened in court; he laugh and said the Judge said as a 15 year old that I was old enough to consent to sex and since the sex was maturely, statutory rape could not be charged. I was so happy, even though I did wonder how a Judge could of came up with that decision without me there, but now that it was legally put out there, I was able to have sex with him and no one could say a MUTHERFUCKING WORD, ALL WAS GOOD!!!

I was relieved, Devin made it clear to all, who dare stepped to me, would be dealt with. I walked on a red carpet dye in blood labeled as D-girl with many perks and respect that took the street over like a drive by; filled with fear and silence. Nicole had mentioned how Ivory and some of her friends made it a point to inform her, so she could inform me that Devin and Ivory were sleeping and living together and she was pregnant with their second child. I asked Nicole what she thought I should do about it and she stated if she knew one thing for sure it was Devin loved me but she also mentioned Ivory was definitely pregnant and leaves room to question the process of elimination so me and Nicole put a plot into action.

One of Devin's boys named Tank who was locked up for almost 15 years due to HEAVY drug charges; ended up in our small town setting up shop. At first Devin was hesitate to bring me around because he didn't like me being in the environment where him and his regular boys hung out at because the men around Tank and even Devin were heavily armed. The reputation Tank had I did feel safe, even with the tension of the police breaking down the door at any time. Tank was not a man of many words until he got to know you. I noticed his operation was organized and the time I spent around him learned how moving drugs and guns was set up like a military operation, everyone had their posts, drop offs, pickups, and timelines.

Tank had girls, money, drugs, guns hell one would think with spending 15 years in prison he would keep far away from this life, but maybe he felt he mastered it. I believed he could have had a payroll that employed the police force and sheriff department since he was ahead of any raids. His connections crossed state lines from Virginia, Maryland, DC; it wouldn't have surprised me if he had connections that poured over to the west coast as well as overseas. From shot houses to crack houses I see why Devin and I didn't spend as much time together as I would of liked because this side of life was now beyond the flipping of a remote control and the people I saw and who saw me really were not there...

I saw those I would of never figured to be an addict. I wasn't there to judge them by any means but knew now not everyone is as who and what they seem. This small town dark secrets were well hidden behind a smoke cloud of weed, cigarettes and crack pipes followed behind a bottle of liquor. I felt dirty and sad that I couldn't find a way to help but as a 16 year old I was in no position to tell these grown ass men and women about the D.A.R.E. program. I wanted to spend more time with Devin and he did warn me but some shit I just rather not have known. I will say though, even in the most dangerous situations I always felt secure and protected with Devin.

Devin on the other hand, had to watch his back constantly not because of drug bust but child support, it seem both his babies mommas had put out an arrest on him for back child support which I sure was nothing but pure hatred for being with me. My Aunt Sandy actually called me one day and said Harminme, girl I was watching an episode of COPS and guess who I saw, I'm like, who my Aunt Sandy said, Devin. She said "he was running from like 5 Police Officers and 2 dogs and let me tell you that boy can run, never knew a man who could outrun two dogs". I laughed for a brief moment, and said thank you Aunt Sandy for the 411, but she was on the other end laughing it up.

When I hung up the phone my laughter and smile turned into deep and penetrating thoughts, for the first time I had fear, I had doubt. Devin and I had been together almost 2 years and it was a constant uphill battle; the law, ex-girlfriends, baby's mommas, his family, my family and his boys. At the end of the day I wondered would I had tried so fucking hard to stay with Devin if there was no one trying to keep us apart, but the thought of not being with him made my heart feel as though it had dropped. He excited me and it was more than the sexual part of our relationship but the emotionally, he had cared for me like a mother should care their child . . . unconditional. It was love. When he said "I love you" I not only heard it but FELT IT, I KNEW HE MEANT IT.

Devin, me, Nicole, my cousin Keira, and two of Devin's boys all took a walked downtown one Saturday night. We had started the earlier part of the evening drinking so we were feeling really "nice". We all sat in the gazebo talking and joking around. I was sitting on Devin's lap and he was touching me under my shirt and I'm trying to stop him since we were around people. Devin stands up and takes my hand and we walk over to the walk way overlooking the water, he mentioned no matter, he would never leave me. I smiled and said nothing, for I knew he meant it. Devin then picks me up holding me over the water, he tells me to tell him that I will never leave him no matter what. The wind was blowing hard and the water with crashing waves, made such a loud sound.

I screamed and told Devin to put me down, he said I will once you promise never to leave me. I told him, no I'm not going to do that. Devin said please, and the next thing I saw was Devin and I falling into the water. My soul had left my body, and while in the water I could still feel Devin holding me, trying to swim up. I was fighting realizing we had fell in and it's like I could hear Devin saying stop fighting. I could hear voices overhead Nicole my cousin and Devin's boys yelling our names. We finally made it to the top and my cousin Keira and Nicole grabbed me out the water. Keira takes my hand and starts running, I'm trying to catch my breath and yelled stop running!! Keira stops running and I fall to the ground she is hugging me asking if I am alright.

I said yes, I'm fine. Devin comes up behind us and asked Keira to give us a moment. Devin bends down and he says Harminme I am so sorry, I lost my balance and please say something. I slowly stand up and Devin stands up as well, now I'm no longer scared but angry. Out of nowhere I raised my right hand and slapped the hell out of Devin. He grabs me and pulls me into him and in my ear said I deserved that, but don't do it again. The rest of the crew walked over and now once was fear became laughter. Devin's boys was like damn, Devin what happen. Devin mentioned he had lost his balance and felt us about to fall but I wasn't going to let her go. Which that was really the highlight of the whole incident was the fact I never left his arms, Devin NEVER LET GO OF ME. I was thinking my mother may of not got Devin's ass for statutory rape, but defiantly would of went to jail for murder if I didn't come up.

The plot I and Nicole had put into place weeks back had finally come around to take action. Nicole had been in contact with Ivory, who was supposedly pregnant with Devin's third child and claims he was in love with her and told her he doesn't want me and he has moved on. What I and my girl Nicole had planned was to pretty much corner Devin with me and Ivory face to face to see exactly what truths would come out. One day while Devin, me and Nicole was chillin over Tank's place Nicole had went out down the road to get Ivory who was also accompanied by her cousin and a maturely friend of both of ours named Kay. Devin and I was inside the house while a few guys were outside the house smoking and drinking.

Nicole comes in the house while Ivory and the others waited outside. I looked at her and said are we ready, she replied "YES", I told Devin our presence is wanted outside, heading towards the door we go outside to see Ivory and her friends. Devin looked at me and asked what is this, I replied, a means to an end. Since apparently Ivory feels you and she are in a committed relationship I feel it's time for the truth to be bought forth. So, Ivory since you had so much to say, talk now. Ivory looked at Devin and said, are we not fucking and are you staying at my place. Also you mentioned you wasn't seeing Harminme anymore so why you here with her. I stood by waiting for his answer.

Devin said fine, since everyone wants to know the truth here it. Yes, I do stay with Ivory from time to time and yes I am still having sex with her. I looked at him and was like REALLY, so is this baby she carrying yours. Devin sighed, I can't really say for sure because Ivory you are fucking someone else too. I just stared off for a moment and said to Devin, all this time you been lying to me and her absolutely since she thinks we're not together. I said to Devin, if Ivory is what you want then you can be with her I'm too young for all this drama, and start to walk away with my girl Nicole. Devin called out to me yelling WAIT HARMINME, he stated since you two went through all this trouble to corner me you minus well hear the rest.

Devin stated, I'm sorry for lying to you both, I didn't want to hurt either one of you and so I lied to spare your feelings. Ivory I do love you and my son very much but the truth is I'm IN LOVE WITH HARMINME and that's where my heart lays. I didn't mean to lead you on thinking we would be more but the truth is I'm not in love with you, I'm in love with Harminme. Ivory yelled and I could tell holding back tears telling Devin to get his shit out her place. Ivory, her cousin, and maturely friend Kay walked off heading back to her apartment. I admit I felt bad for her and tears filled my eyes as well because if the situation had not went in my favor I'm not sure how I would have reacted.

Devin looked at me and pulled me into his chest and held on to me tight apologizing again for what he had done. I could feel his heart racing and knew though we were happy together, our love brought pain and mad jealousy to others. That night Devin and I had the best sex me we have had in a while, he went in hard on me like he was punishing me for cornering him in front of his boys. Devin had always been gentle for the most part but that night he did not hold back and I know the whole house knew that shit was payback for earlier J As soon as I could get up Nicole, Tank, and Tank's girlfriend were all downstairs; I couldn't look them in the eyes just focused on Devin sitting on the loveseat smiling as I came down.

Now that Ivory knew the TRUTH she made it a point to see Devin get locked up for being behind on child support, same bullshit his daughter mother would do when Devin pissed her off. You know what they say "if I can't have him…" Devin was in and out of jail back to back and word resurfaced back on the street he was fucking Ivory again and to be honest I guess that was the way to keep his "freedom" but it really didn't faze me as much since she knew who was number 1. I eventually got tired of the lying and had no more trust. I decided it was time to let Devin go.

My girl Nicole waiting in the same spot she was at, when she first saw Devin years ago riding by on his bike and here we were today in the same place where it all started I figured it be best to also end it. Devin walks up to me on the merry go round and gives me a kiss and knows from the look on my face something was wrong. I told Devin it's been 2 hard years and I just can't do it anymore. This love is a constant battle and I'm tired of fighting. His eyes filled with tears and he was like Harminme, you know I love you we can face anything together. I stated no Devin, with your boys on the other side of town, a third child, ex-girlfriends spreading rumors, you being locked up every other month, I'm sorry but we have grown apart.

He said he understood and we hugged each other one last time. I buried my face in his bare chest which my tears rolled down; he said "you may have left me Harminme, but know I haven't left you"; we both said I love you, and then he walked off. Nicole came towards me with tears in her eyes as well and sat on the merry go round and she just held me while I cried. It was so much pain… it felt like someone died; the shit hurt physically and I cried so hard I gave myself a headache. When I got home my mother and Nick knew something was up because I hardly every went out anymore and just went to work and school and wasn't even grounded. My mother made the comment so, so, you found out Devin won't no good hu. I looked at her and in my mind was like "bitch, go to hell". Then here comes Nick while I'm curled up in bed wanting to talk to me and be my "friend" and find out what happened.

Nick, started to spend more time with me driving me around, talking with me about "life", boys, and sex. He mentioned since I didn't have a father figure in my life that he would always be there for me to talk about "anything". I just listened with no reply. Nicole kept me informed with what was happening on the street. She mentioned Devin always asked how I was doing and to tell me, he loved me. After about 2 months I got past the depression faze, and set in motion my revenge against Devin. There was a new maintenance guy that worked in the apartment complex, he reminded me a lot of Devin. He was built, had muscles and every girl and woman in the apartment complex wanted him!!!

My next door neighbor, Linda who was a year or two older than me, whose mother never let her leave the house became part of my action plan to get Mr. Maintenance Man. Linda, though imprisoned in her mother's home was no stranger at being resourceful. I told her I wanted to meet with the new maintenance man and have a talk with me, I put in a fake maintenance order to have him come by, it just so happened he responded to the call right away and my mother wasn't home. Linda and I was waiting inside in the living room area, when he knocked on the door. He asked which bathroom toilet needed fixing, I looked at Linda and smiled and asked her to keep watch at the door for my mother.

I introduced myself and said my name is Harminme and I do have a job for you to do but it's not fixing a toilet. He looked at me puzzled, and asked "what do you want me to work on" I laughed, and said me. There was a moment of silence and he said "ain't you D's girl, with a smirk on my face replied. . . no, NOT ANYMORE. I mentioned I'm looking for a little payback on Devin for his lies and betrayal. Jerome, the maintenance man said "you know word on the street is you have a tight hold on Devin", yeah I said apparently not tight enough since he can't seem to keep his dick in his pants, and increased his child support payments. Jerome was like damn. . . I hope she was worth losing you over, I smiled and said no and that is what REALLY PISSES ME OFF!!!

Jerome said yes to my offer which I was sure he wasn't going to turn down unless a course he was in love and had a girlfriend or wife and honored his values...shit, not likely. Let's be real there ain't too many men in the world that can read marriage vows, needless to say going to follow them. Jerome, asked how old I was I said 17 and I asked so how old are you, he smiled and said 35. I was like okay, honestly, I didn't think you were much older than Devin. Jerome stated, don't worry I'll be gentle, I smiled and said NO, JUST BE GOOD. After that things got interesting at the apartment complex with Devin still staying with his mother off and on and Jerome being the maintenance man, all three of us in a circle... literally. I told my girl Nicole the plot I had put in place, she made sure word hit the streets for Devin to hear, I had a replacement.

Sex with Jerome was ok but not as good as I have hope being older and more built than Devin. Another thing that distracted me was his scent he smelled like the outdoors which was a turn off smell to me, but I kept telling myself fucking him will surely hurt Devin. I actually avoided seeing Devin because being near him brought on a weakness I could barely fight. It was about 4 weeks when I ended up face to face with Devin and he was so mad he actually showed up at the school during my lunch period where he knew I hung outside under the tree. My back was actually turned when he approached, he whispered in my ear "you know you playing a FUCKING dangerous game".

I was so fucking scared to move because I didn't actually think he would show up on school grounds, this mutherjumper done crossed a line I didn't even draw out for him to cross. I was sitting at the table underneath the tree and he lean across me with his chest pressed against my back and held my wrists down on the table and though I was scared my body overheated with excitement wanting him to fuck me right then and there. He said "you know I love you and I fucked up, but you fucking this guy going start some shit you can't control". I calmly said, can you let go of my wrists and he said "next time, not only will you not see me coming, but there will be no one around", he kissed me on the cheek and left in a car.

Tears came to my eyes and since me and Nicole did not have same lunch time I didn't have her there to console me. In minutes my feeling of fear turned into anger, thinking who the hell does think he is, telling me not fuck someone else, I fuck who I want to fuck. One thing about this situation that made it risky was if anyone could go up throw for throw with Devin, Jerome was it. I figured that's why Devin came to me instead of him. Both men were known for carrying guns and knives and not being afraid to use them. I avoid Jerome for a few days after Devin had stopped by the school. I see now Devin, was willing to go anywhere to get his message across.

Jerome kept calling and I actually avoided riding the school bus home when I didn't have to work so he couldn't catch me coming off the bus. He got smart the fourth day and caught me early in the morning going to school, I eased out the back door and there he was waiting in between the buildings. I was thinking oh my God please don't let this be a morning Devin is looking out the window. Jerome asked "is something wrong it seems like you been avoiding me". I told Jerome I haven't been feeling well and been having issues with my mother so I've been laying low. He looked at me and ask are you sure there's nothing else, I said no Jerome. He said "I miss you and licking that pie of yours", I smiled and said no worries you'll get my cream filling very soon. Honestly, Devin done put the fear of God in my ass, I was planning on shutting down "the bakery".

Jerome and I met up that weekend when I was getting off of work, we went to an open field, sat in the car and talked briefly. He stated he saw Devin earlier and was watching him like a hawk, he definitely had something on his mind which I'm no dummy I knew it was about you. I wanted to tell Jerome about the school visit earlier in the week but did not want to make this situation I now had lost control over fall out any further. I put my hand down Jerome's pants and started stoking his dick and kissing his neck to get him off the topic of Devin. We had sex and for a brief moment Devin was obsolete. I fucked Jerome that night as if he was Devin and he came hard. He stated "I'm glad Devin fucked up and now I got you".

When Jerome made that comment all I could do is smile because deep inside I knew though Jerome may have had my body at this moment in time, BUT Devin had my mind, heart, and soul and YES I WANTED HIM BACK. I was fighting with myself knowing I could get Devin back if I wanted. That night when I was at home laying in my bed here comes my mother's boyfriend Nick, wanting to talk and see what I was up to. I told him I was just working and going to school. He asked "so you not with anyone, you don't have a boyfriend". I said no just Chilin for now. He put his hand on my thigh and stated anytime you want to talk, remember I'm here, you can come to me for anything...

Though Nick seemed to be a down to earth guy, I started to see had thoughts and desires no man dating a child's mother should be having. It became awkward being home with him alone when my mother was at work. I would hang next door to Linda's place where surprisingly enough her mother started to let loose the chain she had around her. Linda could now walk down the road and her mother and stepfather not freak out. One day while walking down the road we got stopped by a guy in a little pink car, the first thoughts that came to mind was this guy is either gay or is very secure in his manhood. He asked where we were headed; I mentioned nowhere just walking. He asked if we wanted a ride, I mentioned no, not tonight we can't go too far we have to head back soon.

So he asked where we stayed and I told him down the street in the apartment complex down the road, he mentioned I know the place; how about tomorrow I swing by and visit. I said sure no problem. Linda and I was chilling at my place, my mother was getting ready for work and there was a knock at the door, apparently she put in a maintenance call for the kitchen sick and Jerome came ready to fix the problem. Jerome stayed for about 30 minutes fixing the sink, my mother was getting ready for work. As Jerome left out we made eye contact and smiled. My mother was on the phone with my Aunt Sandy and was talking about Jerome who just left and told my Aunt how she thought he was so sexy, Linda and I just looked at each other and tried hard as hell not to laugh, for in my mind

I was thinking, yes mother, he is and if you only knew who pipes he was really fixing.

Sure enough the guy in the pink car came by the next day and me and Linda got in the car for a ride around town. I sat in front and Linda in the back so her mother or stepfather wouldn't see her. Kurt was fun to hang around he did make his move on me but with what I had going on with Jerome and Devin I really didn't need a third wheel and plus I really wasn't into light skin men; I prefer my men like my relaxer, dark and lovely. So Kurt went on to option number 2 which was Linda but that was with its challenges a course being she was trapped in the house 80 percent of the time, unlike my mother on the other hand who would let me out but best believe she was out tailgating my ass.

It was always a cat and mouse game with me and my mother. The store my mother worked to was robbed one night and luckily she wasn't working. Word on the street was Devin was somehow involved with the robbery but at the moment police had no one in custody. I sure Devin was capable of many things but robbery was not something I saw in him, so I just blew it off. Nicole and I had been distance from each since she was involved with a new guy which apparently seemed to have her whipped. I picked up more hours at both jobs so really only hung out on the weekends. I isolated myself, at least I tried but I still had Nick who would come in my room and try to make conversation.

I was laying down watching t.v and he touched me on my ass; it just so happened that day I was on my period so he could feel the pad underneath my clothes and made the comment, you on your period. I just looked at him sat up on the bed crawled up in the corner and said yes, and I would like to be alone and he left out. Linda and I would chill together and hang out with Kurt riding around but since her mother was strict on time we I couldn't hang out late with her like Nicole. There was one night when we were walking back across town to home where I knew we were not going to make it but the time her mother had set but luckily a car came to a stop and a man named Tykeem gave us a ride.

It was funny how it was so easy to catch a ride especially from a man who I know had bad intentions on his mind. We got to the apartment about 10 minutes past time but it just so happened Linda's mother was not home, no one was. The three of us sat in Tykeem car and talked a bit, and then I cut it short and decided to go in the house Linda mentioned she would stay in the car a little longer I was no problem see you later. As soon as I stepped in the apartment the phone rings and its Jerome asking who I was talking to in the car I just got out of; I laughed and said oh are you jealous, Jerome stated, should I be. I mentioned it was a guy that gave me and Linda a ride home and what you doing in the apartment complex this late, shouldn't you been off.

Jerome mentioned there was an emergency maintenance situation and he was answering the call. Jerome stated he wanted to see me and to meet him at the playground, Nick was upstairs and my mother at work. I met Jerome at the playground, he quickly grabbed me and started kissing on my neck, since I have a rule about not kissing in the mouth this is how he would show affection along with playing with my breasts. Jerome and I sat on the swing the playground was empty and dark. I sat on his lap and he fingered and fondle me and I afterwards stoke his dick and kissed him repeatedly on the lips and whispering in his ear how I wanted him inside of me, until he came. Jerome mentioned he wanted to spend more time together but I really wasn't looking for a deep close relationship like that.

I just wanted a hit and run for now, since my real intentions with him was to make Devin jealous. I did for a girl of my age desired older men, but Jerome being in his 30s was more than what I was seeking age wise. The advantage of being with older men was they had more sexual experience and knew their way around the female body inside and out. Nicole called me the next day wanting to meet down at the waterfront. I headed downtown, but when I got there Nicole haven't arrived yet so I sat in the gazebo. I was looking out onto the water just thinking about everything going on in my life; sex, men, school, work, friends, family, everything. I heard footsteps approaching and I turned around with a smile only to see it wasn't Nicole but DEVIN. That mutherjumper was right, he said next time I would be alone and not see him coming. I stood up quickly and he just smiled like yeah BITCH got you now. He moved in close to me, and asked what you going to do Harminme, run.

I laughed I said no Devin as much as you want to choke the shit out of me, I know you won't hurt me. I said, besides the Police station is right behind us and word on the street they're looking for you for an armed robbery that took place, so I'm sure you not going to show your ass and draw attention to yourself. All Devin could do was laugh saying you always have a backup plan don't you, yes I said more ways than one. Devin mentioned he missed me and wanted to see me and talk to me. We sat in the gazebo and talked about things and he asked was I serious with Jerome, I emitted I was just having sex with Jerome to get back at what him for, lying, cheating, and getting HER pregnant.

Devin wanted me to stop fucking Jerome and be back with him, he mentioned missing me was driving him crazy. I mentioned I would need time, and I told him I missed us too. Devin and I left the water front, he grabbed me by the arm and pulled me into his chest. He kissed me on the lips and said "I'm taking you back now, you're mine". We ended up in the woods where he laid his jacket on the ground and we had sex. In the way he touch and kissed me I could feel his soul was sad and lost, while he was in me he kept close to my body bearing his chest down on my breast and firmly pressing his hips against me. I held his back with both hands, pushing my hips up to him, breathing deeply and then crying because it was just so emotional I couldn't hold back my feelings. I felt sad too, and my body missed his body, it was so overwhelming; now I knew the difference between fucking and making love.

After that night I thought about how I would approach Jerome with the news Devin and I were back together. Even though Jerome knew his purpose, I felt bad just dropping him. Late in the week I saw Jerome outside the complex. I pointed to the playground and within a few minutes, he came over. I was sitting on the swing and he sat in the empty swing next to me I told him Devin and I met the other day and we are back together, Jerome actually didn't get upset or mad. Jerome mentioned he and Devin had a run in a few weeks back and knew this day was coming. I said why didn't you tell me you two had talked. Jerome mentioned something took place that required him and Devin to get things out in the open. Jerome stated he will still be around whenever I needed him and can still be friends. I didn't reply because I knew being back with Devin that shit won't going to happen.

Reuniting with Devin, I figured to be a happy occurrence but instead Devin went back into hiding, not for child support but the local Police was looking for me him for the armed robbery. Instead of walking around town like we use to we travelled by car or I met him at a friend or cousin's house. He also stopped going to Tank's place to avoid Tank's whole drug operation being exposed. One night, while North Carolina was under a hurricane warning, hurricane Bertha, Devin had called the house and wanted to know if I could leave and be with him. I asked my mother if I say with Devin and she said yes I could go. Nick seem surprised my mother's answer but I was 18 so I was legal now.

Devin picked me up from the apartment complex and we headed back to his cousin's place which happened to be the same apartment complex Ivory lived at. He took me up to his cousin's apartment which was a female he introduced me and she took my overnight bag and made me a drink. Devin headed back outside to wrap some things up with his boys and about 15 minutes later Devin headed back upstairs. We curled up on the couch drinking alcohol and watching a movie. His cousin headed back into her bedroom with her man. Half way into the movie our attention turned to each other and with the rain pounding on the windows and the wind blowing hard made it a passionate night and a night of intimacy, I didn't want the night to end.

Unfortunately, the night did end and our little small town took a hit, trees and debris were everywhere. Devin had gotten up before me and headed outside where there was people standing around talking. I showered, put on my clothes and headed outside to join Devin, when I came out of the building all eyes focused on me. Apparently Ivory's cousin and friends were all whispering. I took my place next to Devin and one of Ivory's loud mouth cousin yelled to Devin, "this is who you were with last night damn, while Ivory and your kids were alone in the apartment". Devin just turned to her and smiled and kissed me on the lips. Ivory's cousin went to Ivory's apartment to tell her the news, Ivory came outside where we were at and made a big scene yelling at Devin saying you were laid up with this BITCH last night during the hurricane when I'm a home with your kids.

Devin's cousin came out to pull me back into the apartment I heard Devin tell Ivory, you know the deal don't try and play me; I told you who I loved. For Ivory to make a scene told me she absolutely was still giving up the pussy to Devin but really I won't even mad because all bitches knew I was number one and have been for 3 years. I finally realized Ivory and others that Devin had been with wasn't mad at the fact he wasn't only with them but he was with me. What was it about ME that pissed them off, maybe the fact he loved me in a way he never loved them or anyone else. I felt a power with his love that just made me feel untouchable and our bond unbreakable.

A few weeks later I got a phone call from Devin, the police had finally caught him. He mentioned his court date was in a few weeks and not to worry he would be out soon. The days drag on I kept busy with work and during the week and on the weekends would hang out. I felt Devin was set up, but by who, the list was long and motives not known. Tykeem was one on the list but after spending time with him, really did not flag as a threat. He made it clear he had a sexual attraction to me. Tykeem for whatever reason, didn't force his sexual advances; he got off in other ways, word on the street or at least from Devin when he found out I was socializing with him was he had HIV/AIDS. I was interested in Tykeem for other reasons, just like Tank, Tykeem had a drug operation as well but his operation was a little different from Tanks, and I was all making money and gaining knowledge. A man I can learn a trade from though it was illegal still had value in learning.

Tykeem would put a condom on and watch women masturbate and play with each other, or he would go down on women, eat them out while he jacked off. I would be nearby watching briefly and then roam the house, but always had a shadow on me. Tykeem would always give his soldiers orders to make sure I was ALWAYS KEPT SAFE!!! I saw he required physical interaction differently which made me think the rumors about him having HIV/AIDS and being bisexually could be true. Tykeem shared things and stories with me, we had an open relationship like best friends. He knew my heart belonged to Devin and respected that and I didn't do anything I didn't want to do nor did I do anything that would piss Devin off at least not sexually with Tykeem. I admired men with a sharp hustle and keep people, money, and time organized. Though it WAS NOT MY INTENTIONS, I always ending up hanging around dangerous men, men that kept a gun on them at all times and at any time a gun could be aimed at them.

The court date for Devin had finally arrived and I was already making plans for when you got out. I was in school thinking about him all day and when I got home received the call I've been waiting for. It was Devin and he said hey babygirl, (I loved it when it called me that), what you doing, I said waiting on you. He laughed and said I knew you would be, but can you wait 7 to 10 years. I said what, Devin stated he was found guilty of armed robbery and was sentenced 7 to 10 years. Tears filled my eyes and I kept saying NO, NO, NO he told me that he loved me with every beat of his heart and I will always be his heart. He said to live my life to the fullest and not hold back on account of him. I asked where would they send you, he mentioned he wasn't sure but would always let me know where he was at.

We hung up and I felt sick to my stomach and not long after I hung up with him Nicole call and mentioned she heard the news about Devin being found guilty. I burst into tears and within the hour Nicole was there with a shoulder to cry on. I was in disbelief hoping Devin was just fucking with me and I would see him across town. About 2 weeks went pass and Devin called me from jail again, he called to inform me they were going to be transferring him to a prison and made arrangements for me and him to visit one last time. When I arrived to the jail it was just me and Devin towards the end of our visit Ivory and the kids had showed up.

Nicole and I left the jail and once again felt like I was in a daze and this was all a dream and when I wake up tomorrow Devin would be outside with his boys waiting for me. Needless to say, the nightmare was real and not only was Devin no longer outside, he was no longer in town. I did what

I could to take my mind off Devin. I got back into writing music again and hanging out with different people from school since a distance also came between Nicole and I. At one of my jobs there was a new manager that was hired and I could tell he had an interest in me. I wasn't really drawn to him at first but as a white guy he had a street demeanor that made my mind wonder to usually places.

During a shift together he would make it a point to push up against me or talk to me in a deepen tone that made hold my breath till he finished. The flirting and intense body structures went on for weeks. I was trying to be good but he was making it really hard. He called the house one night he was supervising and mentioned someone didn't show up for their shift it was busy as well with a game going on at the high school and he really needed me. I wasn't doing much of anything any way so I told him give me about 45 minutes and I'll be there. The place was busy not long after I arrived 2 school buses of football players, cheerleaders and coaches arrived.

Once the game crowd disappeared I went in the lobby to clean up. Once we locked the doors for the night Tony was recounting the registers and I was shutting down the front. I noticed he had sent just about everyone home and there was only me, a grill person, and him. I headed back to the breakroom and in seconds Tony was right behind me. My back was turned but I knew it was him. He thanked my again for coming in and helping him with the buses and wanted to know what I was doing after I got off. I mentioned I would be going home and getting in the bed. He asked if I wouldn't mind just having a drink with him at his place and talking for bit. I smelled and said just talking, he laughed and said, I won't make you do anything your uncomfortable with. I'm not sure why I said yes, but I did. After we shut down the restaurant, I got in my car, and he got in his and I followed him home. When we arrived to his place we went inside and I sat down on the couch and he sat next to me.

He asked if I wanted to take off my coat, I mentioned no, I'm fine. I don't plan on staying long, he asked if I wanted something to drink I was like sure. Tony had whisky and gin which I was not a fan of either, so I just ask for gin he handed me a glass with ice and gin only and I took a sip and with the expression on my face he asked is it too strong I said yes, he mentioned hold on I have some soda you mix with it, I was like thank God. We sat and talk and he bitch about the management team at the restaurant and how everyone is so fake and cut throat there. He sat back next to me on the couch and continued to talk, which I could tell Tony did need someone to vent to about shit at work.

Tony had about 3 full glasses of straight whisky and then by the third glass the conversation shift to him and me. He asked if I had a boyfriend I said it's complicated, he asked what that meant. I mentioned the man I love is doing time in prison and won't be out in about 7 to 10 years. He said damn, that tough there but honestly as a man here with you now I'm not sorry. Tony moved in for a kiss which I did allow him to do and as his body moved in on me I raised my hands and firmly pushed him away. He looked at me and asked if something was wrong, I stated I don't think I can do this. He looked at him and stating he had been fantasying about me for weeks and my fat ass on his face, wanting to see my ass out of clothes and uniform.

He stood up in front of me and I looked up at him still sitting on the couch thinking what is he about to do. He took the empty glass I had between my leg got down on his knees and said, I mentioned I wouldn't make you do anything you are uncomfortable doing and I mean that, he came in towards me again for another kiss and this time pulled himself away. He got up and said the choice is yours, I will be in the other room on the bed waiting naked for you to come in and if you don't, know there is no hard feelings I won't bother you again. Sure nurf he got up and went into the other room I put my head down thinking OMG, is this shit happening, girl here's your chance get up and leave.

I stood up and headed towards the door, I grab a hold of the door knob and though my mind said the open it my body said no Harminme, stay. I had to been standing there for about 2 mins going over in my head the pros and cons of this situation. I was 18 I'm an adult now I can do what I want to do. I turned slowly around and walked toward the bedroom where Tony sure enough was laying on his stomach naked on the bed. I sat on the edge of the bed looking away from him, he said take off your jacket, I stood up and took off my jacket. Tony said take off your shoes, so I took off my shoes. Tony said, now take off your clothes, I didn't move part of me still wanted to run towards the door, thinking this is a mistake, what the hell am I doing here with this white man.

He lift semi up from laying down and said again, Harminme, I said take... off...your...clothes; don't make me ask again. Right then I was turn on immediately thinking, this mutherjumper like to give orders, hell we ain't at work. I slowly started taking out my clothes he just watched and when I got down to my bra and panties he stopped me. He told me to come lay on the bed face down. I walked over to the bed and laid face down like he instructed and waited to see what he was going to do next. He told me to close my eyes, and I started to say something and he went in to kiss me and said baby please, close your eyes, so I closed my eyes.

I heard him get off the bed and open up the dresser next to it, then he got back on the bed positioning himself across my lower back, he unsnapped my bra and the next thing I felt was a cold liquid dripping on my upper back slowly rolling down. Tony massaged my back spreading the cold liquid which then turned warm on my body. The tension I had, was slowly being released with every press of his hands up and down my back. He kissed the back of my neck going down the lower part of my back. Tony then slowly lowered my panties half way on my ass where he put the cold liquid and started rubbing it in. He then pulled my panties all the way down to my feet and let them fall.

He continued to rub the oil all down my body following behind it with him kissing every spot he put the oil. He kiss my ass repeatedly and when got to my ankle was then standing at the edge of the bed. He asked me did I like that, I smiled, opened my eyes and said yes, very much. I said can I turn over now, he paused for a few seconds and said he, not yet. He grabbed my ankles and spread my legs open, I like oh shit here we go!!! He told me to slide down to the bottom of the bed, my mind is like going crazy right now like what the fuck is he about to do. But his ass has curious, so slide down the bed still on my stomach to him, he told me to lift my ass up, so I lift my ass up and he placed two pillows under my stomach. I laid on the pillows and the next thing he did was take two more pillows and placed them on the floor where he kneeled down.

Tony placed both hands on my ass and spread them wide open, he placed his face between my hips and began eating me, and I was in amazement. It felt so good and seeing he took his time with much anticipation before this point I was wet and wanted him. He slide one then two fingers into me stroking with both his fingers and tongue. I thinking wow never been eat out in this position before, I wonder why... then all a sudden it was starting to feel too good I tried moving up toward the head of the bed then he wrapped his arms from inside my thighs and pulled me back down. I was like OH SHIT this mutherjumper done set me up in a trap, sister can't run for the border in this position.

Not only was I intrigued, I was more aroused even more because Tony wasn't just fucking with me physically but mentally as well, he had a strategy when it came to sex which once he brought my guard down his defenses were up, ready for any counterattack. But he was about to find out my body is very stubborn and won't give in. Though I couldn't run from his ass, my body wasn't going to cum either. After about 30 minutes he stood up and said, you're hard as hell, I flipped over somewhat out of breathe and said yes, and from the looks of it you're hard too. He looked down at his dick and back and me and we both laugh.

He claimed on top of me and started kissing me and sucking on my breast, he then got up and stood at the end of the bed I look like, ok, why did you stop. He said, do you want a drink, I looked like a drink, are we not in the middle of something here. So I just came out and asked why you stop, he said I wanted you to want me like I wanted you and now you do. Next time, I won't have to tell you to take off your coat, or take off your shoes, and lay on the bed, you will do everything without being told and come to me on your own. There was a built up outburst I wanted to let out on him sooooo fucking bad but damn it he was right this whole plan of his worked like a charm.

The following weekend, me and Tony didn't closed together but he called me at home and he asked me to come by again tonight for drinks. I watch the clock eagerly waiting for the time to meet him. He called and said he was at the house and I can come now and the door will be unlocked. I arrived at him place and walked in. I was shocked to still find him in his working clothes, he stood next to the bed with a glass of ice and whisky he just looked at me and smiled. I was waiting for him to say something, but he didn't. My mind is now wondering what is it, what he wants me to do. A thought came to mind and I smiled back, I took off my coat, I took off my shoes, then I walked over to him.

He took a final drink out his glass, and I took the glass away sitting it on the dresser next to the bed. I walked back over to him and started to undress them slowly while smiling and looking into his eyes. I loosen his tie, unbutton his shirt, unsnap and unzip his pants and let them fall to the floor. I started kissing him and with his underwear still on rubbing his dick. I stop and step back from him and I began to undress myself, I got down to my bra and panties and stop. I waited to see what response I would get from him, and he just tilted his head like ok, why did she stop. I walked over to him and took off his underwear and then I took his hand and walk him into the bathroom. I turned on the shower and in the bathroom removed my bra and panties and told him I want you clean from head to toe.

We got in the shower and I took soap and a bath towel and washed him from head to toe. He looked at me with the look I had last time... amazement. He took the bath cloth away from me and soap and washed me down as well. When we got out the shower I dried him off he took the towel from me and said I want you wet, go lay on the bed. I laid on the bed and once again he mentioned lay on your stomach, so I did. He took the towel and dried me off, he got up and left the room. Part of me wanted to get up to see what he was doing, but another part of me said no Harminme, just wait. As he walked back in the room he turned off the lights leaving only the light from the bathroom as a guide for sight.

He said, we are going to play a game, I'm going to place 5 objects on your back and you have to guess what they are. I will give you three chances to guess each object. I asked and what happens if I get them wrong he leaned over and whispered in my ear...a spanking and you have to drink a shot. The first object he placed on my back was wet so I said water, he said close but no so I said gin and he said yes. The second object was soft and tickled and I'm what in the world did I see in this house that fits this.

35

So my first guess was his hair brush, no he said, that's not it. My second guess was a cotton ball, he said no, so with final guess I just gave in because nothing came to mind. I turned on my side and in his hand was a feather.

I laughed and asked where in the fuck, did you get a feather, and he replied not everything in this house is out in the open. So I took a shot of gin which was nasty. On to the third object which was heavy, cold, and hard. I laughed with my first response which was is it your dick. He said your funny and that answer counts as one, my second guess was a hand weight, he replied no, you have one more guess, so I'm going through my mind like what in the world could this object be I said a cup of gin, he said wrong time to drink. I turned to my side and the object in his hand was a gun. I replied I hope that shit is unload, he opened it up and there were no bullets.

The fourth object was a warm liquid like substance, and my first guess was hot chocolate syrup. Tony replied no, your next guess, my next guess was pancake syrup, nope he replied last chance, so I gave in and just said hand me the shot when I turned on my side he had a bottle of honey. I'm like really you couldn't have given me that one, I was in the ball park. So I turned back on my stomach for the fifth and final object which was soft, and light weight, thinking could he be tricking me and this be a feather again. My first guess I did say a feather, he laughed and said no I wasn't going be that predictable. My second guess was again with the cotton ball he said nope, at this point I was like fuck it I'll take the shot I turned to my side took the shot and in his hand was a rose. My heart damn near stop.

This man was creative and sweet wow…I leaned forward and kiss him. I took the rose out his hand and laid it on the night stand and we had sex and this time it was with such passion. My body wanted him 100% and took him all in without a fight or any hesitation. Tony and I working together being in an intimate relationship made work fun and dangerous. There was a black female manager named Carla who I was really close with, a lot of employees thought she was mean and bitch but to me, she was stern and hardcore and wanted to be like her one day but at the same time Carla did not seem happy and had little to no love life. Carla was all work and no play I admit on the outside looking in she seemed lonely but she was an attractive black woman.

There was also the head manager that Tony had issues with named Howard. Howard was a white male as well but unlike Tony Howard was a bit of tight ass and in my opinion a little racist. Tony and Howard were where night and day. It wasn't long being in a small town that my mother caught word of Tony and I having "relations". My mother really didn't seem to mind the relationship and her asking around found that Tony actually really only dated black girls and had a baby on the way with one. My mother made a comment Tony obviously like black girls with big asses because his future baby momma has a big ass as well. I wasn't sure to be freaked out or flattered my mom was taking a POSITIVE interest in my sex life. But part of me knew the way Tony approached me it wasn't his first time in the chocolate factory.

Tension started to build at work among the three managers and I needed a break from this small town so for a few weeks during the summer I went to Camp Lejeune where my father was currently stationed. I went and stayed with my father and his wife and 4 kids. While I was there I worked at a bacon factory with my stepmother and Golden Corral. While staying with my father I made an attempt to go see Devin at a prison they moved him to which was about 2 to 3 hours away but when I got there was unable to see him due to the strict dress code where shorts were not allowed. I later wrote him to let him know I had drove up to see him and he mentioned one of the guards had let him know I had come. I was so ready to go back home, the environment here was never peaceful with HER 4 kids and my father and stepmother ALWAYS arguing about something or nothing. On the outside looking in I viewed this a loveless marriage with no purpose.

My senior year was approaching and I knew what I wanted to do but with my mother who offered little support to my dreams didn't seem as though my dreams would come true. My mother did reach out to a family member who happened to have his own recording studio in his home and made a phone call for him and I to meet. My mother took me over to his place over the weekend Larry was his name. I was so excited to finally be recording one of my songs the song I wanted to do for Devin but with my mother being there I ending up changing the second verse since I didn't want to sing the original lyrics that was "at night I dream of you and all the nasty things I want to do", so I changed it to "at night I dream of you and all the things I know will interest you."

Once the song was recorded I sent it to a nearby college "Elizabeth City State University" where I received a phone call from one of the engineers with access to the recording studio on campus and Larry and I rerecorded the song. I was so proud of the song. That experience got me back into writing music again. I got my job back at the restaurant seeing I was one of the best workers there I knew a spot for me would always be saved. When I returned Tony was still there but not happy, he was actually looking for another job since him and the other managers were always getting into it. It was about 3 weeks later and I was on the schedule to work and the manager scheduled for the shift was Tony but when I got to work he was not there. I asked Carla where Tony was and thought he was the closing manager for tonight, she mentioned Tony was fired.

I was floored like damn, what the hell happened. I waited till break and called Tony from a payphone. I mentioned to him I heard he was fired he said yes over some bullshit. He mentioned after I got off work to come by and so I did. When I arrived Tony was on his second bottle of vodka when I walk through the door he was all over me. I put my hands up to his chest and firmly pushed him back. He asked what's wrong, I said nothing but I want to know what happened. He mentioned Howard had opened up the restaurant on Tuesday morning and found in the middle of the floor a pile of ketchup and mustard, he called him and said he was fired.

Tony and I both knew if any ketchup and mustard was found on the floor than Howard put it there, and since Carla wasn't a big fan of Tony she wasn't going to stand up for him. I took the drink out of Tony's hand and walked him to the bedroom, I took off the tank top and gym shorts he had on. He laid on the bed and I undressed myself and began to kiss him starting from neck down to his inner thighs and then I sucked the top head of his dick and slowly worked it all the way in my mouth. I could hear him breathing deeply and exhaling I could feel all his stress and tension going away with every stroke of his dick up and down in my mouth.

After about 10 minutes I came up to his neck and whispered in his ear asking if he enjoyed that he turned his head and said yes very much, I continued to stoke his dick with my hand laying my head on his chest until he came. I got up went to the bathroom and got a washcloth to wipe him down. He got up turned off the lights, turned on the radio and we laid in bed together naked in the dark listening to music till we both fell asleep. The next morning, I headed home while I was pulling in Jerome was outside and saw me. When I got out the car Jerome came up to me with a hug and asked how I was doing. I mentioned I was fine and living life day by day.

He asked so where you coming from so early, I laughed and said now, now Jerome, you're overstepping. (**Song: Here we go again**). Evening though Jerome and I were no longer sexually involved he always seemed to make a point to stop and talk to me and pass on some wisdom. Things at home were still tense since Nick seem to always want to make small talk and wanted to know about my sexual partners. My mother apparently told him about the white guy Tony, my mother being at work and I was down in the living room watching t.v. he made a comment so you moved on to white guys now. I looked at him like why the fuck you care. He held up his hands like no offense just was asking.

Later on in the week Tony calls me and wants me to come over because he has something he wants to tell me. In the back of my mind I had an idea of what it was but wanted to hear it from him. On Friday night I headed over to Tony's place he had order some Chinese food and we sat on the couch and watch television and talked. He tells me he is leaving and wanted me to know, I told him I figured that was what it was, and I understand. This small time has little to no opportunities and as soon as I graduate I'm leaving as well. He asked me where I was going and I said the military will be my best escape plan, maybe be a Marine like my father. Tony laughed said Marine hu, I said yes, I love their uniforms.

Tony and I then had sex which lasted longer than usually maybe because we knew this could very well be the last time. Saturday morning and throughout the day I pretty much hung out at the apartment complex and socialized with the neighbors. Linda who happened to be pregnant with Kurt's baby hung out with my as well with the other neighbors and went back and forth to the playground. Jerome was working on maintenance calls and while me and Linda was on the swing set came over and spoke he asked what I was doing later on tonight I said nothing planned at the moment he mentioned good I want to see you, I smiled and said sure Jerome.

I took my mother's car and picked Jerome up down the street we headed to the waterfront downtown where we sat and talked. He wanted to know what my plans were after I graduated and I told him I was thinking about the military, he looked surprised he mentioned he was in the Army for a few years and enjoyed his time in. He asked why the military, I said it's the best escape plan really and what is it you are running from. I'm not sure how I was going to respond so I just sat in silence then Jerome turned my head and said Harminme what or who are you running from. I put my head down and closed my eyes then when I opened them they were filled with tears.

I grab the door handle and got out the car. I started walking quickly towards the walking pier and Jerome quickly ran up behind me and grabbing me by the waist and pinning me to the pier, trapping me in between his arms and body. I had no way to escape. He looked into my eyes and said I am here for you, please tell me what you are crying about. I took a deep breath and asked could you let me go first I need some breathing room, he said ok but if you run I will catch you. I walked over to the bench and Jerome sat next to me. Looking down on the ground I said my mother's boyfriend touches me.

Jerome stood up and got in front of me and said, touches you how, in what way. I said he touches my butt, my breast, and makes comments that are sexually in nature. After I said it I felt a huge weight that was somewhat lifted off me, Jerome with his back against me was silent with his hands gripping the pier. He turns back around and asks how long has this been going on. I said since I was 15. Jerome then asks, dose your mother know?

I quickly stood up and said NO!! Why not he asked, I said because my mother loves this man. Jerome replied, so what more than you, I mean you are her daughter, I'm sure she loves you more. When he made that statement, I didn't give it much thought at the time, I just replied with I don't want to hurt her, and this would hurt her.

Jerome just took me in his arms and held me tightly, I almost couldn't breathe. That night I laid in my bed going over the conversation Jerome and I had earlier. I had a sense of relief that I finally told someone about Nick and I also was glad it was Jerome. If I had told Devin even though he is locked up for armed robbery, I know if I told him about Nick touching me, there would have been a murder. A few days had past and one day when getting off the bus I saw Jerome out on the grounds just watching me as usually. I went into the apartment and my mother was sitting on the couch, I didn't think anything of it so I headed upstairs. My mother called me half way up the stairs so I turned around.

She asked, do me and you need to talk about something. First thought that came to mind was, well I didn't skip school today so couldn't be that. I replied no, not that I can think of. She asked, did you tell Jerome something a few days ago about Nick. I felt sick to my stomach, OH MY GOD HE DIDN'T. I took a seat on the couch across from my mother and with my heart racing said, yes I told Jerome something about Nick. My mother asked, what did you tell him, so many thoughts were racing through my head and was like maybe I should just lie and say Jerome was jealous or angry with me and he made a story up. I didn't because this was the time for my mother to know the kind of man Nick REALLY IS. **(Song: Child Molester)**.

I told her that Nick touches me, when she's not home and has sexual conversations about what I do with other guys. She asked, it touches you how, I said sexually on my butt, breast, hand on my thighs and when in my nightclothes. She asked how long has this been going on, I said since I was 15, so for over 3 years you let this go on. I looked at her with dismay like, what do you mean I let this go on. The tears started to flow and she says I know me and you never really got along but I would never thought you would tell a lie like this, and on a GOOD MAN. I couldn't believe my ears did she just call me a liar. She stated what a grown man like him would want with a child, when he can have any woman out here. In my mind I was thinking "less mileage" but figured this was not the time for one of my smart remarks.

She asked why I told Jerome the Maintenance Man. I told her me and him are friends. She said a friend you having sex with, I said no, but we were in a sexual relationship at one time. My mother replied isn't he the same age as Nick, I said no... actually Jerome is older than Nick. A switch in me went off, here I was this whole time holding things in to protect my mother's feelings and I see now she could have cared less about mine. I wanted that mother instinct to protect her child to kick in but instead I saw a desperate woman before me, who would rather have the love and acceptance of a man or should I say child molester than the love and respect of her daughter.

I couldn't find ANY words yet created to described this hurt, hate, and lost I felt for this WOMAN who I no longer saw as a MOTHER... it was then I knew what it meant to be a motherless child, I always thought of that phrase as a mother in death but really it's a female with no soul to nutrient or protect a child SHE GAVE LIFE TO. The night seemed so long like it would never end and the sun would not come to bring a new day. I wasn't angry at Jerome for telling my mother but now the walls in this apartment seemed to be closing in and felt even more trapped and this time no safety net. I felt like Devin, both of us serving time in prison.

The next day in school I could not focus and did not want to go "home" ever. When I got off the bus Jerome was in front of the apartment complex waiting for me. He asked if we could meet later and talk. I said yeah, meet me at the playground when you get off. I met Jerome at the playground a little after 5pm. I was waiting on the swing set, he came over and sat next to me. He asked if my mother mentioned anything to me. I looked at him and with sarcasm, and said do you mean the fact she said how I let this go on for years, and what would a man like Nick want with a child. Jerome looked at me with disbelief and I said yeah, I know that look, what happened to a mother wanting to protect her child.

The tears started to come and Jerome wiped them from my cheek. He apologized because he just knew the outcome of this situation would be different. Yeah, I said, so did I. He asked me what was I was going to do, I laughed and said really, part of me wants to kill her. He then looked at me and said you don't mean that, I said no Jerome that's where you're wrong I do, I want to get a knife and cut her throat, silence her the way he silenced me for all those years. I felt I needed to be rescued and no sound came out, for I wanted to spare hurting the mother I hated and love. I made myself endure the touch and company of a predator. I guess deep down even though my mother and I had a complicated relationship I loved her beyond the hate of my existence. Wishing to be dead so she would have a life of no regrets...

A month had past and pretending to act as if things were somewhat "normal" again eased the ability to go "home" and sleep. I figured Nick would keep his distance from me since I could tell by the way he no longer looked at me or came into my room, my mother must of said something to him. I was downstairs watching t.v. one day when he came home from work. I figured him to walk upstairs or pass by me without acknowledging I was there but he stopped in the living room and asked if I had a minute. The first thought that came to mind was what in the world would he need to say to me after a month. I looked at him and said yes, Nick what is it.

He sat on the same couch as me with a cushion between us. He said "your mother told me about what you said I did, and to be honest I thought you and I had something special. I thought you and I could have our own little secret, I see I was wrong, and I see now I can't trust you." I can truly say it was the will of God that prevented me from going into the kitchen and pulling a knife out on him. I was thinking, no, DEATH would be too easy, too simple, and escape not to one day answer for what he had done. With me being 18 years old I could be tried as an adult. He had already taken my freedom internally, he won't take it externally as well. I sat there until he finished and continued watching t.v. as if the conversation 10 minutes ago never happened.

I was thinking like wow this muthafucker got some nerve blaming me, trying to make me feel ashamed. He absolutely had **NO REMORSE** for his thoughts or actions. The hate and angry I felt towards my mother and Nick turned into strength and determination to get the fuck out this house when I graduated in May. It was around November and December I started prepping for my escape, I wanted to join the military since this was likely my best chance of freedom. My mother was talking about moving into HIS house in another county and I was like REALLY if he would do what he did to me under her roof, there's no telling what he would feel he's entitled to do under his.

I first talked with my father about joining the military since he was in the Marines. He asked me what branch I was considering I said, the Marines like you. He smiled, and then said "Harminme, I have worked side by side with many women in the Marines, and knowing you I think the Navy, Air Force, or possible Army may be better". I asked him why he thought that he said most women he has come across in the Marines are not happy being in the Marines and are not as "feminine", and we do a lot of physical training. So I took the ASVAB test to try to join the Air Force, but to join the Air Force you had to score on the ASVAB a 40 or 41 where in the Navy and Army you just needed a 33.

After multiple attempts of trying to get a high enough score for the Air Force with no success I looked now towards the Navy or Army. I ended up around March of the next year choosing to go with the Navy, they were actually on a back log on entry so it would be the beginning of next year before I could join. I graduated in May and continued to work at the fast food place until it was time for me to join the Navy. I received a phone call from my recruiter one day and she mentioned there was an opening for me if I wanted to leave before next year. I was so excited to hear that and I asked when I would be able to leave. She said I could leave as soon as November which was only a couple months away. When I got home I was so excited I told my mother the news.

She seemed shocked at first, then I was like yeah, I'm really leaving. She then asked when, I replied November 15th. She replied before Thanksgiving, they didn't have a time you can leave after the holidays. I looked at her and the thought that crossed my mind was really I figured you would be happy with me leaving. I just said no and headed to my room. My mother and Nick drove me to Norfolk where I was supposed to catch my flight to attend boot camp. When I arrived I went to the building to check in and was told my plane was down for parts and it would be a few days before I could fly out. I was then given the option to go back home with my family for those few days or stay at the barracks till the plane was ready.

Without, even looking at my mother, I told the man I wanted to stay here at the barracks until the plane was fixed. My mother asked Harminme are you sure? She offered to bring me back, I said no, I'll stay here. So, the man gave me paperwork to fill out and directions to the barracks I would be staying. I got out the vehicle and said goodbye and my mother stopped me and said "Harminme I know we had our differences but I want you to know I love you" and she gave me a hug. In that moment my heart felt as though it skipped a beat, and I wondered did she really mean it or was it the proper thing to say due to the situation and occurrence of events.

Even though her words had a brief moment of impact, my heart had harden and soul tainted from years of mental and physical abuse, I suffered from being HER child. I waited in the barracks until it was time for me to leave, I then saw a part of the Navy that made me wonder what the hell!!! They put me in the barracks where the pregnant female sailors were assigned to a ship but could not go out to sea because of their condition. I listened to their stories on how they been in the military for 3 or 5 years on sea duty and have NEVER been out to sea. They apparently had a system to where a few months before the ship was scheduled to go out they would become pregnant.

Some girls were on baby number 3 or 4 and others would abort while the ship was underway and say they miscarried. I was like wow these bitches are stupid and crazy, then I was like is sea duty that fucking bad to risk a life changing event of 18 plus years for something that is temporary and will only last 6 months. I wasn't sure what these women home story was but for me home would be where ever the Navy sent me, for there is no REAL HOME for me to go to. The time came for me to final leave and I was so happy and at the same time scared but I was starting a new chapter in my life where not knowing what to expect was more hopeful then knowing the outcome of my life by not joining the military.

Boot camp for the Navy was in Great Lakes, Illinois and when I first arrived I was like wow this is going to be intense. They pretty much strip you down to nothing erasing all which identified you as you. There was no privacy in boot camp, you showered and went to the bathroom in front of other females and a boot camp shower was run the water, turn it off, soap up, rinse off and get out. Boot camp was an environment where they would use lack of sleep and a lot of exercise to weaken you. It was the process of elimination and I saw females breakdown they just couldn't hack it and they were either held back or sent home. I really didn't feel pity for most since the journey of this 8 week trail just started.

During the short sleepless nights and the nights on watch, out in the freezing cold with a foot of snow on the ground I would think about the life I finally escaped from and wondered about the life that lies ahead. In my thoughts, I wondered with my mother planning to move in with Nick, if he would make a move on my sister, but really unlike me she wasn't a bastard child and she had her REAL father in her life, so I'm sure Nick wouldn't risk being confronted with a Marine who wouldn't hesitate I'm sure to cause bodily damage. My sister was also my mother's meal ticket in many ways so if there was one daughter she would rather give up I knew it would be me.

In week 4 of boot camp things started to become easier since most of us got in line with the routine of things. We were "rewarded" with free time, longer showers, being able to buy hair products, and make up. In the last week of training we had a running course where we had different stations where we had a task to complete at each station in order to graduate. I knew it was going to be the hardest exercise that I encounter while here, fortunately the gas chamber was broken so THANK GOD FOR THAT. I hate running and I had under a mile to go before my legs became heavy, my breathing was hard to grasp, and my will almost gone. I could hear the other girls in my unit cheering me on but really it wasn't helping and I wanted to stop.

I walked for a minute or so and this inner voice was talking to me saying Harminme do you really want to crawl back home to your mother and Nick as a failure. You know your mother is likely depending on you to fail so you can come crawling back and have nowhere else to go and no one else to depend on but her. You will not give that woman the upper hand in your failure. It was then in that moment I started back running even though my feet and legs felt numb,I felt light as if I was being carried... After that event I wanted to sleep for 2 days. To celebrate our victory we had steak and lobster for chow. The next ending phase in our exiting of boot camp was the ceremony and the assignment of orders to where we would be stationed.

It was 2 days before we were to leave and one by one we were called into the office and told where you would be stationed. A lot of the girls were scared of being assigned to a ship but my thought was bitches this is the Navy. I for one did not care where I was going because I knew it wasn't back to North Carolina. About 2 weeks prior we all actually filled out what is called a "wish list" of the places we would like to go. I put down Texas, Florida, and Hawaii yes all places that were HOT as hell since I hated the cold. My name was called and I jumped up trying to keep my composure, when I walked in the office all 3 unit chiefs were present.

I took a seat and waited, I was handed a piece of paper and a sticky note that said Iceland. I just stared at the paper for about 30 seconds and one of the unit Chiefs asked is something wrong. I was like YEAH, what happened to Texas, Florida, and Hawaii. They told me that based on your family status such as whether we had any children or not, played a part in what orders were given. They stated anyone with children depending on what coast they were on east or west were placed state side in that coast. Any females in the unit that did not have children were all given orders overseas. They tried to smooth me over by saying that Iceland is actually warm and Greenland is actually cold, and that the locals switched the names to keep down outsiders.

I left out of the office still in shock. I mean damn I wanted to get away from my mother but not that far. What's the saying "be careful what you ask for, because you just might get it". While I was sitting on the deck thinking, one of the Instructor came out and said Oh I forgot to tell you the drinking age in Iceland is 20...after hearing that I smiled and said well if that's the law there, I must obey and we both started laughing. Before going to our new command we were offered leave to go wherever before checking in. I only had one place to go which was back home. I was going to ask if I could show up early but decided since I was going to be so far away to go ahead and fly back home.

I flew into Norfolk International Airport and from there rented a car and drove home. I got in late so when I arrived everyone was asleep. I went to my old bedroom and laid down and in no time I fell asleep. The next morning, I woke up to Nick, my mother, and sister Danielle. Nick made a comment that him and my mother had a bet going on whether or not I would make it through boot camp. Nick mentioned he bet I would make it and my mother had bet on me failing. I smiled but in my head I was thinking yeah I knew she would. Those 2 weeks back home my mother and them treated me like I wasn't even there, they went on with their lives like normal.

I ran into Jerome who seemed happier than anyone to see me. I told him I had orders to Iceland, he laughed and then said you and cold weather I know you're dreading that. He asked if I would pack him up take him with me. The day had finally came to take my flight to Iceland. It was a military aircraft I was flying on and while on flight I came to find out the perks of flying on a military aircraft overseas was free alcoholic drinks. That was great, since this was actually a LONG ass flight at least I could get my drink on. After waking up from a semi-international hangover I heard the military pilot over the intercom saying 30 miles out arrival at Keflavik Iceland.

When I arrived I had two representatives there from the department I was going to be assigned to, which must have been a small department since one of the people who came to welcome me was a Chief. I was thinking I'm sure a Chief had something better to do than pick up new comers on a Saturday morning. I checked into the barracks which the set up was nice. There was two people to a room with a wall dividing the sleeping area with a shared bathroom and cooking area. My roommate was a white girl with red hair named Mindy. She was very outgoing while unpacking she introduced herself and ask where I was from and what I would be doing. I told her I was from North Carolina and apparently I would be working out of the career counselor office.

With excitement she said Oh my God how in the world did you land that position, what's your rate I mentioned I was an Airman. She stated well you lucked out because that is a great position to be and you are right next door to the Commanding Officer of the base. She invited me to go out with her and her friends to the base club. I wasn't really a club person and quickly said no, she said come on you should get out and meet people it will make your time go much quicker here, and believe me that was something I wanted. I went to the club with her and her friends that night which was packed it was a small base and it felt like everyone was there. The base also opened up the club to the locals so there were a lot of Icelandic there but mostly girls which was no surprise.

The music was split up in the club to appeal to most types, there was country on one side and R&B and hip hop on the other. I actually bounced back and forth between both sides as that's what my roommate did. I stayed close to her for about 45 minutes then I stayed on the R&B and hip hop side where I sat at the bar and order rum and cokes and long island ice teas. There were a few guys who came over and spoke and as soon as the conversation began, they asked can I take you home or in this case back to my barracks. I quickly shot them down and said thanks, but I'm not interested. It was about 1:00am when I found my roommate and told her I was headed back to the room, she said ok I'll see you later.

Though there were taxis outside the club to take people to their destination I walked since it wasn't that far. On Monday I reported to my department at the career counselor office, there I met the people I would be working with which was the Chief that picked me up at the terminal and a Senior Chief who was not only black but fine as hell. I was like Oh shit but luckily he was married so it brought the temptation down some... Senior Chief Watson was his name and he was the first black Senior Chief I seen since being in the Navy and he had a gold tooth; I'm like he apparently must have been "hood" back in his day. My job consisted of helping undesignated sailors like myself who did not have a job specialty help place them with a job specialty they were interested in.

Working at the career counselor office I came into contact with a lot of people on the base since we also were responsible for awards and promotions of all personnel on the base. One day while working I met Stacey who was stationed here with her kids which I had no idea people could bring their family here but apparently so. We chat while she waited to see Senior Chief Watson and hit it off. She invited me over to her home Friday night to hang out. Friday night arrived and Stacey and I had a couple of drinks, we sat back and talked about life, men, and sex. It was fun having girl talk even though Stacey was a woman in her early 40s she didn't seem to mind I was 20 and there was a 20 something year age gap.

Spending the next several months with Stacey I came to know her and her boys which were some of the best well manner kids I have ever seen. Stacey did not play with them; her disciplinary actions were hardcore and old fashion, sometimes I would come by and they both would be standing in a corner holding weights or I would come by and they are stripped down butt naked getting their ass whooped, I can also recall her making them do push-ups. I admire Stacey she was raising men, not boys. The boys and I became close they called me Aunt Mica and when Stacey had a date I would babysit them. I spent more time at Stacey's than at the barracks.

One night while at the base club with my roommate, I felt like my mind was playing tricks on me. There was a man in the club who looked EXACTLY like Devin. I watched this man for hours, I wasn't the only one aware of his good looks because he had women all around him. I don't know what came over me but the bull in me came out and I got possessive while he was out on the dance floor I made it a point to dance as close to him as possible. Even in a dark night club my ass, and I mean literally could be spotted. Dancing side by side with other people around us I saw an opening and quickly took occupancy. Now me and this man who had the face and body of the man I LOVED was face to face and I was going to make him mine.

A slow song came on and I was like damn, I hate slow dancing but when I stopped to walk away this man I now made a target had grab me by my waist and pulled me to him. I felt so weak and so emotional in that moment. I had danced with my back to him pretty much till the end of the song because slow dancing to me was really intimate and though I wanted to be intimate with this man I just met my body tensed up being sooooo close to him. It was close to the time for the club to close and I asked one of the guys I saw this man talking to what was his name and where is he stationed. He mentioned he was part of the deployment (squadron crew).

The command in Iceland had a rotation of every 6 months where a squadron would come in and help with command operations. He mentioned this squadron had about 2 months left before the new squadron came in. I was like damn, which means I don't have much time to work with, there was a designated barracks that the squadron was put in and after the club made sure I would be there. Luckily the squadron crew after the club went to the barracks and went to the breakroom to play pool or watch t.v. this guy whose name was Damon was in the breakroom as well sitting on the couch by himself; finally I caught a break and had him all to myself.

I sat next to him and he smiled because he knew I was the girl from the club. He made a comment that he was like are you stalking me, I quickly said YES, YES I AM. I told him why I was stalking him and how he looked just like the man I was in love with but at the moment was in prison. He said really, so what is it you want me to do to fill this void, I smiled and said something that he can't do at the moment. So we exchanged phone numbers and throughout the week we talked on the phone because I did want to know a little something about this man before having sex with him. He mentioned he was from Georgia and he was married with 4 kids when he said that I got real quite on the other end.

He picked up on the change in the flow of the conversation and asked if something was wrong. I took a deep breath and said no...I mean part of me figured this man as good looking as he was had to be in a relationship with either a girlfriend or wife. I guess part of me was wishing more of a girlfriend but it really did not matter since he was just a substitution to me and not the REAL DEVIN. I said wow that's a lot of kids, what do you have; he mentioned he had 3 girls and 1 boy He stated his wife had the 3 girls from a previous marriage and the little boy was his. After talking on the phone during the week we made plans to meet at the club Friday night.

OMG Friday night couldn't get here quick enough, I had talked with my roommate earlier in the week as well to get her plans and to let her know I would have someone coming over and she mentioned, no problem I got you. At the club Friday night Damon was there with his girl groupies but I knew tonight he would be in my bed. That night at the club I was with Stacey off and on and on the dance floor. I actually tried to keep my distance from Damon just so later on that night would be a little more special. Damon a course noticed I was distancing myself I had no idea where he came from because I was on the dance floor and he was nowhere around, and then all of a sudden, I felt someone dancing behind me and whispering in my ear, why you running.

I smiled knowing exactly who it was. I didn't turn around I just continued dancing and he grabbed my hips and pulled me closer to him. There I was sandwich in between two men and the one Damon who was behind me was the one I wanted on top of me. When the song ended the guy in front of me left and I turned around to face Damon, I finally answer him and said I'm not running just enjoying you from a distance. He said are you ready for me tonight, I smiled and said yes very much so. The club was closing and he mentioned to give him a half an hour and he would meet me in my room. I got to the room and quickly took a shower and pulled out the condoms.

Damon knocked on the door a half hour later and I let him in dressed in my night top. We sat on the bed and he went in to kiss me, I pushed him away and put my head down. He asked was something wrong. I told him, I don't mind kissing but no tongue I DON'T kiss in the mouth. He just looked at me like really, he then asked why. I told him I don't like it and it's too personal, but really the reason I don't kiss in the mouth it's the thought of sharing salvia with someone turned me off. So we just kiss with no tongue, and we started taking off each other's clothes. In my mind he was Devin and therefore I wanted him so bad my body temperature was rising.

He got down to his underwear and laid on the bed. I had just my panties on while he played with my breast. I leaned across him kissing his lips, his neck, and his chest, down to his rock hard abs. I then took off his underwear, OMG!!!! I rubbed his penis a few minutes and I'm thinking Devin must have come across a voodoo doctor while locked up and told him any man I come across that looks like him I want to fuck make his penis small as hell. I know Damon could tell by the look on my face that I was really trying to conceal that I was somewhat puzzled. He said if you suck it, it will get bigger, holding my comments inside I was thinking dude my name could be Ms. Hoover and I couldn't get this up.

I swallowed my pride and took a deep breath like I was diving in a pool of water and began sucking his dick. It was soooooo awkward because I was used to being able to grab a man's dick with one or both hands and stroke it up and down. This man here I had to use my index and thumb to hold his dick. My lips were bigger than his dick and when sucking it I thinking like wow it would even reach all the way in my mouth and I feel like I'm with a little boy right now and not a grown ass man. He got up a little which was no improvement and he was ready to perform. I was like damn, these magnum condoms I brought is going to fall off.

Luckily he also had condoms on him which was a relief. He put the condom on and got on top of me and proceeded or should I say attempt to fuck me. The lights were off expect for the t.v. and lamp. As he was pumping away like he was really doing something I put on an academy performance and did some low moaning because I really didn't want to hurt his ego and tell him, sweetie you still in the entry way, you haven't even stepped foot in the house. I'm thinking his wife either cheated on him or used a turkey baster to get that boy unless his "soldiers" can jump without a diving board. He was breathing hard and laid on top on me like he just had a hardcore gym workout. I went in my mind to my favorite movie and recalled the phase "how did he die... on top of me." (The Color Purple).

As soon as he left I called my girl Stacey and told her about what the hell just happened. Stacey was on the other end of the phone cracking up laughing so hard she was crying. I on the other hand was mad and disappointed as hell but hearing Stacey laughing on the other end I too started to burst out in laughter. The only upside to this and I mean that literally was he would being leaving in about 6 weeks and things would not be awkward when I see him around the base or club. I actually avoid his phone calls and going to the club which was really the only thing to do on base for fun. I'm pretty sure he got the hint by week 4 of not returning his calls.

Working in the career counselor office I always hear information ahead of the rest of the base and an order came through that the deployment squadron was leaving early and this week would be their last week. I was so relived and decided I was going to the base club that weekend even if Damon was going to be there since obviously this was going to be his last weekend of me seeing him anyway. I called Stacey and told her the news and we were going out to the club that weekend. When the weekend came everyone at the club was on extra high mode for seeing the squadron crew off. I did see Damon and Damon saw me, he asked for one last dance I said sure dancing close to him this time I had a big smile on my face because I was thinking sometimes there are small things in big packages and this one was being returned to sender.

One day I got a phone call from Stacey asking if I could go to the house and wait on Z-man; which was a nickname for her youngest son. Come to find out Christin had got into some kind of trouble at school. When she arrived home with Christin she went off on him, I mean like I never seen before. I actually intervene with this session which is something I never had done before but I could tell there was something deeper and the anger that was coming out of Stacey was scary. I yelled to Christin go to your room and I grab Stacey by the arms and said what did he do that was so bad. Stacey looked and me and said he hit a girl; I was waiting for more but there wasn't that was all she said.

I looked at her and asked he's a little boy that what they do. She started to cry and I just held her, and started crying too even though I had no clue what I was crying about, I just knew she was in pain. After the moment of embrace we both walked over to the couch, I put the t.v. on mute and just waited till she was ready to talk. She mentioned when she was married to the boys' father, he took her through some things. He was very abusive and had beat on her, talk down to her, and even when she was pregnant with Z-man pushed her down the stairs. She mentioned he would force himself on her sexually and the boys were all witness to this physical and mental abuse.

She mentioned when she heard about Christin hitting a girl that she went off because she doesn't want her boys turning out like their father. I understood where all this pain and angry was coming from now but explained to her this was not the way to prevent it. I told Stacey that she was an amazing woman and mother and how her boys have the upmost respect for her, but if she was to continue to raise them by the sins of their father she could very well be creating the environment and behavior she is so determine to erase. I saw that Stacey needed a release and took her to the base club for dancing and some drinks.

Stacey and I were on the dance floor dancing up a storm, I took a break and headed to the ladies' room, while I was in there two other girls entered. They were local girls from off base who came for some fun and drinks. One girl sparked up a conversation with me and stated I had lovely skin, I said thank you and she saw me on the dance floor and mentioned I could dance, I thanked her again for the compliment and said see you later and left out. I headed to the bar and ordered a run and coke for me and a long island ice tea for Stacey. I went out on the dance floor again and about an hour later headed to the ladies room. While washing my hands the same girl from before comes in and I looked at her and smile and said she said hi and as I was turning off the water she gave me a paper towel.

She asked me if I was here with my boyfriend I said no, I don't have a boyfriend. She moved in closer and said I like you, and said she wanted to meet up later after the club. I admit I may have a buzz going but I know when someone's trying to pick me up. I smiled and she rubbed my face and I slowly pushed back. This chick total caught me off guard I mean I know how to derail a man from coming on to me but NEVER a girl. I told her I am flattered but I am here with someone and she said you have a girlfriend, I paused and said yeah_____ that's right I already have a girlfriend and she's waiting on the dance floor for me. Stacey was standing at the bar talking to some guy.

I quickly walked over to her, not looking back and when I got to the bar I told her what happened in the bathroom and to play along we are "GIRLFRIENDS". After Stacey finished laughing her ass off for about 2 minutes she said ok. She introduced me to Don we spoke briefly and he asked me to dance, I said sure and we went on to the dance. The girl from the bathroom was still lurking but I just made sure homegirl wasn't in a close dancing proximity to try to get a feel up on a sister. That night after the club Don and I exchanged phone numbers and made plans to meet up next Friday at Stacey's place.

Don and I had talked on the phone throughout the week before meeting up at Stacey's place on Friday. The conversation on the phone with him flowed and I enjoyed the conversations we had. Friday came and Don and his buddy Lopez came over to Stacey's. We hung out at Stacey's talking, playing cards, drinking and eating. We headed to the base club around 2200. At the club we continued drinking and Don and I tore up the dance floor. Don's friend Lopez was trying to holla at Stacey but she wasn't feeling him. After the club Stacey heads home and Don accompanied me to my room in the barracks where we laid on the bed, he goes in to kiss me and I put my hand up and push him back and told him my spill about how I don't kiss in the mouth.

Don commented that kissing was something intimate and something he enjoyed doing. I told him I felt tongue kissing was awkward and I don't like how it feels. Don stated who ever I kissed before must not have been doing it right and wanted me try to it with him. So I attempted it and just like I said...I don't like it. So we fondled around with one another's bodies and this time my hand went quickly down his pants because I was not about to waste my time trying to make a dime out of less than five cents. Luckily Don had a nickel and two pennies to work with so his dick would make it pass the "entrance way".

Don had a lot of female associates on base but I didn't care, he made me feel important, which is all that mattered. After about a month of carrying on with Don one of his female associates was in the career counselor office one day when I came back from lunch waiting to see Senior Chief Watson. She spoke and said hi and I said hi as well. She mentioned seeing me and Don at the club the other night dancing and noticed we had left together, she mentioned they used to talk a few months back but broke up due to issues with his wife. Trying to hold back the eagerness of response to the word wife I asked what do you mean what happened with his wife.

She then went on to tell me he was living with his wife and son on the base and she was in the Navy as well. I said well Don and I are good friends so I have no issues of him having a wife (but REALLY I did). As soon as this bitch left, I called Don from the office and told him to stop by my room when he got off. I was pacing the floor back and forth looking at the clock waiting for the knock on the door. My roommate was gone which was perfect since I'm sure there was about to be some heavy cursing going on. The knock I was so eagerly waiting for had finally came, Don walked in and I was looking out the window and soon as he entered the room I turned around and said, you got a wife.

With no hesitation he replies yes, AND, I looked like what the fuck you mean AND. Why didn't you tell me that your family was stationed here with you? He told me to calm down and things are not as what they seem. He mentioned yes, his wife and son was here but they were going through a separation, he then went on to say before they took orders here they were stationed in Florida and talked about getting a divorce after taking orders to Keflavik. He mentioned she was seeing other people as well, and thou they live together they were sleeping in separate beds and maintained a cordial relationship for their son.

I heard him, but still didn't see why he couldn't have told me this a month ago. I felt as though if he could hide this whether intentionally or not then he could be hiding other things as well. As the weeks went on and time with Don was consistent I didn't even think about his wife and son living here on the base, that was until one day her ass showed up to the career counselor office. I knew who she was because Don had mentioned her name on several phone calls they had and not many women on the base had the last name of Freeman. She looked nothing like I would have pictured Don's wife to look. She looked and talked like a man, there was no lady likeness to her other than the fact she had tits and I'm thinking a vagina...let me find out this muthafucker on "that crying game".

The reason Ms. Freeman was in the office was pertaining to her next duty station. Apparently she was leaving in less than 2 months and was heading back to Florida. She mentioned her husband Don was also going to Florida too but to a different base. One thing I quickly learned about the military and being stationed on short term duty is people come and go out your life very quickly. I had fun with Don but the trust in him was dead and buried, I would go on with our last months together just riding the clock and his dick till the final take off.

The day had come for Don to leave, he was leaving early in morning and we hung out the night before at Stacey's place where we had a party with some people from the base. There was an older guy there that was all over Stacey named Greg, who I for some reason did not like. In the morning before Don's flight he stopped by my room and we said our goodbyes, he knew I wasn't a morning person and wasn't about to get out of bed and get dress to see him off at the terminal. When he left I laid in bed thinking wow first Damon, then Don, and then next Stacey she was due to leave in 3 months. My birthday was approaching and I figured I would take a flight to North Carolina to visit my family. Stacey offered to join me and I said yes, I would love that but be forewarned this is a small town with very little to entertainment other than fishing and going out to eat.

I had called my mother and informed her I was bringing a friend and her two boys, she was fine with that. On the flight we had laughs, drinks, and told life stories. She opened up more to me about her abusive husband and how she was thankful to get away without something happening to her and the boys, because the time she lived with him figured each day would be her last. We landed in Virginia and purchased a car rental so that I could drive the rest of the way to North Carolina. When we arrived my mother was the only one at home, my sister was over a friend's house and Nick at work at the shipyard.

The boys were still trier from the trip so they took a nap while Stacey and I drove around town and I strolled down memory lane. It was Monday morning and my sister Danielle was getting ready for school and I was heading to the bathroom and noticed she was throwing up, at first I thought nothing of it until I noticed her throwing up every day that whole week. On the day before we left I told mentioned to my mother that I think Danielle is pregnant she just looked at me and said WHAT, no Danielle is not pregnant. I was like really because she has been throwing up all this week before going to school and wearing bagging clothes or her coat to cover up her stomach.

My mother went in on me like I was just trying to start trouble intentionally. She still saw me as an outsider to her home and took NOTHING I said to be truthful. I decided to let it go and this was not my battle to fight because in several short months Danielle will show what I have spoken into existence. The plane ride back to Iceland was not as fun as the ride there, even though the free alcohol did ease my mind somewhat I still had this overwhelming hatred for my mother not loving me and protecting me like I wanted, like I needed and even years later still sharing a bed and living a life loving a man who touched me in ways no MAN should be touching A CHILD.

Once back in Iceland my personal life had change from me not being intimate with anyone since the clock was starting to count down for me as well I didn't want to start something new. We had a ceremony in the career counselor office for Senior Chief Watson for being promoted to Master Chief. After the ceremony was over Master Chief Watson called me into his office to talk about my career plans while in the Navy. I told him I was interested in something administrative and fun and I was actually interested in several career options but since hanging around Stacey I wanted to give being an Aircraft Controller a try. Master Chief Watson set it up where I would do some job shadowing with the Air Traffic Controllers (ACs).

Stacey and I were friends and now working side by side. We had lunch and sometimes dinner together, I also kept the boys while she and Greg would go out. I kept my distance from Greg because it was just something about him that had me on guard. Greg was way too friendly with the ladies and Stacey just didn't see it as being a problem and I did. I also did not like the way Greg looked at me like he was thinking about fucking me in the back of his mind. Stacey and I actually got into an argument about

Greg when I went to the terminal one morning to pick up a new check in I saw him at the terminal with a girl and they seemed really close. I told Stacey about it and asked her specifically not to say ANYTHING to Greg especially with Stacey leaving in 3 weeks I didn't feel the need; but as a friend I wanted to her a heads up.

I had to admit I did have another motive for telling Stacey and that was loyalty. A week had passed since I told Stacey about Greg and the girl at the terminal and with Stacey and the boys having only 2 weeks left before her transfer to Texas felt we would cross the finish line. Stacey, Greg, and I headed to the base club Saturday night to make sure Stacey had a good time before leaving in 2 weeks. I was at the bar with a drink and Greg had came up and sat next to me, I looked at him and smiled and continued drinking. He touched my hand and I looked at him, he said Stacey had told him about what I saw at the terminal with him and the girl being close. I pulled my hand away I said...really, nice to see where her loyalty lies.

Stacey was lit up that night and though I was disappointed I had an overwhelming angry inside me as well. I was silent the rest of the night while watching Stacey dance and carry on and Greg hugging and kissing all over her. I decided not to go in on her due to the fact I wanted her ass sober and remember everything I had to say. The next day Stacey called me she could tell by my lack of conversation on the phone something was off. My entry moment of attack finally came when she asked me, what was wrong. I said why you crossed me and tell Greg about me seeing him at the terminal. She laughed it off and mentioned Greg said the girl I saw him with was just friend nothing more.

I told her that was not the point; the point was you keeping your word and promise to me and not putting a man before your best friend. She of course tried to downplay what she did and I couldn't get her to see things from my perceptive just like she couldn't get me to see it from hers. The call ended with me wishing her and the boys the best but our friendship was official over and hung up. Stacey did try calling back several times but I wouldn't pick up the phone. Things were more tense when she would come by the terminal where I was doing my job shadowing with the ACs and just ignored her and she would speak I just said good morning or good afternoon and kept it rolling.

The time had finally came for Stacey and the boys to take flight and leave Iceland for good. I was sadden that I wasn't able to say goodbye to the boys because they were like nephews to me but the bull that I am couldn't see past RED, couldn't see past the betrayal. The damage my mother had done had left me scarred and I promised myself to not tolerate a woman who puts a man before me. **(Song: Hello to tomorrow).** Now I was alone in Iceland with no romantic partner or best friend for distractions I focused on my time leaving this place which was under 90 days and Master Chief Watson with his connections got me into A-school for Air traffic controllers out of Pensacola Florida. While at the base club that weekend I went with my new roommate just to show her where she would likely be spending most of her free time.

At the base club it felt so unfamiliar since the majority of the people I knew had left. I was at the bar when a girl that use to hang around Don had approached me, she spoke and I spoke as well. The topic of Don came up and she asked if Don and I were in a sexual relationship. I looked at her with a bit of confusion and asked her why she was asking me this question. She mentioned her and Don were together and when she would ask him about our relationship he would mentioned we were just friends. I really didn't see the point of bringing this shit up now since Don was long gone; but I told her the truth and yes Don and I were sexually involved.

She stated "I knew it" I could tell how you two acted around one another and how you two danced on the dance floor something more than friendship was there. I couldn't put my finger on it that night but could tell the deceit bothered her more than it bothered me. We actually started to hang out after that night at the club we had lunch together and got to know a little bit about each other. During a dinner date we had she had opened up to me about why she needed to know the truth about Don and I and what she had been through with him. She mentioned when Don left she reached out to him to let him know she was pregnant; as soon as she said that I put my fork down and stopped eating.

I asked her when did this happened she mentioned she found out a few weeks after Don had left and she called to tell him and he was so emotionless about the whole situation. She said he told her, he didn't want another child and I can do what I wanted to do but he wasn't going to be in the picture. I really felt bad for her and she had stated besides the pregnancy that Don had given her gonorrhea. I was like OMG she got quiet for a minute and she was like you didn't catch it. I told her NO, besides Don and I NEVER had unprotected sex. She stated wow you were fortunate. I said I guess but the truth is I never loved Don and my heart belongs to another.

I explained how the man I truly loved was in prison and it's not my intentions to be IN LOVE with anyone but him. My time had finally came to depart this volcanic rock and head to A-school in Pensacola Florida for Air Traffic Controller. I was just happy to be somewhere hot for a change. The A-school for Air Traffic controller was about 5 months long. I found a group of guys I was in class with and we hit if off like we knew one another for years. We would joke and laugh and hang out together going out to eat and walking the base. I did meet a guy while in A-school who was more than a buddy and I gave him the spill like all the others about not looking for a committed relationship and my heart belonged to another.

I was doing pretty well in A-school until towards the end where we were learning about precision approach radar (PAR). I struggled with it and the instruction was talking about holding me back to retake the course. I didn't like that idea and wanted to graduate with my class but it was made clear the choice really wasn't up to me. I'm sure it was God's doing but for some unknown reason the Commander of the base got word of my situation and called me into his office and the conversation went like Harminme Love where do you want your naval career to go from here and take being an Air Traffic Controller off the table.

I told him there was another rate I wanted to be other than Air Traffic Controller but I couldn't get it because the rate was overmanned and they weren't taking any more people, so that's why I choice AC. He asked what rate I was referring to and I mentioned AZ (Aviation Administrator). He stated "yeah that rate is closed but let me see what I can do". I left the office thinking what other job I could see myself doing in the Navy or was I going to be an undesignated Airman forever. Four days had passed before I heard back from the Commanding Officer. He once again called me into his office, my heart was racing waiting to hear what news he had for me.

He was still on the phone when I was directed in his office, and from the sound of the conversation it had something to do with a report date to an A-school. When he hung up the phone he looked at me and smiled and said, "I have some great news, I made a few calls and I got you in the AZ A-school in Meridian Mississippi and you leave next week. I was so astonished I was at a loss for words and just kept saying thank you Sir, I will be the best AZ I possible can I won't let you down. He smiled and stated "I Know you will be a great AZ". As the days counted down for me to leave, I read up and studied the job description of being an Aviation Administrator (AZ).

I ended up driving from Pensacola, FL to Meridian MS which wasn't far. This was my first time in Mississippi and even though I had been hard on my home state of North Carolina, I would choose North Carolina over Mississippi each and every time. This place had an eeriness to it where safety was always a concern on and off the base. My class was small with about 12 people and there was only 2 females in the class me being one and another black female. I studied hard during the week and on the weekends I would drive to Biloxi Mississippi where there was an all you can eat seafood buffet and gambling. I made sure I left when it was light out and was back on base before dark; because even if the police pulled me over I still wouldn't feel like I was out of harm's way.

The racism in Mississippi was like the passing of a category 5 hurricane storm, you prepare and brace for the worst hoping when it's over you'll recover and be alive in one piece with some sanity still intact. Mississippi was a place where you didn't SEE ghosts but you FELT SPIRITS... The AZ A-school was 8 weeks long and I was so ready for my time here to be over. The only reason I can say I was glad, that I did visit Mississippi, was so I know NOT to come back. I studied hard to stay among the top of my class not only because I was fortunate and appreciative to be here but students got to choose their orders based on their GPA. It was week of the final test which was a big part of our GPA and the instructor had the list of orders our class was to choose from.

That night I could hardly sleep waiting for tomorrow to come and find out where I was going next. The next day we all waited patiently in our seats while the instructor wrote our names on the board. The instructor then handed us a piece of paper faced down and mentioned not to turn it over until instructed to do so. I turned my paper over and saw my GPA of 91.9 ranked 4 out of 11; we started with 12 but one guy got kicked out for behavior issues. So with being ranked number 4 in the class I got to choose 4th for orders. As each student chose the location where they wanted to go the instructor wrote it next to their name on the board.

The first person chose Virginia, the second person chose Texas, and the third person chose California. It was my turn and looking at the list I knew right away where I wanted to go and that was either Texas, Florida, or Hawaii again looking for somewhere hot. I ended up choosing Florida, Mayport to be exact. I was so excited to being stationed in Florida, my command was a helicopter squadron HSL-40. I will start by saying not too much occurred here at this command. I had a GREAT chain of command a caring and supportive Master Chief and a wise Lieutenant. There was another black female AZ I worked with and we for the most part got along and were even good friends until she pissed me off then she became just a co-worker.

This job was very important and I took it very seriously because the AZs were responsible for ensuring all the maintenance and inspections were done on all aircraft for a safe flight. My direct Supervisor Robert was a black male from Alabama, he was an AZ2 married with no kids and owned a dog. My Master Chief Franco was cool he took Toni and I the other black female AZ under his wing and kept the peace whenever she and I would get into it he would sit us down to talk things out. He had a cookout over his house one holiday weekend and Toni and I were invited. His wife mentioned she felt like she knew Toni and I already since Master Chief Franco had talked so highly of us.

There was also an older woman at the command that I hung out with named Diana she lived off base with her husband and son. She invited me over to her house one night for dinner and drinks, she opened up to me about her marriage and the issues she faced with him. I saw a picture of Diana and her husband and will say he was fine. She told stories of how her husband had cheated on her several times with several women, she mentioned behind his cheating she had contacted several sexually transmitted diseases even while she was pregnant. I stood up like WHAT, why the hell you still with this sorry man, and she said because "I have known him all my life since high school and I love him, really love him".

I told her I understood having a long history with someone and told her about my love Devin who is currently in prison and how I was in love with him. I told her even love has its limits, your husband has made a fool out of you and has put you and your unborn child in harm way not once, not twice but several times. This man has obviously lost his love and respect for you and by you staying about after his lying and cheating he know he has trapped you in some way. I love Devin but I'll be damned if I tolerate him disrespecting and cheating on me bringing lies and diseases. It's one thing to be a cheat but to be a cheat and careless is a heartless man I won't share my bed, body, or life with.

I found it kind of strange I was a 22 year old telling almost a 30 year old woman how a man should be treating her. I'm sure by age standards this conversation is supposed to be the other way around. Needless to say I didn't spend much time with Diana because she definitely was not the female role model I wanted or needed in my life or career. She was a sweet lady and I pray that God would bring a good man into her life but like I've heard many times in my life, in order to receive what God has for you, there are times you must let something go. I kept a neutral relationship with Toni and Diana for the sake of the chain of command being we all had to work together.

I received a phone call from my father, which was a little strange since I didn't really talk or reach out to my family that often I figured someone must had died. He mentioned my sister Danielle had a baby, I stated yeah I knew she was pregnant when I went home last year, I'm just little surprise I'm just now getting a call and getting it from you, did my mother not want to face me and deal with the fact she was wrong. My father didn't comment I guess he knew it wouldn't do any good since I was right. Danielle having a baby had no effect on me since my sister and I were never close to begin with. Seeing the baby was born in December and it is almost June the information was bleak.

After about 9 months of living in the barracks I decided I wanted to live off base. My lieutenant tried to talk me out of it saying why go from living in the barracks where I didn't have to pay rent, cable, and light bill. I mentioned I'm not a teenager anymore and I wanted to see if I could handle the responsibilities of adulthood. I had put in my request to move off base and with the final approval from my Commanding Officer I went looking for an apartment. I found an apartment complex about 10 minutes from the base and moved in. I had money saved up to buy furniture which Florida was filled of flea markets so I got a good deal.

While, dropping Toni off at the base one weekend from hanging out shopping, I stop for something to eat on base. I'm not sure why I chose to go in verses going through the drive-thru but I did. While eating a guy at another table caught my attention since he was staring at me like I was on the menu. When we made eye contact I just smiled and turned away letting him know pretty much this was NOT an invite to come over. Well, this mutherjumper didn't catch my settle jester and when I turned back around he was standing in front of my table. He spoke and introduced himself his name was Marcus and he was stationed on the Cole ship which was in the area for about 2 weeks for repairs.

He asked to sit down, not wanting to be mean to a fellow sailor I said yes. He asked if I was married or had a boyfriend, I was like damn, you get right to the point don't you. Marcus just laughed and said yes I don't just stop and talk to girls at random but there is something about you. I laughed and asked is that your pick up line. We talked for over an hour and he asked if I wanted to leave and spend the rest of the day or night with him. Since, I had nothing to do I took Mr. Marcus up on his offer. We went to the mall, and the movies I dropped him back off at the base about 2200 hours and we made plans to hang out again, we exchanged phone numbers and that was how the night ended.

During the week we would meet up for lunch and talk about family and our naval career. He was from Alabama and was an AD which was an Aviation Machinist Mate. He had one child and was not married, and planned to stay in the Navy till retirement. I told him I wasn't sure of my plans yet but so far I am enjoying what the Navy has to offer. Marcus and I spent over a week together and when we met up for lunch one day he stated the ship was almost fixed and he would be leaving in 3 days. I replied I'm was happy that the ship would be fixed and I did enjoy our time together. With Marcus leaving part of me was like I'm sure he wants to have sex with me before he leaves and though I am not one for one nighters I again was single and had that right.

I actually waited the day before he left to seduce him just in case he ended up being another Damon I wouldn't have to deal with the awkwardness the next day. When we started to have sex he was so eager like he hadn't had sex or seen pussy in years. Thinking back to one of many conversations he did mention being out to sea for months before pulling into Florida. I grabbed a hold of him and told him to slow down a bit, we have 8 hours before you to go back to the ship. I then rolled him over to his back and took off his pants, where I proceed to exam the dick. He passed the hand test so he was sure to make it in.

I felt in that moment like I was having an outer body experience, I mean I really wasn't into it maybe because I was doing it out of the sake of doing it but not really wanting it. While, Marcus was exploring my body I was staring up at the ceiling and my thoughts just drifted away. I was thinking about how it was a good idea that the health department in my hometown decided during a pap smear to hang up an attractive man on the ceiling to take your mind off being examined and was thinking what man would I have on the ceiling at this moment and though I missed and loved Devin I pictured my fantasy husband K. Sweat. This is the second time having inattentive sex and I must say I was glad when it was over. He asked did I cum I said "no" but that is normal for me it takes A LOT for me to cum; so don't feel bad.

I drove him back to the ship and we said our goodbyes, he wanted to exchange information such as my address so he could write but I mentioned I don't think that will be necessary. I went back to focusing on work and studying as well since the second class AZ test was coming up soon. When the test results came back I found out I made it, I was a Second Class Petty Officer AZ2; Toni had made it as well and AZ2 Robert had made first class we celebrated at AZ1 Robert's place where he had a cookout, he was also celebrating his recent separation from his wife and we had drinks, laughs, a good time and Toni and I went home. I've heard as you get promoted that things can get competitive.

The way Toni was acting towards me I sense a change in her like I was now more of a threat. I not only noticed it but Master Chief Franco as well and we were assigned to different shifts. I ended up on the midnight shift which I didn't mind since I was more of a night owl and not a morning person. My Lieutenant called me in his office one morning before leaving off my shift and stated I would be coming up for orders soon and I needed to reenlist if I wanted to be able to go anywhere else because if I decided not to reenlist than I would finish out my time here due to it being more cost effective for the Navy. I told him I did want to reenlist and he mentioned I would have to do so within the next 3 months.

With my enlistment within weeks away a thought came to mind, why not just have my father reenlist me, a father and daughter reenlistment him in his marine uniform and me in my Navy dress whites. I called my father and told him my idea he was thrilled and onboard with doing the ceremony. My reenlistment event was emotional and history making, since no one had ever had a father and daughter reenlistment done at that command before who were both serving in the military. My father and stepmother stayed the night over at my apartment which my father compliment the place. In the morning, I got up and cooked breakfast for them before they headed back to their home, they were arguing about something which is always the case, these two were like oil and vinegar but still hanging on to "I do".

The time had finally come for me to choose my orders, I put down Spain, Texas, and Hawaii. After about a month of waiting my Lieutenant had called me in his office and mentioned I had orders cut. I was so excited but still wondering where would I be going next. He said AZ2, you are going to Atsugi, Japan; I just looked at him like did he just say Japan hummm that wasn't on my list. He mentioned that even though we (sailors) are asked to write down where we would want to go the end result is what the needs of the Navy. I started to cry because I was not happy with this selection my Lieutenant tried comforting me by telling me his experience when he was stationed in Japan.

He mentioned that I had orders to CAG staff CVW-5 which when not out to see with the ship which was the U.S.S. Kitty Hawk we would be working out of Atsugi base, you get COLA and it counts as sea duty which each rate had a sea and land duty rotation. I tried to bring myself to terms with it but all I could think about was waiting on my first flight to Iceland where I waited in the barrack with the girls who got pregnant to avoid this very type of tour. I was like yes, now I see why but the pros still does not outweigh the cons trading 18 years of the rest of your life for 2 years. I told myself, this is God's plan and everything happens for a reason and I need to suck it up.

As the weeks went on I did extensive research about Japan, the culture, food, language, and travel system, since they drove on the opposite side of the road compared to the U.S. One night during my shift AZ1 Robert came in and was doing some back up and downloads to the system, he called me in the office and we were talking and out of the blue, Robert stated he was interested in me and had been fantasizing about me for a while even more now since his separation. He wanted to know if I wouldn't mind if he come over one night and make these fantasy of his come true. I smiled and was kind of flattered I didn't give him an answer right away, instead I asked him if I could think about it and get back with him. He agreed.

I knew my answer the first week since Robert asked but I decided to let him wait two weeks. While exchanging shifts on Friday morning I told Robert he could stop by tonight if still interested. Robert smiled and said yes he then asked why it take so long, I replied because I want you to see how much you wanted it by watching you wait. He stated he would be by at 2000, ok I said; 2000 came around and so did Robert right on time. We started the night watching t.v. on the couch and he started touching my breast, I then turned my attention to him and started kissing him he unfasten my pants and started to fingering me. I unbutton and unzip his pants and started to stroke his dick, and yes he passed the hand test.

There was heated tension and passion between us that I hadn't felt in a while with a man. He was kissing on my neck and just when things were able to get real turnt up he throws his head back and said I'm sorry. I said "what" he repeated again I'm sorry, I said "what for" he stated I came, I looked down and there was sperm dripping all over my hand. I looked at him and he replied I am so embarrassed I just really wanted you, I got over excited. I'm thinking this mutherjumper here done got the oven all hot and he can't put nothing in it, HELL NAW. I just smiled and told him "it was ok maybe next time", but I knew in my mind there was not about to be a next time.

My sex life was really sorry in my 20s compared to my teenage years. Can't get a dick with the right size, stamina, or performance and toys were not an option for me because I only take the real thing. Luckily things were not too awkward at work since when Robert was coming on I was getting off. My Lieutenant called me in his office one morning while getting off my shift, he mentioned he had received a phone call from Japan and they wanted to know if I would come early due to them going out to sea. Part of me wanted to say HELL NAW since I didn't want to go there in the first place but I knew either way I was going to Japan so might as well be a team player and fulfill the needs of the mission, so I said yes.

They wanted me to report to Japan next month so I had little time to play with. I ended up giving away and selling most of my household goods and gave my car (Gea) to my father. Once again I looked forward to the benefits of flying international in a military aircraft FREE ALL YOU CAN DRINK ALCOHOL. Just like Iceland I really wasn't looking forward to being in Japan knowing most of my shopping would be online because I was sure they wouldn't have stores there to fit this fat ass. When I landed in Japan there was someone there to greet me from my command, I checked in at the front desk at the barracks where they gave me a key to my room.

When I entered my room there was a couple sleeping in what should have been my bed. The girl stood up and asked who I was I stated, I am AZ2 Love the new AZ for CVW-5, she stated she was sorry and that she thought I wasn't supposed to be here until 2 more months. I smiled and said nope they wanted me to report early. This chick which was a Yeoman YN3 third class decided her and her boyfriend was just going to shack up in my room till I arrived. Looks like the honeymoon suite is no longer vacant. She asked if I would give her a few days to move all her stuff out I smiled and said no problem. I shared rooms with her used to be and about to be again roommate which was also an YN3.

Jennifer was the girl I was sharing a room with, until, Rhonda the high yellow chick sleeping and fucking in my bed moved her stuff back. The first week I did the regular check in around the base along with orientation. I had to attend a driving course since in Japan they drive on the opposite side from the U.S. I also had to learn the traffic signs and we took a trip off base and rode on the train, which I have to say this was my first time ever on a train and even though I was sure Japan had a lot to offer and see their train system was too confusing for me and this would most likely be my first and last time on a train while here, unless of course I'm with someone who knows where they hell their going and how to get there.

Rhonda had inform me while we upstairs in administrative office where her and Jennifer worked that she would be all moved out today. I said ok no problem, I spent most of my night that night unpacking and getting settled in MY ROOM. I actually didn't unpack a lot since we were due to go out to sea in about 3 weeks. One day while leaving out to walk the base I happened to be walking out the same time as Rhonda I spoke and said hi she didn't reply back, I just bushed it off and went on my way. A few days after this incident I spoke again and she didn't speak so part of me was like ok I need to find out what's up because I didn't nothing to this chick.

I said umm Rhonda are you ok, she turned to me and said I'm fine. Ok because when I speak to you I noticed you don't speak back did I do something, and why in the world did I ask. This trick went off talking about, I don't need to speak to her outside of work we are not friends and I don't like you. I smiled then laughed and said ok YN3 Jackson no problem, I turned to open my door and that's when I heard her say "you bitch" I thank God she had entered the room and was half way into mine because she was 3 seconds away from meeting my alter ago who would of pinned a bitch up against the wall and ripped out that good hair on her pretty little head.

The next day at work I went to my new Chief, Chief Mantas and told him what happened, he then called her chief and we all meet upstairs behind closed doors. She admitted to calling me a bitch and yelling and me being senior over her the Chiefs asked if I wanted a formal write up on her. It took everything I had good and decent in me to say no, I stated I'm sure I just caught YN3 Jackson on a bad day and I'm sure I won't have any issues from here this day forward. I held my head up high and walked out with my chief. As we were walking away Chief Mantas stated you better than me I would have had that ass written up. I just smiled but in my mind, I was thinking that bitch better not be walking alone somewhere on or off base and I be in one of MY MOODS...for there will be scars.

Jennifer approached after work and told me she heard what happened and that Rhonda is a little stuck up and plus she thinks Rhonda was mad I showed up 2 months early and was kicked out the room. I laughed and wanted to say shit why the bitch mad at me for cock blocking, she needs to pass the advancement exam and make rank. I just told Jennifer I was sorry to hear that and hope she pass the YN2 exam next time around so she can get her own room.(**Song: Don't Hate on Me**). It was the day before leaving to go out to sea and tomorrow morning, we were to take a ride down to the ship and get settled in our berthing (sleeping) area.

I went to the office location and loved the fact when you stepped out and turned left you were right outside overlooking the sea. The first night on the ship was nerve wrecking I didn't know whether to be excited for the new experience or scared as hell to be surrounded by so much water. The female berthing area was underneath the catapult area on the ship, and for those of you that don't know what that is, it is the area the aircrafts launch from, it was so loud and there was a vibration for each launch. I'm like how in the hell are people supposed to sleep, the other females in the berthing area were like don't worry you won't hear it after a while because you will naturally block it out. After about 2 weeks, OMG they were right.

As the CAG AZ I received reports from all the squadrons so I got to know all the chiefs, Master Chiefs, and other AZs very quickly and they got to know me especially if their report was late, my Commander would get IN THAT ASS!!! My Commander was Dan Hunter and his last name suited him. My new Master Chief was a character as well I swear I think that man had something more in his coffee every morning besides sugar and cream. Being out to sea I had a lot of down at time after my morning reports were done and checking messages for any alerts and mission changes. I held a secret clearance so there was a lot of stuff I came across that people on a need to know bases were privileged to.

Being on the ship I was able to write Devin more often and I looked forward to his letters as well on the ship. For the female heads (bathrooms) the cleaning scheduled was altered every week between the squadrons. During your assigned week you had to make sure the bathrooms were stocked up on toilet paper, soap, clean the toilets, floors, sinks, and showers. It wasn't until I had to clean up behind other females that I found out how trifling females can be. One chick took a shit in the shower, I mean REALLY some of these bitches act like they were born in a barn somewhere, luckily that was not CAG 5 week to clean. Some people can be so vindictive.

We had been out to sea for about a month now and I was starting to get stir crazy and bored, the newsletters that the ship had were entertaining and I found out shit that went on that I really didn't want to know. For example, there was a cartoon showing an Officer heading back to his stateroom from working out and when he walked in he made a comment stating, I don't remember turning my lights out and when he hit the switch he yelled apparently there were two sailors making out in his bed, though that should be been funny as well, it won't because the two sailors were male...now if that had been a male Officer walking in on two female sailors going at it we would of never heard shit, because that twosome would of turned into a threesome J

There was another cartoon in the Kitty Hawk newsletter where all the squadrons where in a boat with paddles in their hands stroking back and forth except for one squadron and the message below read "do you feel like someone around here is not pulling their weight". This came from one of the squadrons aircrafts being down for an extended amount of time due to repairs, the shit was funny but at the same time my CAG Commander was PISSED and him and the Skipper (Captain of the ship) had words but really we are considered company on HIS SHIP sooooooooooooooooo really Commander Hunter had to suck it up.

Needless to say there was not only a tense relationship with the CAG Officer and the Ship's Commanding Officer but with the squadron sailors and ship sailors there were tension, mainly because when we pulled back in at homeport we got to get off the ship and only return when time to pull out again, soooooooooo yeap there was a bit of jealousy. Though the Kitty Hawk was my first ship, it really wasn't bad and she didn't breakdown too often... One day while getting cleaning supplies for the berthing area since it was CVW-5 week to clean I was pretty much accompanied by some guy who apparently noticed me a few days back and was searching the ship for me.

He wasn't the best looking fellow but he was kind and helpful and gave me extra supplies and even help carried them across the ship to the female berthing area. I asked him when and where he saw me, he stated he was standing in the chow line and when I walked passed I caught his eye. I said so you didn't see my name tag. He state my coat was covering the back of the pants showing my name but he remembered my hairstyle, umm so you saw me from behind and remembered my hairstyle. I rolled my eyes thinking yeah this nigga saw my fat ass and apparently got hard up. He asked what time I took lunch and if I would eat with him so we could get to know more about one another, I said sure because one thing learned about being on a ship having an SK (storekeeper) as a friend can be very beneficial...

He was an SK3, his name was Chris, and we had lunch and dinner together on the ship every day after we met for about two weeks. We were coming up on our first port in a few days and he wanted to spend time with me and take me out on a real date. Our first port was Hong Kong we pulled in at the Fenwick pier; on day one it just so happened Chris had first watch and would get off later that morning, so Jennifer and I hung out and got a hotel room together. I told her I was meeting up with Chris later and she made plans to hang out with another YN from one of the squadrons. Chris was supposed to get off watch at 1200 and was supposed to meet me at the hotel at 1400.

It was a little after 1600 and I haven't heard from Chris. I was about to head out the hotel room when the phone ranged it was Chris, he was down in the lobby. At this point I am heated because he is over two hours late. My plan was to let him wine and dine me and send him on his way. When we met up in the lobby he was just as upset as I was and he was telling me about his difficult journey trying to get here and the money he had to pay the taxi. I told him he could have took the ferry and he got even madder because yes, that would have been quicker and cheaper. We went out to eat and there was still tension from me for him being late and tension from him of paying almost $60 to get to the hotel.

I ordered a pasta dish and had two glasses of wine to try and ease my nerves. Chris ordered a drink and a sandwich he stated he was still too upset to eat. We had very little to say and conversations were not like the ones we would have on the ship. After we finished eating I asked him where he wanted to go to next, he mentioned he was tired and just wanted to head back to the hotel room. When we got back to the hotel room we sat on the bed and talked for a bit and then he made his move. I wasn't in a romantic mood but with all he been through today I figured sex would make it better...for him at least. With no hesitation I went for the dick to perform the hand test which is a routine and must for me after Damon, most women don't even see or feel the dick till a man is in and on top of them me NO, I need to plan an out or sorry but this won't be happening again speech.

Chris though eager he was gentle in undressing me and kissing my neck and breasts, a few minutes had passed and I couldn't wait any longer. I reached for one of the condoms on the night stand and handed it to him, he got undressed and put it on. When he first entered me I was like oh my God, he was so hard and big like he grew from the time I performed the hand test till actual penetration. He lasted about 10 minutes which I figured since he was so anxious it was likely going to be a brief encounter. He took the condom off and as I started to get dressed he grabbed me and said "NO I'm not done". I held back the smile but was also really shocked he grabbed a second condom and proceed to round two and this time he lasted longer.

I was sexually satisfied with Chris, he made an impression. The rest of the time out to sea hitting ports such as Guam, and Singapore we met up and went shopping, site seeing and getting a hotel room to have sex. On the trip back to Japan Chris and I still met up for lunch in the chow halls and I received extra supplies for the female berthing area. With less than a week out before hitting our homeport Chris asked how we were going to be when back home. I told him, this is not a relationship and you can fuck whoever you want when we pull back in, I don't belong to you. The look on his face I can tell he felt some kind of way about that statement but it was what it was sex nothing more.

I told Chris we can still hang out from time to time but my heart is spoken for and I love only one man. Chris would call me or email me daily, he asked to go out and there were some dates I would turn down, not wanting him to think we were exclusive, so I would tell him I had others dates even when I didn't. The dates we did go on Chris and I enjoyed each other both in and out the bed, he satisfied me I am not gonna lie but I had to keep it on a contract basis and stick to the agreement, this was not a commitment or a boyfriend/girlfriend relationship. I was a free agent and to prove it to myself I told myself I needed to start dating other people.

The ship had finally anchored in Yokosuka Japan Chris went his way and I went mine. He called that night wanting to see me, wanting to come to my room, I told him I was pretty tired and wanted to rest but we would get up in a few days. The next day I went to the stores on base and did a little shopping and I ran into another supply guy that would hook me up with supplies on the ship, him and Chris actually worked together just on different shifts. Ervin was his name and he was from Jamaica and I asked what he was doing on this end and mentioned he was visiting some friends from the squadron. He asked if I wanted to grab a bit to eat at the food court I said sure and afterwards we went shopping.

Ervin walked me to my barracks and he asked to take me out for brunch tomorrow at the E-club; I said yeah that sounds great The next day Ervin picked me up from the barracks and we walked to the E-club when we got there we ordered our drinks and then started to the buffet lay out. This was my first time coming here and I was really impressed with the food and service. We sat at the table and pretty much talked about work and relationships, then he asked a question that caught me sideways. He asked if I had fucked Chris, I paused for a moment and looked down at my plate then back up at him and said, what I do with Chris has nothing to do with you. I could tell he was not pleased with that answer but I really didn't give a damn.

Though I tried to go on like he didn't hit a nerve but he did. I tried to lessen it by thinking maybe it was a likely question since him and Chris did work in the same department on the ship together but at the same time really felt it was not his place especially on the first date. On the walk back to the barracks he asked to come up to my room, I really wanted this date to be over with but at the same time didn't want to come off as a bitch. When we got in the room a switch turned on in him and he couldn't keep his hands off me. I kept pushing him off letting him know I was not in the mood, then he took my hand and put it on his dick.

I looked down with an expression I was really trying to hold back. The print of his dick over his pants was like, this couldn't be real and this couldn't be him. I mean this dude wasn't nothing but sticks so skinny that the width of this thing was bigger than his leg, I had to see it. I unzipped his pants and all at one time I felt excitement, fear, and disbelief. This was the BIGGEST DICK I had even seen in my life like this shit belongs on a baby elephant. I asked him did you have a surgery of some type to enlarge your dick, he laughed and said no, this is all me. I asked him ok be real with me do you currently have a girlfriend.

He claimed he did not, but he did have one a month ago but they broke up, part of me was wanting to send her a get well card if she took all this. I just sat on the bed holding his dick with both hands since the other one was getting tired I kept stroking it, he was touching my breast and I knew what he wanted, but there was no way in HELL he was going up in me. I quickly stood up and told him, I can't have sex with you he stood up his pants fell down to his ankles and asked why. I told him, you have the biggest dick I ever seen and I know us women talk shit about men and wanting a man with a big dick but every woman has her limits and you have surpassed mine I mean even half your dick I may be able to take the length but the width is still...WOW!!!

Then he said "well, suppose I only put it half way in", yeah...like I'm going to trust you to commit to that. It took a few extra seconds but I eventually forced my hands to let go of this massive dick. Ervin pulled his pants up and I walked him to the door and told him, that we will have no need to see each other after today, Ervin asked why I said because it just wouldn't be any point of us hanging out knowing you want something I'm not just unable to give and it wouldn't be fair to you. He said he understood and left. I thought about him for weeks Ervin's big black, long, thick dick would cross my mind along with the women who have conquered or failed or women like me that just knew walking and peeing would be uncomfortable for a week or so.

While doing laundry one day in the barracks I caught the eye of Isaac. I had seen him a few times at work because he was attached to one of the squadrons under CAG-5 and also stayed a few doors down from me. We would speak and he was attractive but he a had feminine persona about him that made me think he couldn't dominate me in the bedroom, and to keep me in line and by your side your sex game must be well made. I kept him at a distance which for some reason drew him in even more. He would hand walk reports over to my office which was odd considered he was an AD and not an AZ which is who would normally bring me the reports if they were for some reason were unable to submit them electronically.

After about 3 weeks Isaac finally got up the nerve to ask me out I told him I wasn't looking for a relationship, he said that was fine he just wanted to be in my company. I am not one to turn down a free meal so I told him he could take me out to dinner on Friday. Since Isaac had a vehicle so he took me to dinner off base, we went to restaurant not far from the base and we ate and talked. He asked me, what seemed to be the number one question most men asked, and that was if I had a boyfriend. I told him like every man who asked that question before him, I'm in love with someone, in which I am unable to physically be with, and let's just leave it at that.

We talked about the military, family, and relationships; which again is the norm of conversation for most people on a date. He mentioned he was from Africa and his family moved to U.S. when he was a teenager and he has one brother and one sister. I told him I was from North Carolina and I moved back when my parents divorced when I was about 13 years old. I have one sister and 2 stepsisters and 2 stepbrothers which I really don't claim. My father is a Marine and so I traveled somewhat in my lifetime. He then asked about Chris and I since he had seen us on the ship hanging out together, I asked what about him, Isaac asked if we were a couple. I looked at him and told him to please refer back to the commit I made earlier about the man I'm in love with I am physically unable to be with at the moment.

He laughed and said wow you are forward and I said and you need not be overly concerned. I'm not looking for a boyfriend. The conversations from there on dealt with military and family. On the drive back he ask if I wanted to go anywhere else, I mean it's not like I am familiar with this country so, I really can't give you an answer to that. So we headed back to the base, from there we caught a movie and went back to the barracks. He walked me to my door which was really not necessary since he was only 3 doors down on the opposite end. I knew he was likely going to try and make a move, men are really predictable. I stood in front of the door and he said he had a good time, kissed my hand and went to his room.

During the week Isaac and I met up about every day for lunch at the food court and for dinner or to go to a restaurant whether it was on or off base. After 3 weeks of being well behaved, Isaac asked after a date on Friday to come in my room to tuck me in. I smiled and said; I'm old enough to put myself to bed. Isaac laughed and said well, can I make love to you before you go to sleep. I took a deep breath, he was good looking, and smelled good and part of me was like you can do this, have more than one sexual partner, hell men do it all the time!!! I opened the door and Isaac followed me in. I sat on the bed and Isaac sat at the desk. I asked are you waiting for an invitation, he got the hint and walked over to the bed.

He went to kiss me, I pulled back and said, and I gave my routine spill about how I don't kiss in the mouth, he said no problem. He seemed nervous so I didn't go in on him like I would normally do by performing the hand test. I let him go at his own pace which he was very solicitous and gentle. I started taking off my top and pant, he started kissing my breast, which is usually not a sensual area for me but when he sucked my nipples I could feel myself getting wet and my body temperature rising. Isaac kissed me down to my navel and began eating me, Oh my God, he was so into it and I was really surprised of how well he ate my pussy. He was down between my thighs for about 30 minutes and I was freaking climbing the walls, I wanted to yell out and believe me if I did this whole barracks would be at attention!!!

I couldn't take it anymore I opened the dresser and grab a condom and handed it to him and told him to put it on. He got undressed and put the condom on when I saw him dick and I was like, OMG another one slipped through. It wasn't as small as Damon's but after fucking Chris this poor fellow would be lost in this black hole. I was trying to be optimistic thinking he may have a few tricks up his sleeve, Isaac went in and my arousal gauge went down. I took a deep breath and while he was stroking away went for the lamp light because I did not want to see this. How in the world he eat me out like a buffet no hands and the utensil (dick) can't stay on the plate.

I swear this was like a WWF moment where I wanted to tag Chris in and let Isaac go on his way and say thank you for starting the engine but you can't drive. Luckily he came quickly. I sat up, and got dressed in my sleep wear, he got dress and I walked him to the door, we kissed and said goodnight. I felt bad because Isaac was really sweet and such a gentleman but not sure if he had it in him to be the aggressive lover I at times need. After that night Isaac blew up my phone, if it wasn't Chris it was him. Isaac had asked me out to a movie, I really didn't want to go but I could hear the eagerness in his voice.

Isaac and I went to the movies Friday and after there went to the bar on base where they were having a special event since it was a holiday weekend. We had a few drinks and socialized with people from base and the locals. Ervin was there and came over where Isaac and I were. We talked briefly and Isaac went to get me another drink. We left about midnight and headed back to the barracks, he walked me to my room waiting for another invite. I took pity and invited him in granted his dick got lost in the sauce, but he ate pussy like a professional. So best to have one pleasure meet out of the two.

Early the next morning, I got a phone call, thinking it was Isaac, but turned out to be Chris. He asked me what I was doing today and then asked me what I did last night, which I thought was strange but told him the truth that I had a date. He then asked, did you and Isaac have a good time. I stated really Chris, is this what this phone call is for 9 o clock in the freaking morning. Then I asked who told you, he said I have eyes on you, I know where you go and who you're with 24/7. Though pissed off I have to admit there was a slight attraction on the fact he was monitoring me. Chris mentioned he would be here within the hour, I said, I don't remember inviting you over, he just hung up.

I took a shower and got dressed, I laid across the bed watching t.v. waiting for Chris to show up, Saturday morning Chris arrives and we head off base, we ended up going to his cousin house which was about 15 minutes from the base. His cousin girlfriend was Japanese and they were expecting their first child. We sat at their home for about an hour and talked, Chris and his cousin spoke back and forth to each other in their own language, Chris was Nigerian.

His cousin asked if Chris and I were planning on a family in the near future, I laughed and said not likely. His cousin asked why, I said because it's not an option for us. The look on Chris face and the non-English conversations between them, I could tell Chris was directing his cousin to ask me certain questions about our relationship which I didn't want to discuss. Chris spoke on Devin and how I was in love with a criminal, I'm sure he knew it but that bitch hit a nerve. His cousin stated "my cousin,

I'm sure is better than a criminal". I smiled and said, no comment. Chris was talking down about Devin and I go up and went outside.

Chris after about a minute came outside where I was at, I told him I wanted to leave, and he looked me and said "no". I looked like, what this mutherjumper just say. I said again, I want to go, Chris leaned up against his car and, again I said no. I took a deep breath and said fuck you and started walking I got to the end of the road and I heard a car ramming the engine behind me and it was Chris. He pulled up beside me rolled down the window and told me to get in, I kept walking he said how you going to get back to the base, I yelled Japan do have taxicabs. He drove up the road and turned the car around streaking the tires he started speeding back my way, and while not moving out the way thinking to myself I know he ain't trying to run me over.

Chris swung the car around several feet in front of me, got out the car, grab me by the arms and pinned me up against the car, at this moment I was scared because looking at him, he was pissed. I didn't move or say anything, just looked at him, then he asked "why don't you love me"; tears filled my eyes even in this intense moment I couldn't lie to him. I replied "I love Devin". Chris released me and opened the car door, I sat down, while he returned to the driver's seat. We sat in silence for about 2 minutes and he reached for my hand and leaned in for a kiss. I kissed him back not wanting to upset him even more, because it was then I knew Chris had a temper.

He put the car in drive and we went off, my base was about 15 minutes away and when we passed the road leading to the gate, without turning to look at him, I asked where we are going! Chris with one hand on the wheel and other holding my hand, didn't say a word. In my mind, I'm asking is this son of a bitch about to kidnap me, hell I'm in an un-Americanized country with a black man who knows more of the Japanese language than I do. I needed to play this out smart and calmly, my second thought was I could jump out the car, if he wasn't holding my hand so tightly. After about 20 minutes into the drive I figured we must be heading to Yokosuka from the street signs.

We arrived at what I assumed was his apartment, he got out and I sat in the car, he went around and opened the door. I got out the car and he reached for my hand again, with a firm grip. We went into the building to the 6th floor and he opened the door to his apartment. I went in, sat on the couch waiting to see what was going to happen next. He asked if I wanted anything to drink, I turned my head away not responding, he walked over to me, got down on his knees, and gently with his hand turned my face around, my eyes closed and tears flowing, he wiped them away. He said, I'm not going to hurt you Harminme, I just want to talk.

He asked me again, if I wanted a drink, I answered no I'm fine. Chris stood up and went to the fridge and got a drink for himself. He sat on the coach across from me and for a few seconds just stared at me. He asked, what was it about Devin, I loved, I told him, Devin and I have a long history together, and people were always trying to break us apart, that in returned brought us closer together. I felt protected with Devin, even in the most dangerous of storms, I felt at ease. Devin, I know without a doubt loves me, and it's not in the words but I feel it inside my heart, inside my soul, there is a warmth, a fulfilment that loving him makes my life worth living, and giving my life for him would be worth taking. It makes the loneliness and emptiness that was once a part of me at bay, I belong to HIM because I know he belongs to ME. I hold this man heart in the palm of my hand, and when I look into his eyes; I see... and feel... HARMINEME.

Chris took a drink, and tears coming down his face, said, "Well I guess I will wait". It was an overwhelming and emotional moment, I stood up and walked over to Chris and wiped the tears from his face, and got down on my knees, and my alter ego came to surface. I spread his legs placing myself between them, and I kissed him on his lips, saying please let's not fight, don't make me choose, enjoy us now. I unbutton and unzipped his pants, and took off his shirt. I started kissing on his neck and licking his chest, I could feel his dick getting hard, I pulled his pants down, I started sucking his dick, and he laid his head back exhaling with relief and moaning with pleasure.

After about 10 minutes he raised his head, leaning forward and reaching down to take off his shoes. He grab several pillows and placed them on the floor, I took off my top and laid down while he took off my skirt and boots. He licked and sucked on my pussy for about 15 minutes, then I started begging for him to please put it in. I reached for the condom, he put it on and I could tell from the thrusting moves and him pushing my hands away he wanted me to feel him. I could tell that I had hurt him emotionally and physically from the way he was bearing into me. Chris was bigger than any of my past lovers and though we had sex many times before, it was tonight that I knew that my body truly had opened up to him that below the surface this pain he felt he wanted me to feel as well; I also felt gratification and was holding him, pulling him closer, deeper into me.

The next morning Chris took me back to Atsugi, he told me he would be back for me later tonight and he was heading over to his cousin's place to run some errands. Once in the room I took a shower and air dried on the bed. It was then I knew I had to let Isaac go, for Chris would surely be a problem for him. When I woke up, I called Isaac and told him that we could be friends but as far as having a sexual relationship, well that can be no more. Isaac wanted to know the reason, and I told him I was involved with someone here and I didn't want things to become complicate. He agreed to us being friends and that he was just a few steps away if I ever changed my mind. Chris called and mentioned he would be by to pick me around 2000 he said we were going to the club where his cousin works. Chris arrived on time at 2000 and I met him downstairs. It was about an hour drive to the location where his cousin worked. His cousin was a security guard at the club, Chris mentioned this was just one of the clubs he worked to and from time to time he would help out with security.

Chris and I were seated in one of the V.I.P. sections of the club overlooking the dancefloor. The club was playing R&B music so I felt right at home in some way and for a brief moment thought I was back in America till I seen all the Japanese girls on the dance floor. Chris whispered in my ear he had some business to take care of and that security was keeping an eye on me. If there was one thing I could say positive about Chris is that he never left me unattended even with him away from me. I stood for a few minutes listening and watching the crowd, there was a good blend of people black, white, and Japanese. I made my way down the stairs to the dancefloor and started dancing. Right away I was surrounded by men and surprisingly women too.

About the second song in I turned to see Chris standing in front of me. He stood there with a smile on his face and started to dance with me. He whispered in my ear you got moves, I laughed yes, this hips do amazingly in and out the bedroom. This was my first time seeing Chris dance as well and I was surprise to see, he could really move as well. The night consisted of me dancing and drinking, I had a good time with Chris, we left the club around an hour before closing and headed back to his place. I was tired but still I had to have him. Sex with Chris was good he was big and by no means never held back which at times he was overwhelming even for me but I always managed to make him come before gaining real control.

Things were going good, and we were preparing to go out to sea again. This time around at sea Chris and I took advantage of ever port. Chris mentioned he was up for orders, and was trying to stay in Japan, but we both knew that wish list the Navy tells you to fill out is just that and for the most part, you end up where the Navy needs you which is opposite of where you want to go. While out to sea the results came back for the advancement test and Chris made E-5, now he was an SK2 (storekeeper). The next month Chris got word his orders to stay in Japan was approved so he had another 2 years to stay in Japan. We both were happy and part of me sad since this was going to be our last cruise out together.

When the cruise was over Chris and I went back to our routine of hanging out together. One night while playing pool at Atsugi Isaac walked in and saw Chris and I playing pool. We made eye contact and he spoke then he approached Chris and they started talking. I tried not to ease drop but when you have two men before you that you had sex with talking you kind of wonder what they're talking about. It really didn't seem as though they were speaking in English, I mean Isaac was from Zimbabwe and Chris Nigeria, so it was hard for me to make out some things they were saying because of their accent. Isaac had left and Chris and I continued our game of pool. I couldn't resist so I asked Chris what him and Isaac talked about, he smiled and said you know just guy stuff.

I smiled slightly and just decided not to dig any further into because I didn't want Chris to get suspicious and start questioning me about Isaac because I wouldn't lie. It was back to the work week and just like any day during the week I would receive letters from Devin. I usually read Devin's letters right away but on this particular day at work was hectic so I didn't get a chance. When I returned to the barracks I opened the letter from Devin, I stopped reading after the first paragraph and just laid on the bed in complete disbelief of what he wrote. He wrote that he wanted to hold off from mentioning anything but he was up for early parole and would hopefully be out in a few weeks.

My heart dropped I was excited and somewhat sad because now, I knew I had to tell Chris. Later on that night Chris called to check on me and see how my day went. I didn't mentioned the letter Devin had wrote and figured it would be best to tell him the news face to face. Friday night Chris and I went out to eat at one of our favorite spots off base, I figured this would be a good time to let him know about Devin's early release. When we got to the restaurant there was Isaac there with his date, I was praying Isaac would not invite us to join them. So much for that, because he did and I quickly turned the invitation down and told him Chris and I had some things to talk about and maybe next time.

Chris just gave me a look but, agreed to what I stated. I chose a table on the opposite end of the restaurant from where Isaac and his date was. Even though I was trying to act "normal" Chris picked up on how usually quiet I was. He asked me was there something wrong, I stated not really... he asked what is not really. I told him I got some news today that I need to tell you, Chris stopped eating and gave me his full attention. I said I received a letter earlier in the week from Devin and there a chance he will be getting out early. Chris just leaned back in his chair and asked what's early, I said in a few weeks.

There was a dead silence for a few moments, and he stated you must happy, you been waiting on him for 5 years. I thought of how I would response to his statement, and I said yeah, 5 years and I am happy he is getting out. He told me, he loved me and even though I didn't love him back he wanted me to be happy. I knew he was hurt, but he can't say I wasn't up front with him about where my heart was. I cared a lot for Chris and if Devin wasn't in the picture I'm sure I could love him, but Devin has always been in the picture, from the age of 15 to now at 23 Devin from behind bars had my heart and soul locked in there with him. Though, my body roamed free from man to man, none could take something in me and from me Devin had in his possession.

From the restaurant Chris and I went to Yokosuka Base to the base club, when we got out the car he gave me the keys and told me I would be driving later on tonight, I knew then his ass was about to drink the pain away. In the club there were a lot of people from the ship, along with Ervin who wasted no time approaching me. Chris was already at the bar ordering drinks, Ervin with a smile on his face saw who I with and made a sly comment stating, so I take it you found a man with the right size, one you can handle. I replied back with, and the reason your ass is here by yourself is because homegirl in the ER, couldn't walk. He busted out laughing saying I was a trip and quick on the draw, yes so I've been told.

Ervin and I hugged and laughed it up, Chris came where we were, Ervin and Chris spoke briefly and I found a table to sit and people watch. Chris was talking with a few of the guys from the ship catching up on old times seeing he no longer was attached to the ship and was on shore duty. I headed to the dance floor, in my own world not really paying attention to those dancing around me, though I should of. There was a guy behind me and his dick was hard, I tried to move and he would just grab my waste and pull me back on him after like the third time I just turned around to see who he was, I just shook my head, muther fucking Ervin!!! I didn't go off because he and I both knew this was the closet he was ever going to get to feeling this pussy.

A few minutes later, Chris came on the dancefloor, and dances with me and Ervin. Here I was in between two chocolate men who both wanted me in and out my clothes. I could see it in Chris eyes he was tipsy. I figured he was entitled and I let him enjoy himself. Ervin left not long after Chris joined us, Chris was feeling all on me, with my back against him he spoke in my ear, and said I want to fuck you now, and takes my hand and we leave the base club. I drive off base to his apartment which was not even five minutes away, the whole time stroking his dick with one hand and the other on the wheel.

When we get into the apartment our clothes started coming off as soon as we stepped through the door. Again, I could tell Chris wanted me to hurt physically as much as was mentally at the moment, which I'm not going to lie he was good at. I know the neighbors heard me and with him tipsy, for some reason seemed to have lasted longer, I was praying for him to come soon, he finally reached his moment and laid on top of me and fell asleep. I rolled him onto his back, took off the condom and covered him up. I went into the living room and watch television since I really wasn't tired and couldn't sleep knowing Devin would be out soon.

An hour and a half of watching television, I started to get tired and went in the bedroom and laid next Chris, who automatically shifted to hold me and went back to sleep. In the morning, we went shopping on base for food and items for his apartment. For lunch we went to one of our other favorite restaurants to go to which was the beef bowl. Towards the evening, we headed back to Atsugi base he mentioned he was going to his cousin's place and from there out to the night club where he worked and helped with security. Chris asked if I wanted to go, I told him I was still pretty tired and I would just catch him tomorrow.

When I got to the barracks, I laid on my bed and in moments fell asleep. Time seemed to drag by, me waiting impatiently for the word of when Devin would be set free. The news was put out we were to prepare for another deployment which meant if Devin was released in a matter of weeks it would be several months before I could travel to North Carolina to see him. I tried not to be too upset about it saying everything happens for a reason and what's a few more months on top of years that I have already waited. I went to my room and packed up for deployment which not only delayed my chance to see Devin but also Chris wouldn't be there as well. This was going to be a long and boring cruise.

We set sails as usually and I went back to my routine of working, eating, working out, and cleaning female berthing area. Luckily Ervin was still attached to the ship so I still got my hook up with the supplies even though I turned down having sex with him. By Chris not being on the ship I had a new social group mostly AZs from other squadrons. One AZ which I was kind of surprise we clicked was Kisma, she was a black female with over the top standards. I ain't say she's a gold digger but... she was entertaining to be around. She dressed to impressed, even in uniform, the girl would doll herself up like she was going for a model interview.

After a few weeks of hanging out every day I finally just asked her, Kisma, why do you go to the extreme on everything, from make-up, to clothes, and how you carry yourself. Her answer caught me off guard, Kisma stated she had a 5 to 10 year plan where she was to marry a white rich man, never have to work ever again, and trap him with babies and a non-prenup marriage. I had a moment of silence then I asked why does the man have to be white, there are plenty black successful rich men in the world. Then Kisma comes out of left field with "I don't want no dark babies". I told a deep breath and in my mind, I thought does this BITCH not realize her ass is black, but what I said was "you do know you are black..."

Kisma mentioned she had a tough time growing up and faced A LOT of racism, from both black and white people. She stated she had very low self-esteem and when she became old enough to wear makeup she piled on the foundation, lip stick, mascara, eye lashes, eye liner, and transformed herself to be as close to an off-black girl. Talking about it tears filled her eyes, and honestly I could related, being a dark female and even darker than Kisma I felt like I wouldn't get a certain job or certain man. It was the reason why I didn't care for light skin men because I felt they were out of my league and I wasn't good enough; which is strange considering I was with a white man back in the day.

Though I didn't agree with Kisma's methods, I did understand it. As a friend I learn and/or try not to judge so I did not give her the third degree and now I saw her passed the make-up and she was a hurt black woman, looking for love and acceptance from the outside in. I wanted to be the counselor but what she needed was a supporter. I hung out during down time at her work station where there was another AZ there I spoke to a few times on the phone but had only seen today in person. Nathan was his name and in the first 15 minutes of being around him caught on to he was also gay. Nathan was a good looking black man, which in my head was thinking damn another one gone.

All three of us sat in the office and talked about basically everything, Kisma and Nathan were really close friends and so Nathan and I had clicked in a matter of minutes. We were coming up on our first port in a couple of days which was Hong Kong and we made plans to hang out. Kisma and I got a hotel room together and since Kisma had watch the first day, Nathan and I hung out. I checked into the hotel room and Nathan had the front desk call the phone for me to come down. There was a restaurant in the hotel and so we decided to stay there and eat and drink. We had ordered some drinks while waiting on our food to come, and after the second drink, Nathan felt the need to confess...

He opened up with, "I don't know why, but I feel I can tell you this". I turned my attention completely to Nathan and said OK, tell me what. He said "I'm gay"; I smiled and said, yeah I know. Then he busted out with, "did Kisma tell you" I said no, I caught on to it by myself, from the way you talked, dress and the usage of your hands while explaining things. Nathan took a drink and had a look on his face like I stole his thunder, then he asked if I had any questions for him. I smiled, took a drink then called the waitress over and ordered two more drinks, Nathan mentioned oh no wine for me, and I said no, both drinks are for me.

I took a deep breath and was thinking man, if I knew my day was going to end up like this I would have had a pad and pencil on hand. So trying not to come off like a eager little kid, whose mom just said go at it in a toy store, I eased in with the most likely question, "how did you end up or know you were gay". He stated by saying he was seduce by a teacher, he went over to his house one day after school had a few drinks and the teacher gave him a blowjob. He stated they meet up a few times and each time they went further and did more and he enjoyed it. My next question I asked Nathan was had he been with a female. He said yes he had slept with at least 3 females and he didn't like it, even when they gave him a blowjob it didn't feel the same he prefer for a man to do it.

He said being inside a woman to him was like being in the ocean and he didn't get any pleasure from it. I was like WOW OK... I was thinking damn, most men would love being in wet pussy. So I stated, so... if we were at a spa you would prefer the feel of a mud bath over a hot water bath. Nathan laughed and said he never heard that analogy before, but yes, that would be accurate. I asked next how did his parents feel about him being gay, he stated they didn't know. His mother till this day brings up when is he going to give her some grandbabies, but he doesn't have the heart to tell her the truth about who he really is, A BLACK GAY MAN!!!

My next question for Nathan was and I had to think how I was going to ask this question delicately, so I used a phrase of, do you prefer to be the catcher or pitcher, and strangely and awkwardly enough he knew what I meant. He stated he preferred to be the CATCHER, but he does do both!!! So now I was just blunt with it, and said so you enjoy taking it up the ass, Nathan smiled and said yes very much. It was then the food had arrived but after that question and answer I really wasn't hunger anymore. I sat silence as Nathan asked me was that all I wanted to know, I took a drink and said yes...it...wasJ

Nathan just like Kisma came out of left field, and apparently had some questions for me. I wasn't sure what he wanted to know but I figured since he shared so much of himself with me I didn't really see the harm in sharing myself with him. Nathan already knew some things with the long talks in the office so wasn't sure what was left on his mind. The first question Nathan asked me was if I had ever been with a woman, I laughed and said NO, and then he asked if I ever fantasize about being with a woman, and laughed again and said NO. I'm not sure why Nathan was hooked on sexual preference even after the first two questions, his ass came up with a scenario.

He told me to close my eyes and imagine I was blind folded laying on the bed naked about to have sex with my man. He gives me a massage with heating oil rubbing it all over my body and he sucks my toes, kisses and rubs my legs, and licks the inner part of my thighs, kiss my stomach and caress my nipples then he starts eating me out and I'm moaning with pleasure enjoying his touch, his tongue. Nathan then says to me, take the blindfold off and look down and see that it's not your man but a woman, what do you do. Oh HELL no he did not...this moment made me think of the time on the weekend when you leave your front door open and you're in the living room cleaning your house and two Jehovah witnesses knock on the door, and yes they already seen you so YOU MUST ANSWER!!!

I cleared my throat and bluntly said hell if she is doing that good of a job why would I stop her. Nathan with a big smile seemed pleased with himself and my answer and said "see anyone can be persuaded". I replied NO because best believe she won't "persuade" me to go down on her, it's my actions I can control not someone else's. Nathan replies "never say never" and I sat in silence not even going to entertain this conversation any longer. I did understand what Nathan was insinuating because I could see how a young girl being abused by men over and over would find comfort and safety with a woman and how a young boy being giving attention from older boys or men feel drawn to the desire of being wanted and a sense of being accustomed to a certain role or behavior where the "abnormal is the prevalent".

I came to a realization sitting there talking with Nathan that the "monsters" in the world are not born as monsters but turned and created. We ask ourselves why certain things happen to us, what we did to bring certain things and people into our lives. I thought of Nick, and maybe he did what he did to me because it was done to him. Sometimes cycles keep going because the lesson is never learned or the habit is too hard to break and if it wasn't for the pain and hate towards Nick and my mother I would have never joined the Navy to escape them. Nick's weakness gave me strength to conquer the physical and mental challenges that got me where I am today. Though I will never forget or forgive... I don't regret.

As for my mother, we had more of a sister relationship it seems more than a mother and daughter one. I think her being the only black pregnant teenager in the family and school in the 1960s she took on a role I'm sure she didn't want or even knew how to play. Here I was again making excuses for her actions when really, the truth was I ruined this woman's life by being born and she hated me for it. My mother loved and valued Nick beyond any maternal instinct she had. I knew if I ever had children, some of the mistakes not to make such as putting a man's love before that of my own child. They say experience is the best teacher, I agree.

Nathan who let me soak in my thoughts for a moment came with one last question. He asked me if the love I have for Devin would change if he was having sex with other men while in prison. I had to catch myself REAL QUICK because Nathan was about to get bitch slapped. I replied with the Navy policy... "DON'T ASK, DON'T TELL". Nathan applaud, and smiled, and said well put. Nathan and I said our goodbyes since he was about to head out to a gay club. He asked if I wanted to go with him, but I knew I would not be comfortable in such unfamiliar surroundings. I told him I would pass this time but maybe in the future. I was one where I would try anything once but that was not the night.

So much was on my mind after talking with Nathan, my mother, Nick, and Devin and how sex to females is more of a spiritual and mental endurance and with men it's more of a physical one. Most men for some reason can seem to separate sex and love where women having sex is symbolic of love, we can't have one without the other. As women, our feelings have us fucked up; we fall prey to predators whether it's a husband, boyfriend, or pedophile; emotions lead us, guide us, and FORM us. The next two days in port, one day Kisma and I went shopping and the last day I had watch so Kisma and Nathan hung together. We set sail again to our next port which was Guam.

While waiting to arrive in Guam the ship life was same the routine as usually work for 12 hours, which in that time I would also eat, clean the berthing, and visit the other squadrons. I visited my favorite two people on the ship now Kisma and Nathan. I asked Nathan how was the club in Hong Kong and did he meet anyone, he smiled and said yes. I asked what happen did you two exchange numbers, dance, what. Nathan stated he met a sexy Filipino man at the club, they danced, talked, and then had sex in the bathroom. I was like WOW REALLY!!! I quickly asked, did you use a condom? Nathan replied no, it was unplanned and in the heat of the moment.

It took a lot to hold back what I really wanted to say, which was really, do you not realize the AIDS rate in the gay community and black community is high as hell and your ass is BOTH. Our friendship was too fresh and I didn't want to come off as judgmental instead I said be careful even though you can't get pregnant there are still STDs out there. After I said my peace on that subject I left out and headed back to my office space. While in the office I got a call from Chris, he asks how was my day going and what I did so far at the ports we pulled into. I told him I just caught up on some quiet sleep in the hotel, with the female berthing being at the catapults a restful night sleep is a luxury well missed.

Without Chris being on this cruise my eyes and ears were more opened to my surroundings. For the most part I just watched and observed like in the female berthing area late at night on the way to the head, the distant moans and heavy panting and breathing. There were stories of females having sex with each other and seeking males into the berthing area late at night. I also noticed pulling into port now the local girls and women who waited for our arrival, prostitutes. The men and women on the ship that walked through them like they were purchasing clothing or cars, checking for breast size, ass, color eyes, color of hair.

I heard of stories of how some "women" where not really "women" and usually sailors and marines didn't find out until they were behind closed doors. I understood how this operation worked was two girls came together what is called a "double purchase" they take the guy back to the room, it starts off the she-male taking off their top to show their breast then they begin to give the man head, while the real female gets completely undress showing her full body. The man then starts eating her out while the she-male continues to give the blow job. When the man is ready to have sex he starts off the pussy he was eating. The light room are dimed so when its' time to switch the man is unable to see the other "girl" does not have a vagina.

This person tells the man she wants to only have anal sex, I heard when a lot of the men reach for the front or want to only do vaginal sex they run into a problem and 6 out of 10 times once the guy realizes it's a man he was about the fuck they do one of three things: 1) leave, 2) fuck anyway, 3) go the fuck off and kick the shemale's ass which is why in these situations the "girls" are in pairs with some type of blade or knife to protect themselves if the man becomes hostile. I only heard of one situation that took place where a black guy after fucking the shemale is when he found out beat the "girl" up so badly ended up in the hospital in critical condition. The Navy from what I heard had to do a lot to **"persuade"** the locals to let him leave.

Now I understood the comment the Captain made before pulling into port about making sure to be safe and to check all packages before making a purchase. There were men on the ship that even with wives and children at home just threw caution to the wind and said fuck it and I mean that shit "literally" married men who talked to their wives every day, saying baby I love you and miss you and pull into port rings still on end up fucking 5 to 10 women or men without any subconscious. Again it was how men were able to separate sex from love, to them it's just a body of a woman, no heart... no soul. It was then I was like I really don't think I could marry a man in the service especially the NAVY.

In my subconscious I really wasn't able to pass judgement in a way, seeing I loved Devin mind, body, and soul and still with each duty station would lay down with another man, substituting their body for his. Love in itself is powerful but as humans we are subject to weakness. Love can create and destroy us because we allow it. Everything that has happened in my life is because love in some way shape or form gave weakness to one strength or another and though I felt my life was destroyed by it, another life for me it had created...(stay with me people). Remember when I made the commit we ask ourselves why certain things happen to us, what we did to bring certain things and people into our lives...we loved.

This cruise I called the sea of life, looking out in the water the world seemed as though it was innocent, comforting, and serene. Behind the troubled waters, I see now I was blind to thinking I ran and left my fears and troubles in North Carolina but looking out at the sea on this carrier I realized fear and "troubled waters" surrounded me. I can choose to live above the surface where things are safe and serene or go deep in the waters where fears and troubles manifest, one thing about it once I go in the deep end coming back to the surface I will not forgot what lies deep underneath.

So much shit weighed heavy on my mind, I just wanted to sleep, so I went to the berthing and got ready for bed.

Before going to bed I decided to take a shower. It was late so there was no waiting in line and I had the shower all to myself so a nice HOT shower was likely. As I'm in the shower washing up, I take the showerhead and ran the water all over my body. I lean forward with my head pressed against the tile and my eyes closed as I'm moving the showerhead between my legs the water pressure builds up and my knees go weak, my heart starts racing, and I'm breathing heavily I didn't know what this feeling was but the mental and physical tension was diminishing. The force became stronger I pressed my head harder into the wall and seconds later shouted FUCK!!! Masturbation was introduced.

After that experience I would take showers now twice a day and was a lot more relaxed on the ship. After showering one late night I was in the head brushing my teeth and Kisma had walked in to go to the bathroom. I stood at the sink frozen in shock of what I saw, this was my first time seeing Kisma with absolutely no make-up on and I couldn't take my eyes off her as she stood next to me at the sink washing her hands. She was half sleep still she recognized me and spoke then walked out. Kisma looked like somebody had REALLY fucked her up with no make-up on. I personal don't wear make-up expect for lip stick and mascara but Kisma wore it all, foundations, eye liner, blush, lashes, lip stick, mascara and lip liner and now I know why.

When she left the head I couldn't help but to think if I was a man and seen her only with make-up on all dolled up and been dating for months hell YEARS and I saw what I just saw a few moments ago I would be highly upset. Truthfully I would be pissed. The best analogy I can use is imagine going to a car dealership picking out the car of your dreams with the high gloss paint job, leather interior with all the trimmings and toys you wanted and one day a bad rain storm hits and the paint on the car washing off and you see the original color and it is horrifying and sick looking and even when you repaint it with the glossy shining paint color you purchased driving it won't be the same because now you done seen what really lays beneath the surface.

Yeap I know the saying "beauty is skin deep", "beauty is in the eyes of the beholder" and "it's what's on the inside that counts" but at the same time don't claim to be selling me a luxury car and later I find out it's a pickup. The next day in the office Kisma came by to visit me. I tried not to look at her any differently than before but after what I saw last night needless to say that was a challenge. Kisma and I went to lunch and talked as usual. She told me she was seeing someone and she wouldn't give me much details because the person was a Navy Officer which her being an enlisted was a HELLS NO in the Navy. I didn't push the issue because the less I knew the better and part of me may want to warn him to look under the wrapping paper.

We were less than a week out before pulling back into Japan and then I would be heading home to North Carolina to see Devin. We made it home and Chris was at the pier to welcome me. He had balloons and a stuff animal it was so sweet. He took my things and put it in the car. We went to eat because Chris knew from many cruises that eating real food was the first thing people from being out to sea for months wanted. After we ate we went to his place and as soon as we walked through the door Chris was all over me. We had sex and I being over excited and tired fell asleep. Chris and I later that night decided to stay in order food and watch movies and along with having sex over and over and over again.

I think Chris was trying to literally fuck me to death because he knew at the end of the week I was taking a flight back to North Carolina and I would want Devin less. Chris took me to the airport and before they called for boarding on my flight, he pulls out a condom and said this is for Devin. I just looked at him kind of surprised at the gesture but knew he really was hoping I wouldn't fuck Devin at all. The flight to North Carolina was exciting and I was so eager to see Devin after all these years. Devin and I decided to meet at the playground where we first met. I was so nervous. I arrived at the playground first on the merry go round thinking about the day Devin and I first met the emotions were overwhelming.

A black car pulled up in the playground and Devin exited from the passenger side, I stood up and I wanted to run to him but my feet would not move. He walked up to me and hugged me so tightly and the tears started flowing, all I kept saying was I love you and he said I love you too and kissed me so hard. His ride had left us and we sat on the playground on the merry go round talking about his life behind bars and my life in the Navy. We were like old friends catching up on all the time we lost together. Devin and I left the playground after sitting and talking for over an hour. I knew what was coming next as he said he had a hotel room for us.

In the hotel room I felt somewhat off, Devin started touching me, kissing me and undressing me. I stood there touching him still trying to wrap my mind around the fact I was touching him I took off his shirt, unbuttoned and unzipped his pants. I laid on the bed and Devin climb on top of me. As he was gripping me and sucking my nipples I closed my eyes and for once when I called Devin's name it was Devin physically there with me. When Devin pushed himself inside of me I felt a sense of reassurance. As I laid there with Devin making love to me after all these years I pictured this moment to be passionate, romantic, and mind blowing but it was everything but that.

My body and mind no longer seem to desire Devin, my heart and soul on the other hand refused to let him go. I was at war with myself while making love to Devin I was thinking about Chris. When it was over I sat up in bed tucked under the sheets, Devin looked at me and asked me what was wrong. I smiled and said nothing, just happy we are finally together. I mentioned I had less than nine months left in Japan and I can take orders back to the U.S. and we can be together. He sat on the edge of the bed and said, I wish it was that simple. Devin stated he could not leave the state of North Carolina for at least a year since he on parole.

I yelled at him, I said are you fucking kidding me I put 5 years of my life on hold for you so what to add another year or so. I jumped out of bed and started getting dressed Devin grab me and said to me please, don't give up on us now. I had some much anger and rage in me I took it out on Devin, truthfully I really wasn't mad at him just the situation. It seemed like even now years later we faced road blocks, was this a true sign Devin and I were not meant to be together. I sat on the bed and with tears running down my face I knew I was at the end of my rope, I had to move on. I told Devin, if we were truly meant to be God would bring us together but I can no longer live my life waiting for you.

Devin with his back to me and head down replied "I understand" and just like that the love we had fought for all these years in one swift moment had perished. We hugged another for so long it seemed like we would never let go. I ended up taking an early flight back to Japan seeing my reason for coming to North Carolina was short lived. On the flight back I thought about how everything had played out over the years and by waiting on Devin did I miss out on something or someone. I knew once I got back to Japan Chris and I didn't have to worry about Devin anymore, we could be together now like he wanted because know I knew I felt more for Chris than what I lead on. **(Song: Crush).**

Chris was happy to hear that things between Devin and I went south and he and I no longer had these limitations. I was officially Chris's girl and me not pursuing anyone else, there was no more open season when it came to sex partners now. Not too much had changed between Chris and I and things went on like normal. I was coming up for orders soon and Chris wanted me to stay in Japan with him. I personally thought Japan was a nice country I really did not want to stay here. I told Chris I would do what I can to stay but in the back of my mind I knew if I saw something that I wanted I was going to choose that area. I really was interested in staying overseas because of the cost of living allowance (COLA) and wanted to go to Rota, Spain.

Like the times before I selected 3 locations one being Japan, the others were Spain and Hawaii. Drum roll please and I got slayed to go to...........
........................Diego Garcia.

Where the HELL is that and why the Navy keep sending me to places I have never heard of. I of course was the first to know where I was going since with my clearance I had access to the message center and when I saw my name and the word Diego I was like yes I am going to San Diego California but then I saw the word Garcia and unaccompanied tour and was like where the fuck. Now the real moment I was bracing for Is telling

Chris, I didn't get orders to stay in Japan and put on my best acting skills like I am really upset J

Honestly though Chris and I were together I decided to no longer make life decisions just to be with a man. Since, that obviously got me nowhere with Devin. One weekend Chris and I headed down to Tokyo his cousin was doing some security work in the area, clearly his cousin got around in Japan. The night really consisted of club hopping, the first club we went to was like any club you really would expect to see in the U.S. R&B, hip hop, and Jamaican music. Chris brought me a drink and gave me money for more drinks. Chris sat me at a table and as usual told one of the security personnel to watch me. I would think to myself, was he scared I was going to run off but really Chris was overprotected which was something I admired and feared about him.

Chris, his cousin and I left this club after an hour and headed to another club. I got me a drink at the bar and at this club Chris and I actually danced together he wasn't in the corner or at a table with his cousin and a group of guys talking about whatever they were talking about. The third club we went to was actually a female stripper club, which this was my first time in any stripper club. Seeing this was Japan this strip club was nothing like America would have, the men in here would converse among themselves and paid little attention to the girls on stage. At this club I sat at the booth with Chris and his cousin and 4 other guys.

I was thinking now I would get some insight to what the hell Chris and his cousin were into. Wrong, these mutherjumpers were talking in a difference language and I had not a clue what was being said. Since, I couldn't well ease drop I drew my attention to the women on stage which I noticed a trend after the third one. All these women had the same shape, figure, and ethnic background. When two of the men broke from the group I asked Chris, why all the women look the same. Chris stated all the women were brought in from Russia. After he said that, I sat back in the booth and thought wow, you mean to tell me in a world where I thought they only import and export food, plants, and animals, people are on the list too.

Now instead of looking at these women as strippers, were they really hostages, victims of something at this moment I had no idea about. Sitting at this booth with Chris and his cousin I couldn't shake the feeling that Chris was involved with something illegal and I was there right in the middle of it watching deals and transactions take place, whispers in the dark, exchanges of money, and meeting behind closed doors. I like a race horse chosen to put blinders on and not see the events and people around me. Granted I had been around drug dealers in my day but my intuition knew this was far beyond any drug deals. With, less than 5 months left I was not going to raid this situation.

Chris and I left the stripper club and from there we actually went back to his place. We spent a lot of time together because Chris knew I was coming up on my last cruise and from that deployment would be flown off to prepare to leave for my next command, Diego Garcia. It was time for my last and finally cruise with CAG 5 and wanted to make this the best deployment ever. Our first stop was Guam which though I had been here in the past cruises hung out with a more diverse crowd we went club hopping, bar hopping and shopped up a storm. The second port was where I was to fly out but it was a port I had never been which was Korea. I wanted to get some mink blankets from here which if you tried to get in the U.S. would be 4 times the price.

I said my goodbyes to everyone and flew off the ship. I am always fond of the memories and experiences from each command and gain new knowledge and friends along the way. I usually take a 2 week break and go back home to North Carolina before checking in to my next command but with Devin being out I wanted to avoid the awkwardness. Of course international flight on a military aircraft meant FREE alcohol. I did my research like I do with any new command and the pictures of this place where absolutely beautiful. Diego Garcia put me in the mind of the show Gillian's Island, surrounding with clear blue water, white sands, and palm trees.

When I landed there was someone from the command to show me to the barracks and get me situated. I arrived in my room and unpacked it was a Saturday so I had the weekend to explore before reporting to work on Monday. After I unpacked I headed outside and behind the barracks was the beach, hell water and sand was everywhere. I walked to the small exchange and picked up some items as well as the commissary, there were bus stops I noticed while walking and saw that there were buses that run people around the bases which was convenient since no personal vehicles were allowed here. I was happy to be on an island where winter is not a season and hot days, warm nights all year long!!!

Sunday I didn't do much stayed in my room watch t.v. and prepared my uniform for tomorrow. Monday I got a knock at my door from my sponsor and we headed into work on the buses that transport people around the Island. The first three days consisted of checking in with personnel in the command and around base to the post office, exchange, and getting a personnel tour of the Island and what it had to offer. It was a very small secluded island, with personnel only from the military American and British and the service people who were flown in which were Filipino. There were several benefits to being stationed here one was as a service member hair styles, haircuts, manicure, and pedicures were free but of course we tip them.

After I finished checking in I was told I was going to be the new Central Technical Publication Librarian (CTPL). This job was responsible for making sure each department was using the most up to date publications while working on military aircraft and support equipment. Luckily the previous librarian was still there, bad news, he was due to leave in 2 weeks, so, therefore, I had little time to learn a whole lot of information. The commander was due to leave as well towards the end of April and his relief was due to report in May so there would be no face to face turnover but with emails and phone calls I'm sure things will transition smoothly.

While undergoing my training, my relief had mentioned that I actually would be getting formal training for 2 weeks in Astugi Japan and the next class was in May. I couldn't help but to laugh what are the chances I end up going back to the place I just left for training. When the time came for me to fly back to Japan, I decided not to say anything to Chris and wanted to surprise him. When I arrived I called Chris and told him I was back in Japan, within the hour he picked me up. When he first arrived he just sat in the car looking at me shaking his head and stated "you are full of surprises" I smiled and replied you have no idea.

He mentioned he had plans with his cousin that evening but was going to call and cancel. I told him no, its fine, it'll just be like old times. We first made a stop to his place where we had sex and afterwards he first took a shower. While in the shower I noticed a bunch of papers on Chris's table which was the norm but one piece of paper stood out. It was a letter written by a girl name Kimberly, the letter said thank you for a fun weekend and I am off to work, I will talk to you tomorrow, love Kimberly with a phone number. Chris was coming out of the shower a few seconds after me reading the letter and as soon as he got in my view I asked who the fuck is Kimberly.

With a hesitation, he laughed and said what are you talking about. I mentioned there is a letter here on your table from a girl named Kimberly. Chris mentioned it was his cousin girlfriend and he needed a place for her to stay since she couldn't very well go to the house with his cousin and his pregnant Japanese wife. I asked how long did she stay here, Chris said for a week. I asked how come of our many emails, and phone calls you NEVER once mentioned you had a houseguest. Chris stated he didn't see the point of mentioning it because it was irrelevant to us. Chris gave me a kiss and told me to shower so we can go.

In the shower I couldn't shake the feeling that Chris just lied to me and there was more to this Kimberly girl than he had told. (**Song: A Good Man**). We headed out to the Tokyo party district and like the times before stop at our first club. This club they played mostly Jamaican music, we stayed at this club for about 40 minutes and moved on to the next which played R&B. At this club we sat upstairs overlooking the dancefloor in a VIP room with men drinking and talking with strippers dancing. Chris and sat together on the couch I was handed a glass of wine and watch the women that were dancing in front of me since I didn't understand the language happening around me.

It was in that moment I was thinking to myself, I really need to learn another language. I have been to Iceland, Japan, Hong Kong, Korea,

Guam, and as a child Hawaii and never bother to broaden my terminology beyond the basic of simple greetings. There are people in these countries that know the English language enough to get by. Granted I felt safe with Chris but just imagine if this was a first date with a guy I just met and here he was talking about kidnapping and raping me and my ass is sitting right next to him bouncing my head to the music and having drinks.

We left to head home around 2am we went to Astugi so I could check in at the barracks and we stayed there for the night. The next morning we had breakfast and Chris headed back to Yokosuka. I visited a friend of mine who husband was Chief in the Navy, she worked at the Post Office on the base. She and I would meet up a few times on base and play bingo. Leslie was her name and she cook and we watched movies until about 2200 then I headed back to the barracks and prepared for training tomorrow. The one week of training went by quickly and just so happened my last weekend in Japan was during my 26th birthday. This was the last weekend Chris and I had together before I went back to Diego Garcia.

Chris picked up me after class Friday afternoon, and he paid to get my hair done. A few hours later he picked me up and we went to one of our favorite restaurant's right outside the base. Afterwards we went for a walk, then we drove to Yokosuka where we went on the base and played pool and went bowling. We then took a shower together and had sex. I stayed there all day and night Saturday we hung out on the base and walked outside the base to the local bars. I was tired and mentioned to Chris I wanted to turn in early tonight so tomorrow Sunday I can pack up and be ready to fly out Monday morning. Chris mentioned he would take the day off to take me to the base to fly out.

I told him that was not necessary, but he insisted. Once we arrived to the Air Force base where the flight was, he helped me get my bags out the car and since we had time before the flight we went to the exchange and got something to eat. Chris noticed I was kind of distant and quiet. I have to admit after this weekend I felt uneasy confused about Chris and this relationship. Thinking to myself do I really know him and what is he capable of. After we ate he took me to the terminal and he mentioned he had an appointment so he couldn't stay and wait, I mentioned that was fine I will call you when I arrive in Diego Garcia. Chris gave me a kiss and left.

The flight was due to leave in one hour, I sat in the terminal with flashes of the weekend going through my head. I couldn't shake the feeling that whole Kimberly story was not real, part of me was wondering why I was even thinking about it because she is supposedly gone. In the moment someone from the flight came out and told us that the aircraft had some maintenance issues and would be grounded for 3 days and we will be taking care of with rooms and a meal card to eat in the galley on base. I took out my phone to call Chris but in that moment I heard a voice saying no Harminme, don't call, go to him...so I went.

I was hours away from Yokosuka and taking a taxi there would cost a lot of money, so for the first time since I been in Japan I took the train by myself. I could not tell you how in the world I made it to Yokosuka and in journey there felt God was leading me. I rented a car from base, so I could have a way back to Atsugi. I knew Chris wasn't home and since his car was having transmission issues he didn't drive it regularly. I knew he had a spare key for his apartment in the car, the only thing now was trying to find how to get in. The driver side window was slightly rolled down but not enough to where I could reach in and unlock it. Luckily there was a welding shop within walking distance and though they didn't know what I really needed it I saw a piece of equipment I could use to unlock the car door.

I needed to get the phone number off the letter and find out exactly who Kimberly was. I grab the key to the apartment and ran towards the entry way as soon as I turned to go through the sliding doors, I see Chris walking towards me hand in hand with some white chick. He quickly let go of her hand and stopped right in front of me, I looked at him and said you SON OF A BITHCH!!! His reply was "I thought you were leaving today", I looked at the girl and said is your name Kimberly she said yes, I said hi, I'm Chris girlfriend and if you were wondering why you didn't see him at all this weekend it's because he was fucking me. I then threw the keys at Chris and told him, you better go lock up your car. I turned and walked away.

Tears filled my eyes I couldn't believe what I just saw, I went to the car and sat for a minute. Then I was like FUCK THIS, I got out of the rental car got inside Chris's car and started breaking all his CDs, then I poured water all over the seats, and keyed his door. Obviously this bitch didn't take my warning when I told him to lock up his car. After I finished causing damage to his property, I got in my rental and drove off. Waiting for the light to turn I saw Chris walking to the parking lot where his car was at. Kimberly was still in front of the building, I wanted to run the light because I had some things to tell her but with a Japanese cop car at the opposite light I knew God was saying not to be impulsive.

As soon as the light turned I went around the roundabout and pulled up next to her, I told her, that Chris apparently ain't shit and if you looking for boyfriend materially he is not it, but if you just looking for a big dick to fuck have at it, I told her to have a nice day and drove off. As I was driving off Chris was coming from the parking lot and his ass looked mad as hell, I smiled and waved. I speeded off heading to Atsugi. I was able to check back into the barracks since I told the front desk that my flight was grounded for 3 days. I headed to my room and laid on the bed for about 10 minutes and then decided to go to the exchange.

I was so ready to leave this place now. I knew what I saw was something God meant for me to see, because everything happens for a reason. On the walk back from the exchange a familiar blue sports car pulled up next to me, Oh My God, it was Chris!!! He got out the car and approached me, I kept walking he is yelling Harminme get in the car, I pretend not to hear him and I continue walking to the barracks. He gets back into his vehicle and drives up the road in front of the barracks; I'm like really I do not have time for this shit. He starts walking back towards me and near us at the bus stop there was a girls' soccer team, Chris grabs my hand and starts pulling me towards the car. I yelled STOP!! Chris lets go of my hand and I walk to the rental car because I didn't want him to know what room I was in.

When I made it to the car I unlocked the doors and put the key in the ignition. Chris at this point turns and walks back towards his car, as he is walking away, the tears and anger ruptured and I get out the car go behind him and just start beating him up. The girl soccer team was in shock along with Chris since he didn't see or hear me coming up behind him. As I am throwing blows my cousin that works in the Post Office drives by and stops her car in the middle of the road. Leslie calls out my name and I came back from going WWF on Chris ass, she grabs me and we head to her car. Leslie pulls off and asks what in the world, I just said it's a long story.

Leslie was like Harminme you know you can't go off like that on base and then in public. Leslie takes me to her place, she mentions I should call the base police and tell them what happened just in case someone from the base recognized me and reported it. I waited for about 10 minutes and I called the base police, but in middle of the story he stops me and says, Ms. Love I'm going to need you to come down to the station. I asked why I need to come to the station, the Officer mentioned Chris was at the station and is currently pressing charges against me. HE IS WHAT!!! That son of a BITCH gets caught cheating and he is the one pressing charges. The Officer stated ma'am I understand your frustration but I can pick you up if you like and we can hear both sides of the story.

I gave the Officer on the phone the address to my cousin's house and he arrived in 15 minutes. I sat in the passenger seat which I did appreciate him for doing that, and sat quietly on the ride to the police station. When we arrived they took me in a room with two Officer and told me to explain what had happened. I told them the story and how when I arrived back to Atsugi he followed me. One of the Officers asked about me breaking into Chris's car and breaking his CDs and pouring water on his seats. I looked at the Officer and smiled and said, you know I did pour water on his seats but his window was cracked so I just unlocked the door. I told the Officer technically I'm still not in the wrong because of the events that happened so far.

As for the CDs the CDs were mine I had purchased so technically they belonged to me, it was my property I destroyed NOT HIS!!! The Officer stated well we told Mr. Chris that since, the incident took place off base and there is no proof of any broken CDs or that the CDs were his we couldn't do too much about that. I was thinking I know his ass pissed about that. Since I was no longer stationed at Atsugi, the Officer would have to contact my current Command and see what my CO wanted to do. I was like, shit, the CO at Diego Garcia just arrived there this man doesn't even know my name, or what I look like. He's most likely going to say keep me here.

The Officer called Diego Garcia and spoke briefly with my NEW CO and then handed me the phone. I quietly said "hello Sir" this is AZ2 Love. Commander Jefferson in a soothing tone said AZ2 don't worry about anything, I will take care of it, just stay clear of your ex for the next 2 days and arrive back safely and in one piece. I had a look of confusion but yet relief, like this man just gave me a get out of Atsugi card without even meeting me, and this was not a good first impression I wanted to make with my CO. The Officer went next door and told Chris, no charges could be made and he was to leave Atsugi as soon as possible and not to report back to this base while I was here unless it was for official business.

Chris was escorted off the base and one of the Officers drove me to the barracks. I called my cousin Leslie and told her what happened. She was relieved like me about the charges being dropped, and mentioned when Wednesday came she would drive me to the base where I was due to fly out just in case Chris was going to try something. The flight went off as scheduled on Wednesday and I arrived at Diego Garcia. I went into work on Thursday the next day. Commander Jefferson had called me into his office I explained what happened and he mentioned he understood and sometimes emotions get the best of us and the good news is he can't come here unless he has orders.

Yes, one thing about Diego Garcia, is no one can just take a flight and decide they want to visit, they have to be on official orders or have some type of professional purpose there. When I got back to work, my life started getting to normal as possible. There was a new AZ1 that had arrived while I was going through my training in Japan, she was the CO's new Administrative Officer, and her name was Charlean. She came into my Office I guess to try and see how crazy I really was, but we hit it off and started talking and hanging out every day. It helped having someone to laugh and talk to about what happened in Japan.

Charlean was a black female as well and she was married with no children, and she chose to come to Diego Garcia to save up some money and this command counted as sea time, which is a lot better than being on an actually ship. I was receiving emails and phone calls on my cell phone from Chris but didn't response to either his calls or emails. Then one day, my work phone rung and it was Chris. How in the HELL did he get this number, I was in shock when I heard his voice on the other end. Chris started going in saying how sorry he was and he made a HUGE mistake and if he could take it back he would. I still had too much anger and hate in me for his words to make any difference what so ever.

I said ok, was that it. Chris pleaded for me not to hang up and if I did he would keep calling, which unlike my cell phone I had to answer the office phone since I couldn't very well turn it off. I told Chris it has been almost 2 months there is nothing more we need to talk about concerning that situation and I want nothing more to do with him. He mentioned he was going to take a flight out to Diego Garcia, I laughed and said, he won't make it. Days later I get another phone call from Chris who indeed found out, his ass just can't take a flight to Diego Garcia, and this was one place in the world that was literally cut off from the public. With that now established I felt better he couldn't get to me.

I had got word from Charlean that I would be getting a roommate this weekend, we have a new SK3 coming in. I went with Charlean to the terminal to welcome the new check-ins, the girl who was going to be my roommate was a black chick named Kayla, she was originally from Haiti and looked like a sweet girl. We drove back to the barracks and got everyone settled in, on the weekends there is usually a cook out going on with people playing spades and dominos. I would make rice Krispy treats or fried chicken, and sit back and drink mud slides watching the card game. I got Kayla settled in and took her downstairs and introduced her to everyone.

Of course being attractive the guys swarm around her like bees to honey. On Monday I took Kayla to Charlean's Office who was the point of contact for new check ins. I went to my office and began working on backing up publications, I was in the process of converting the library over from paper to electronic which was a massive task to complete. On top of that we got word that Diego Garcia was shutting down and we would be opening up in a new location, Bahrain to be exact. I really wasn't looking forward to the move since Diego Garcia was starting to grow on me but it's not like I had a choice in the manner. Charlean and I would walk from work to the barracks since this was a place where getting into shape was a goal for most people.

Charlean also was planning to go back home and visit her husband in a few weeks and wanted to drop some weight. On one of our walks we ended up talking about marriage and relationships. She asked me why I haven't try to go out with anyone here. I told her I was taking a break from being in a relationship and needed time to get to know me and what I really wanted out of life, and I was taking a YEAR off from sex; besides, MEN can't be trusted. Charlean being a married woman I'm sure was going to weigh in on that comment, but her response was not what I expected. She mentioned she had a conversation with her husband last week and they came to an agreement dealing with their time apart.

Charlean mentioned she told her husband he could have sex with other women while she was here. Of course there were guidelines or should I say rules, he was to follow such as, it couldn't be someone from work, no one they both knew, not in their bed, and he must wear condoms. It was then apart of me clicked with Charlean like no other. This was a woman of "reality check" she knew the game would be played, so she decided she would make the rules. Bravo. Charlean in the months we had been at Diego Garcia enjoyed herself but wasn't out there like that so she had self-control. As for my roommate on the other hand, this chick was apparently easy to open like a beer bottle.

She would be seen around base with different guys, which I really didn't care, what she did, because it was her body. She also lacked home training, she wasn't very clean and I got tired of being the motherly roommate telling her to pick up her things, and what time her guest should leave. I spoke with my CO and asked if it was possible for me to have another roommate, he mentioned someone would be transferring next month and I could get the room. As if my roommate issues wasn't enough Chris was still calling trying to win his way back into my life, but that shit wasn't about to happen. He called one day and I was in one of my moods, I told him, to say whatever the fuck he had to say so he would stop calling me.

Chris mentioned he wanted to make things right and wanted to apologize and explain what happened. He told the story of how him and Kimberly met, she was taking groceries to the car, she had dropped some bags and he helped her. They sparked up a conversation and they exchanged numbers, he took her out wined and dined her and they had sex. He stated they went out twice and his intentions was to end it after that, but she kept calling him and she had left a message on his phone and... Chris paused for a minute and I was like what, what was the message she left. Chris said Kimberly is pregnant. I said, what did you just say, he cried Harminme I am so sorry, please. I just hung up the phone.

I couldn't believe it, some white bitch he just met and he came in her REALLY!!! I was so hurt and angry, and I hate to admit a little envious because she was now giving something to Chris that I wanted to be the first to provide...a child. The emails and calls kept coming but I didn't want to hear anything else he had to say. I would go into work early and stay late, on the weekends sleep in late and then go downstairs, cook, eat, and socialize. Being downstairs did take my mind off things, the things that were troubling as well as haunting. I had many sleepless nights but on the weekends I found some relief. Then there was my crazy roommate, who was talking to some guy from work and apparently got into some kind of domestic assault, she went all commando on his ass.

I felt bad, for him not her so much because he was a sweet guy and they were one of the few biracial couples on the island. She apparently had bruises on her as well but I was told he was trying to get her off of him. It just so happened I took a walk to the beach behind the barracks, and Josh my roommate's boyfriend was on the beach drinking a beer looking out onto the water. I came up behind him and stated "troubles on your mind" he turned around and laugh and replied yeah, like you wouldn't believe. I told him I heard about him and Kayla and I knew that bitch was crazy. Josh shared with me that he loved Kayla but there was something seriously wrong with her, like one minute she's calm loving, playful, and the next she manhandling him wanting to fight.

I'm thinking OH hell first thing Monday morning I'm going to my Commander and ask about that room. Monday morning came and I did just that; Commander Jefferson told me I could move in to my new room Saturday. Oh thank God because the next fight I'm sure was going to go down would be Kayla and I. I didn't even tell Kayla I was changing rooms, I figured her ass would find out when she saw my things gone. I liked having a room all to myself even though it would only be for a few months since the Command would be going to Bahrain. At the moment I at least had peace, quiet, and a clean room. One problem down, but there still was the phone calls and emails from Chris.

I unplugged the phone at work since Chris would just keep calling and I couldn't have the phone just ringing. It had been over a month now so I plugged the phone back in. Things were quiet for about 2 weeks so I figured Chris must have moved on. Then the phone ranged, it was Chris, damn he is persisted, really I was worn out from yelling and hanging up the phone over and over again, so I sat quietly and listened and figured I would try killing him with kindness. He mentioned how he wanted a child more than anything but wanted it with me. He stated when Kimberly mentioned she was pregnant the first thing that came to his mind was me and how he fucked things up. He went to his cousin and he gave him a pill and mentioned to give it to Kimberly and his troubles would be over.

Chris told me how he called a date with Kimberly and waited for the right moment to put the pill in her drink, for as bad as he wanted to fix or correct this mistake he couldn't bring himself to hurt this innocent unborn child. He flushed the pill. I wish I could say I had some sympathy towards his story but I didn't. The hate and angry flowed through my veins, like the air that I breathe the hate and angry fueled me to move on. I know Chris was truly sorry for what he did to me, but it still doesn't change the fact the SHIT HAPPENED. I told Chris I forgave him and that I wish him and his soon to be new family the best but him and I...were no more. He said he would never give up and that he loved me and hung up the phone.

This whole situation with Chris wouldn't had been a hard pill to swallow if she wasn't pregnant. Having sex...making love there is no difference in the two when both can create and destroy...a life. It was a normal party weekend at Diego Garcia, the guys have been teaching me how to play spades and I was getting quite good at it. My ex-roommate Kayla was over indulging in the alcohol and was being way too friendly with everyone. Charlean kept an eye on her to make sure, she didn't get into any trouble. It was getting late and Charlean and I kind of felt responsible for Kayla's well-being so I told Charlean I would take Kayla to her room and make sure she was safe along with the safety of others.

I grabbed a hold of Kayla and took her upstairs to her room, I sat on my old bed and waited till she calmed down and fell asleep, but that did not happen right away. Kayla took off her clothes all the while talking what sounded like a bunch of nothing. She got in the bed and said "Harminme I am so sorry for being a bad roommate" I replied no problem Kayla your young you still have a lot of things to learn and experience in life. Then she said believe me I learned a lot at a very young age, I lost my virginity at thirteen...and to my brother. I didn't say a word at first, just looked at her with what the fuck did you just say look. She said her family was original from Haiti and she was about 10 when they moved came to the U.S.

She mentioned her family moved to America for a better life for her and her brother. America had so many new things and opportunities, good and bad. She said her brother who was three years older got exposed to porn. Her father had a collection he kept in the bedroom and when their parents went to work, her brother would sneak in and watch them. She mentioned at first he would just masturbate, then it escalated. So then one day, he called her into the bedroom, while watching a porn movie told her they were going to play a game and do everything the people in the movie were doing. She said it hurt and she tried to tell her parents that her brother was hurting her but they did nothing.

It went on for years, and she mentioned she started to enjoy it and in high school had sex with so many guys and still with her brother having girlfriends to have sex with they never stop having sex with one another She said "I knew it was wrong, because at first it didn't feel right but then

I wanted it, my body wanted it but I didn't." I sat across the bed from her with tears in my eyes; I got up and sat next to her in the bed and held her tight while she just cried; I stayed with her till she fell asleep. I couldn't understand, how is it a mother, a father finds it acceptable to let things in their home happen to their own children simply because they either don't want to face or don't know how to face it. This is how victims become predators because those we loved the most failed us.

Now I understood the craziness and unstableness I saw in Kayla because it was a familiar look. Later on in the day I went to check on Kayla, she was hung over but she had remembered what she told me. She said, she was sorry for putting that burden on me, but it was eating her up inside and had to tell someone who she felt would believe her. I told her I did believe her and she needed to get some professional help and talk to a counselor or someone who can help her find a way to live thru this. I said if you don't history is bound to repeat itself and you will turn an "innocent" into a "victim". It's easy to tell other people to face and fight their demons, when I have demons of my own still hibernating within.

It was November and a few people from the command were being sent to Bahrain to prepare for the move from Diego Garcia to there. Charlean went with the first group since she was admin and had to get all the paperwork, orders, and living arrangements into place. It was in December when I and the rest of the crew went to Bahrain. Since we were setting up from nothing here we didn't even have really a building. We shared a building with another Command and a few weeks down the line we got a big white tent and some trailers. We stayed at the hotel Crown Plaza up to 60 days which was the time we were given to find our own place. Some people found villas and houses right away.

Bahrain had a lot to offer when it came to living quarters, most people got 4 to 6 bedroom houses with 2 to 3 levels and a pool. I tried to stay in the hotel until the last week that the 60 days expired and I got a 3 bedroom house with a screen pool in the back, the only thing I did not like was having a gas stove. After cooking on it a few times and toasting marshmallows I came to like it more than electric. Charlean moved in an apartment building with all the amenities pretty much a hotel had, such as a front desk person, a doorman, a pool, even maid service.

The house I had was small compared to what the guys got but I still had maid service once or twice a month, since our schedule in Bahrain was 12 plus hours.

When we got to Bahrain, we all figured it would be like Diego Garcia as far as 8 hour shirts and free time to cookout and hangout as we pleased but we were wrong. Bahrain was by far the hardest and most challenging in my Navy career thus far. We worked 5 to 6 days a week with 12 plus hours, all we had time for was to work, eat, and sleep and no one could take leave except in emergency situations. The morale in the Command was at an all-time low and we had no PRT program in place so the weight was starting to catch up to me before I knew it I had put on 30 pounds. On top of all that I was still on my no sex for a year with no detachable showerhead and the Arabic men in this country were fine, then there were guys at work trying to pursue me but even with all the temptation I didn't give in.

Commander Jefferson had approached me about extending my orders in Bahrain for another year since I had done so well with the transformation of the library he felt it would hurt the progress if someone new came on, and I just passed the audit with flying colors. Though the place had my blood pressure and stress level at an all-time high the cola, pay check being tax-free, and living arrangements were better than being stationed anywhere else. Though I was leaning towards yes, I asked Commander Jefferson to give me till the end of the week for my final answer. On Friday I went to Commander Jefferson with my answer, I told him if he would allow me to take a 2 week leave I would stay one more year here in Bahrain.

Commander Jefferson without hesitation agreed to grant me leave. I left for leave within 10 days, Charlean told everyone I had a family emergency but her, me, and Commander Jefferson knew the real deal. I returned home to North Carolina, I had to get the address from my mother since she moved. Nick also was no longer in the picture and from what my sister had mentioned been gone for a year. I didn't bring it up to my mother since she seems to live in a fantasy world where "nothing bad happened". I went downtown to the library to use the computer, I decided to walk to drugstore downtown where I got an orangeade. I decided to continue my walk and found myself standing in front of a real estate agency with a picture of condos on the water.

The picture brought a sense of easement to my mind. I saw myself on the deck in a rocking chair overlooking the water, my mind at peace. I went inside and spoke to a realtor and asked her about the property in the window. She mentioned it was a new development and they just broke ground, she stated if I had a few minutes she could take me to the location. The ground was absolutely bare, I remember this location and it had nothing but trees. The realtor mentioned the price which was $250,000 but that price wouldn't last long because once they started actually building it will go up. I can't explain but I knew I wanted it, this would be a great retirement spot and I wouldn't have to worry myself with lawn work.

I wrote a check out for $10,000 to lock in the price, selected the condo I wanted and signed the paperwork. I didn't do much else while at home, 3 days before I was due to report back to Bahrain, I mentioned to my mother about buying a condo. She said really, that's good but why didn't you get a house, I told her I didn't want to be bothered with lawn work. Then she said "suppose we got a house together, I'm sure we could get something cheaper and I could find someone to tend to the grass cutting. I figured maybe this could be the turning point between my mother and I and the healing of our relationship would build from this. I told my mother, I would buy a house with her.

Of course I informed her that it had to be a house and not a trailer since my mother was interested in purchasing a trailer at one time, but to me I found them not valuable. I stopped by the realtor and told her I was going in on a house with my mother and won't be needing to purchase the condo anymore. On the flight back to Bahrain, I felt good about this visit and was sure things would be better now between my mother and I. Once I got into Bahrain I met up with Charlean who mentioned that Kayla was sent back to the U.S. She mentioned Kayla had a breakdown and was trying to commit suicide and pretty much found she was bipolar. I told Charlean the story that Kayla told me about her brother and the fact is I don't believe she will ever recover from that.

Being raped repeatedly by your brother, then becoming accustom to it... accepting it. I can't even imagine the turmoil she is going through mentally and physically. I hope that the Navy doesn't just process her out but make sure she gets the help she needs or else she will bring destruction to herself and any man she falls in love with. Kayla was literally coming apart at the seams and I know she felt helpless. I prayed for her and hoped God would give her strength to pick up the pieces. I told Charlean about my decision to buy a house with my mother, and from the look on her face knew Charlean didn't think I made a smart decision. She held back for a while but I kept digging until she gave me an answer.

Charlean stated "after all you have been through with your mother, do you really think it would be wise to buy a home for a woman, who did not make a safe, loving home for you." Though it angered me to hear Charlean speak I knew she was right. I told her I'm trying to get pass the past and Nick is no longer in her life, we can start over. Charlean said "suppose Nick came back it's only been a year do you think your mother would take him e back and into the house you brought". I replied surely my mother would not be so insensitive and heartless to let a man who molested her daughters into a home her daughter, you know what...Charlean I appreciate you sharing your concerns and I will think about everything you said before I make any final decision.

I liked Charlean, for the simple fact she knew how to breakdown my walls and tame me in my most hostile states. People who have been in and out my life would say there are several sides to Harminme Love and if so, Charlean would be the first to subside them all...she was the level that balanced me out which I needed from time to time. She gave me sisterly advice and motherly love, she was truly by my best and dear friend. I still got phones call while in Bahrain from Chris who I have to applaud was keeping on with the fight. I got a phone call from my mother and she mentioned she had found a place, I asked her to describe it to me and as soon as she said the word trailer, I stated, I know I told you and CLEARLY emphasized I did not want a trailer and was not going to waste my money on a trailer.

She kept trying to make her point that it was built like a house would be sturdy, etc. So I let her talk and while she was talking I was thinking this woman, just plainly disregarded what I said and did what the hell she wanted to do. Then I thought about what Charlean said, if Nick and my mother would get back together would he be allowed to come into this house. When my mother was through talking, I asked her, if I decide to go in on getting this trailer, would Nick be allowed to come into this place, my mother with no hesitation said "why not". I could not believe my ears, so I asked, what did you just say, and she repeated why not, Nick and I are still good friends and he's done nothing to me.

I got loud, I said the man molested your daughters is that not enough!!! She said, I don't believe he would do something like that, I told her well then me and you have nothing further to discuss and you don't ever have to worry about me getting a home with you or for you, goodbye mother. I didn't want to cry but it hurt to hold it in, I sat in my office at my desk as tear after tear hit my keyboard. It was in that moment I convinced myself that my mother had died. The next day I called the realtor Lisa and told her I was mailing out a new check for $10,000 and I was no longer get a house with my mother I wanted to purchase the condo. She mentioned the original one I had selected wasn't available but the one next to it was, so I selected that one.

The last year in Bahrain was so different from the first year, I was happy that Charlean extended a year as well and we took this journey together. Commander Jefferson left us and was replaced by Commander Anderson, a black Officer and also a prick. If he was trying to be the biggest asshole in the Middle East he was succeeding. Commander Anderson, ruled with no compassion, no soul, and a heartless man. He was under the impression that signs of feelings were signs of weakness, in my opinion he was more suited for the Marines than Navy. With almost being 50 pounds heavier I went for a consult to have some elective surgery done, a tummy tuck. Recover time was going to be a challenge since it was difficult to get any time off but my department gave me a week, since I told them I would have Charlean as my backup.

Charlean also took a break to go back home and visit her husband but with the new Commander it was like pulling teeth to get him to agree. Since, Charlean like me had no backup in her office she had to train me to run admin while she was gone. Charlean was gone for three weeks, and it was well deserved. She called me once sometimes twice a week to check on me and help me with admin stuff that came up. I was more than anyone happy to see Charlean, running the library and admin was more than one person could bear, but for Charlean I powered through it. Charlean mentioned her and her husband had a great time and she mentioned he wanted them to start a family. I could tell from Charlean's body language this was not something she shared the same excitement about.

I asked her was a child something that she wanted, and she said it was something her and her husband talked about and discussed when would be the right time, they even went to a fertility clinic, it was something they prepared for. I understand but is it something YOU want, Charlean with such remorse replied "no, I don't want children", then I asked why have them. Charlean was a religious and spiritual being and stated in a marriage, you have to make sacrifices and compromise. I told her I understand but a child...a life once you make that decision to become a mother there is no going back, and I don't want to sound negative but 50% of marriages in America end in divorce.

I stated are you prepared to be a single parent because we both know men can walk away from their old wife to a new one and not carry the burden. Having a child can bring changes to your life which also can be a blessing. As a mother you will be stuck with this responsibility for 18 plus years. Then I asked the most underlining question dealing with this topic...why don't you want to have children. Charlean shared with me that she was adopted and it haunted her not knowing why her mother gave her up. Charlean was not even the first born but the third child and found her mother kept the other two. She was grateful for her adopted parents but no household is perfect and she stated "I too turned to the military to escape..."

I was in my 6 month window and was thinking about my next location, but really I was preparing for my transfer out the military. While in Bahrain the Navy apparently was downsizing and anyone that was over the weight limit or could not pass the PRT was being discharged. With, no PRT program here for the past 18 months and 50 pounds of extra weight to carry around, I knew the next command I went to passing the PRT would surely be a defect. Approaching my 5 month window I choice all three locations in Virginia since it was close to home and if was going to be separated I wouldn't have far to go. Charlean came in my office a few weeks later with her hands behind her back and a smile, she said "I got your orders".

I laughed and said where are they sending me this time Egypt she said "no surprisingly enough you are going to the location you wrote down... Virginia." She said I was going to NAS Oceana. I was thinking really after almost 8 years of filling out wish lists and I finally get something on the list. I was approaching yet another end to a chapter in my life. Just like every other command I leave with joyous memories, and take with life lessons that will get me through the next chapter. I got an offer on the land I purchased while in Japan which I made a profit of about $12,000. I also purchased a car while in Bahrain since it would be tax free and I could pick it up once I got back to the U.S.

My last week in Bahrain I stayed with Charlean we went shopping, out to eat, watched movies and talked. She mentioned how proud she was of me and also impressed, I asked her what was it she was impressed about, she mentioned the fact I went 2 years without sex. I laughed yes, here is was May 2006 and on May 16 it would be 2 years that had I no sex. I'm not going to lie the first year was the hardest, but once I got over that hill my body became numb and didn't crave it as much. I'm sure now with me heading back to American, heading back home this time of reflection will be no more. I can say it was a sense of relief not having to worry about any STDs or getting pregnant even though I stayed on birth control the whole time just in case I had a moment of weakness. I made arrangements to live with my Aunt Sandy since the condo would not be ready yet. My sister Danielle had mentioned mother felt some kind of way about me living with my Aunt and not her but I told my sister I really don't give a damn and she's your mother...NOT MINE!!!

My Aunt Sandy stayed out in the country so it was peaceful and not a lot of neighbors around in your business. I drove to NAS Oceana everyday but with me being a road warrior the drive really didn't bother me just the traffic when backed up. I was assigned to production control and was also the Training Officer. The crew here was not like my crew in Bahrain, the personnel here were not as keen and lazy. There was one guy always late to muster, and uniform looked like shit every day. There was young girl as well who was a decent worker but couldn't stay focus for too long so I had to keep her on track. There was another black female who was a good worker and had I little issues from her name was Chanel.

It wasn't long that word got around town, I was back. While going downtown to the realtor's office I ran into Devin. My heart felt as though it skipped a beat when I saw him, he stopped me and mentioned he had heard I was back in town. I said yes, he asked was I still in the military, I stated yes at least for the moment. He asked if we could get together sometime and catch up. I didn't response right away and he saw my hesitation, he stated Harminme, maybe this is our chance, our time to be together. I said well, I did come back...he smiled, I said we can get together this weekend how about Saturday. I gave him my number and proceeded in the realtor's office.

Saturday came and Devin called, I told him I was staying with my Aunt Sandy and I gave him directions. When he pulled up in the yard I was shocked at the vehicle he was in, it was my...I mean my sister's mother old vehicle. When Devin got out the car he laughed and said yeah, I wanted to see the look on your face. I mentioned of all the cars you couldn't find one that didn't belong to Regina. Devin said it was the only thing he could think of that would make him feel closer to me. I'm not going to lie Devin but, that's creepy. I asked where we were going, he mentioned to his best friend house, which I knew actually who he was referring to. It brought back a lot of memories seeing Devin and his boys together again, like he wasn't locked up for 5 years.

Devin and I talked in the backyard he asked how long would I be staying at my Aunt's place. I told him I actually purchased a condo and I should be ready to move in it sometime in August. Devin didn't waste any time asking if we could start over. When August came around they were putting in the last finishing touches and at the end of August I moved in. I called the storage place that had the furniture I picked out while in Bahrain and it was delivered the following week. Devin hung up the blinds, and did minor cosmetic maintenance, which I found he was very handy. After 2 weeks of being back together Devin had moved in with me.

Though I was happy to be back with Devin part of me still felt like something in the relationship was missing. When Devin and I had sex there was more compassion there, then it was the last time. This time around my body, soul, and heart were on the same page... but not my mind. My mind still didn't seem to accept Devin but 3 out of 4 are still good odds. It was also strange that after 2 years and 3 months of no sexual relationship with anyone I would end up back with a man who I once was in love with. It was more of a comfort and safeness being with Devin, since it wasn't a stranger I was giving my body to. Devin was currently unemployed and looking for a job.

While, waiting for a call back from potential employers, Devin did all cooking and cleaning. I was really impressed with his housekeeping skills. When I would come home Devin and I would sit and talk a bit, he would make dinner and then he would leave out to go drink and hang out with his boys. Devin got a phone call for a job, he was working 12 hour shift which ran opposite from my schedule. Devin would go into work between 2230 and 2300 and I wouldn't see him again until I got home that evening which was about 1800. Devin still made sure dinner was prepared for me when I got home. When Devin got paid he would cash his check and give me most of it expect for about $50 which he took out for him for gas and alcohol.

During the week Devin and I didn't spend much time together and on the weekend when he wasn't working, we would spend a few hours together but then at night he would go out hanging with his boys. At first it didn't bother me but then Devin didn't come home one night and he didn't call. I got worried something happened to him and when I called his best friend, he mentioned Devin had left late last night. So I'm like where the fuck is he. When Devin final came home, I asked him where he was at. He stated with his boys, I said I called your boys and you left them late last night so where have you been. Devin mentioned I do have other friends and I was with them, really I said so why did you not call me, anything could of happened to you.

Devin apologized and said, I was right and he should of have called. In my mind I was thinking, strike one. Things were good for about a week then Devin didn't come home for 2 days, this was strike two. It was Monday night when I saw Devin again, I told him that we needed to talk, he mentioned I know what this is about and it was this weekend but something came up and my phone died, I shouted STOP!! You are gone for two days, and even if your phone died I'm sure there was someone around you that had a phone. I told Devin, you were the one who asked for us to get back together, but I am not a teenager anymore you just can't do as you please because NOW I don't have a curfew and have to report back home to mommy. We are both adults and you need to start acting like it and start being responsible because I don't need you here if this is how you're going to act.

Devin again apologized and mentioned he just had a lot going on and was looking into possibly another job to make more money but didn't want to mention anything because it wasn't a sure thing. I believed him since he would always say, when he gave me his check that he wish it was more to help out with the bills. The next day Devin asked me to marry him, I had mixed emotions but I said yes. On my way from work I stopped in Suffolk to get some gas, I went inside to play the numbers and there was Nicole behind the register. I couldn't believe it my best friend from high school. She called the other girl to the register and we walked outside the store.

We hugged and she started to cry, saying how she thought about me and wondered where I was at and what I was doing. I told her I joined the Navy and moved back home, I purchased a condo and Devin and I are back together. Nicole wanted us all to get together and along with her man and do something this weekend. I asked Nicole what she was doing with her life, she mentioned she is the manager her at the gas station and she has two girls and lives here is Suffolk. That night I told Devin I ran into Nicole, he was happy we met up again and couldn't wait to see her as well. The weekend came and we all went out to eat, we talked about the past and it was fun going down memory lane, here I was almost 9 years post grad high school and I was with the love of my life and my best friend, in that moment my life felt complete.

After dinner we went to my condo drank, talked, and took pictures. Nicole was impressed with the condo and couldn't stop talking about the location and the view of the water. It was after midnight and Nicole and her boyfriend Julius headed back since she had to work in the morning. I was cooking breakfast and while eating breakfast Devin mentioned Nicole comments last night about the condo and waterfront property. Devin asked..."so when are you going to put my name on the condo", I looked at him and said with a smile when we are married we can discuss that. I was thinking this mutherjumper don't even got a ring on my finger and want his name on MY SHIT. It was in that moment... my defenses went up.

This man has no idea the stress, the challenges, the lost I went through to get to this point. Being the only black owner in this community having neighbors look at me like I'm lost or out of place. Thinking if one of these white people ask me how much I charge to clean houses...I'm...going... the...fuck...off. I would hate to think Devin was using me for some type of financial gain, but for a man who is bringing little to nothing to the plate, this bitch won't get a free meal off me. I see now Devin not too smart, and with him being on strike two, strike three you're out, is just around the corner. The clock was ticking.

From time to time Nicole and I would meet and have dinner or I go visit her at work once or twice a week on the way home. I stopped by her house and met the girls, I couldn't believe Nicole was a mother with two girls, time has flown. It was one late Friday night as I was heading from Nicole's place, I went home took a bath and got in the bed. Saturday morning, there was no sign of Devin, now the clock counts down. It wasn't until Tuesday when I saw Devin again, I will give him credit he did call Sunday but he also said Sunday when he called he would be home in a few hours. When he came home Tuesday I decided I wasn't going to argue, I wasn't even going to say a word. This was strike three.

I got things in order, I went to the hardware store and got new locks for the doors, and I had maintenance install the new locks on the doors Saturday morning and then just waited. Monday night Devin tried to use his keys to get into the condo, he figured out quickly they didn't work. He knocked on the door, I opened the door, and the first thing he said was "did you change the locks", I said yes, you are no longer a resident here and you have 30 days to find somewhere else to go. I turned walked into the bedroom and closed the door. Devin comes in behind me and starts pleading his case, I told him I don't want to hear it, you and I have outgrown one another and you are not ready to be anyone's husband especially not mine.

In two weeks Devin moved out, I was going through so many emotions, hate, angry, love, and pain. I didn't want to face the truth before that the Devin I fell in love with almost 15 years ago was gone. I would look in Devin eyes and everyday see less and less of the man I loved and the man that loved Harminme. Here we were together with no baby momma drama, no parents keeping us apart, no hiding from law enforcement, we had no barriers...expect maybe his boys. As a wife I would expect my husband to make me a top priority, Devin as a grown man priorities were all fucked up. I'm not sure what happened to him in those 5 years of incarceration but I didn't need a man with just street smarts but common sense as well.

Eventually all us gets old and have to survive and Devin's boys are not going to be there in sickness and health, love and cherish, till death. There would have been nothing I wouldn't have done for Devin but the Navy transformed me into someone stronger, wiser, and defined and no one will treat me less than what I am worth. The shit hurt but now I knew why my mind stood alone from what my heart, soul, and body felt, because I had common sense... and I knew Devin and I wasn't going to work. With 2 years and 3 months with no one I settled.. for anyone. Well I only wasted 3 more months of my life so now I know, we were not meant to be. Now to put all my focus back on me.

The PRT was coming up and despite my best attempts, running with 50 extra pounds was torture. In my mind I had already failed so I started preparing for my exit. I put more into my G.I. Bill, I refinanced my mortgage, started going to college, and paying off all my credit cards. I also decided to have a home warming party and invite the family over to see the new condo now that everything was how I wanted it. I told Nicole about the home warming and she mentioned she would be there. My Aunt Sandy, Aunt Betty, cousin Candie with her boys, my sister Danielle with her son and mother Regina with her friend Tom and Regina's cousin June. My father and stepmother showed up as well.

Regina my sister's mother was on the balcony overlooking the water I stepped out on the balcony as well to enjoy the view and holding the title of a homeowner. The exhilarating moment ended briefly when Regina sitting in my white rocking chair asked "why you want to live out here with all these white people" I turned around quickly and said what compared to choosing the ghetto or a trailer park. I went inside thinking nothing I do will be good enough, or maybe she was jealous because instead of her being a homeowner she was still renting. I gave her an opportunity to own a home but to let the pedophile who ran me out of her home into a home I put my money in, I would board up the windows and doors and burn her and him in it.

After the home warming I cleaned up and started my bath, I took a drink a glass of wine and soaked in the Jacuzzi. Nicole did not make it to my home warming and there was no missed call from her. I called Nicole the next day to see if everything was alright, she mentioned she was called in to work. As the weeks went on Nicole was becoming more absent to events, and dinner arrangements with no phone call letting me know she would not be there. I even brought concert tickets to see my favorite artist. After being stood up 5 times in one month, I decided it time to cut Nicole off as well. **(Song: I thank you for being a Friend).** I went to the store where Regina worked to play the lottery and get some gas. Regina mentioned there was a man who worked at the Condos I stayed at express to her he was interested in meeting me.

Regina gave me his name and number. I called the number on the paper that night and it was a man named Samuel he worked for the developer of the condo community I was in. He mentioned he had been watching me for a few months now and noticed that a certain car was no longer around (Devin's) and figured I was available. I stated I know where you're going with this you're trying to see am I seeing anyone, the answer is no and at this time I'm not trying to get into another relationship. Samuel mentioned he just wanted to get to know me and when can start off as being friends. He asked to take me out to a dinner and movie, I said yes and we made plans for Saturday night. It had been 4 months since Devin left and I figured it was time to check out what else is out there.

Though my Jacuzzi and detachable shower head were calming my sexual urges I was one who prefer the real thing. Saturday came and Samuel arrived on time. I let him in and we talked a bit then we headed out to dinner. He opened the car door for me getting in and out which I was impressed with because I didn't know gentlemen like this still existed. We went to a restaurant downtown near the waterfront. During dinner we talked about being from a small town, relationships, and future goals. I knew right off this man had some depth to him, he was ambitious and hardworking even though I didn't mentioned it to him he caught my attention as well working at the condo since he was one of the two black males I saw working on the grounds.

I even saw him working on the weekends and he would just wave and smile, and me having an attraction to dark skin men he lingered on my mind for a minute. He mentioned he was divorced but his wife and son still live in the area. He asked me how old I was, I said 28, he said Oh, I said what, how old did you think I was. Samuel mentioned he thought I was at least in my mid-thirties I was like really, do I look it. He stated no it's just you don't see many 20 something year olds buying a house or condo. **(Song: Figures)**. Then I asked well how old are you he said 42, I said Oh, ok. Samuel then replied "I'm too old for you Huh", I laughed no...Luckily for you I like OLDER men. After dinner we went to the movies, he drove me home and asked if he could come up.

We sat on the couch watching t.v., and continued talking. He asked if he could kiss me, I smiled and said yes, but just so you know I don't kiss in the mouth. He asked why that was, I told him I always been that way and really having someone else saliva in my mouth is...well let's just say I don't like it. Samuel went in to kiss me, I could feel his heart pounding and pants rising. He started caressing my breasts, he said I don't want to move too fast since this is our first date but I do want you. I said its fine we are both adults, its ok. Samuel took off my top and I laid on the floor, he sucked my nipples as if he was starving, he pulled down my skirt and started to eat me.

He put me in the mind of a teenage boy about to have sex for the first time, not with the quickness, but with the eagerness of wanting something so badly. I unbutton his pants and started stroking his dick, he was really, really hard and had nice size. I asked if he had a condom, he said yes and took it out. He put the condom on and OMG for a minute I felt like a virgin again. I put my hand up to stop him, and he asked was something wrong, I said...no...but...just...go...slow. I'm not sure why I was so tight but as he slowly pushed his dick in inch by inch I got wetter and was able to take him all the way in. He lasted longer than what I expected and about 30 minutes later he said, "I can't hold it anymore, can I cum".

I grabbed a hold of his back and pulled him in closer to my chest and whispered in his ear, yes Samuel, you can cum. I never had a man ask permission to come before, it was a selfless act. He asked if I got mine, I said no, but it is VERY HARD for me to cum, you best not wait on me, if that was what you were doing. Samuel and I talked every day and we meet up on the weekend when he got off work. I went to his house in town, he had a three bedroom brick house not far from the house my grandparents once stayed, and also next door to my cousin Keira. Samuel and I stayed very busy throughout the week with our work schedule.

On top of our work schedule I also was taking online classes working on my Bachelors in Technical Management with a concentration in Accounting. One late Friday night I had not long got off the phone with Samuel, he wanted to come over but I mentioned I was studying and had a lot of work to do. I heard a knock at the door, it was almost midnight and I'm thinking Samuel didn't hear me when I said I had a lot of work to do. I looked through the peephole and was shocked to see it was not Samuel but

Devin. I stood in front of the door with my hand on the handle, waiting. Devin knock on the door again, and I slowly unlocked the door and turned the handle. **(Song: Bad Boy).**

I opened the door, and asked why are you here. Devin claimed he was here to pick up the rest of his clothing in the spare bedroom and needed a coat since the weather was turning. I let him and he walked back to the bedroom on the right. I go back to sitting with my computer, Devin walks back up and stops behind the loveseat and I could feel him staring. I looked up and asked was there something else you needed. Devin ask how I was doing, I said fine. Then he goes in with an apologize, I stop him in mid-sentence and I said save it, I don't want to hear it. We said goodbye once, hell several times already, I don't need a recapture of everything. Devin with a look in his eyes, walks to the door and opens it, and before he walks out says to me, Harminme, just know I will always love you. **(Songs: So Cold).**

I didn't respond, nor did I look up once the door closed behind him, I got up and locked the door. I knew this day would come, which is why he left some of his clothes behind to have a reason to come back. I'm just glad I was prepared and not let him see me cry or breakdown in anyway. Hopefully Samuel will be a new and happier chapter in my life, since we don't have a past haunting us and ripping us apart. Back at NAS Oceana they were making some changes and moving the AZs around, I was told I would be going to check-in and check-out processing. In this position I would be cutting orders, making travel arrangements, checking people in and out of the command on PCS orders.

Before my transfer I had to train my replacement which was the young girl that was a decent worker but couldn't stay focus for too long, Kathy was her name. Kathy was a white female and only been in the Navy less than a year, so she was still getting her "sea legs". I had 2 weeks to pretty much train her on everything but since I was only going like 2 blocks down the road I mentioned to her if she had any questions I was a phone call and walk away. After one of our training sessions we went to lunch together. We sat together in the gallery just talking about work and what she plans to do with her Navy Career. While, in the middle of us talking, a guy she knew came up to the table and spoke to her, I could tell by the way he looked and responded to her, that he liked Kathy.

He asked her out to lunch and she said, sure with some hesitation. When he left I asked Kathy, do you not like him, she said no...it's not that. I said ok, what's the problem, he's black, I said OH REALLY I didn't noticed, I thought it was a white boy with a good suntan. Kathy laughed, and said you know Harminme I am going to miss you and your sarcastic comebacks. I said so, he's black, I been with a white man before. The look on her face was like NO WAY!!! I laughed but then I forgot there is a bit of age difference between us. I said so all through high school you never dated a black boy. Kathy looks to her left and looks to her right as if she did not want anyone to hear what she was about to say next.

She stated she didn't have a lot of black people in her high school... and her grandparents raised her...and they are racist. They told her that black people are hired help only, they are dumb, can't read or write, are trouble makers, and their skin is scaly like a snake and they make a lot of babies they can't take care of. I asked Kathy where she was from, she said Ohio, (ok mental note to myself don't carry my ass to Ohio). Kathy stated the only time she really saw a black person regularly was on t.v. and if they were too many blacks her grandmother would turn the channel. As I am listening to her say all this, I'm thinking damn one of the KKK members' granddaughter done joined the Navy surrounding by all men of different colors, backgrounds, and ethnicity (smiling)...

I said Kathy, you are a grown woman now and you should experience all that the world has to offer. She mentioned she was scared, I'm like WHAT you still scared of black people, no...She said I actually got over that in boot camp. I asked ok...so what happened in boot camp, Kathy mentioned when she signed up to join the military and started boot camp she was surround by a lot of black females. Kathy said she went up to one, one day and asked to touch her skin, the girl, didn't really know why, but she said yeah, ok. So, Kathy stated "when I touched her skin, I said OH your skin isn't scaly" the black girl said, was it supposed to be. Then Kathy told her what her grandmother told her about all black people having scaly skin, she said the girl just gave her a look and walked away. I laughed and said your ass lucky she ain't slap the shit out of you.

OK back to dating black men, what is it that you are concern with, a mean a man is a man all day long, there are dicks of different colors, sizes, shapes but they all can do one of two things, get you pregnant or give you an STD...Shit let me stop lying or BOTH. Kathy then whispers "I heard that black men dicks are REALLY BIG", I busted out laughing for a good minute and a half thinking about Damon. I lean in close to Kathy and whisper...NOT ALL OF THEM!!! I told Kathy and this was really feeling like a mother and daughter conversation at this point but advised her to take things slow, examine the package (meaning dick) to see if it was acceptable to you. This is something I call the "hand test" which I do now since 1998 when I came across a finger dick and not a hand dick.

During the hand test you also want to take it out and check for any discoloration, sores, or shit that don't look right. If you find out during the "hand test" the dick is not acceptable or to your standards, you say something like, "I'm sorry I really want to but my period is on but I can give you a hand job or blow job to make you happy". Men never turn that down. Kathy was mentally taking notes like she was in high school and I was the sex Ed teacher. I also advise her to always have condoms, do not leave it up to the guy to have them, because some will try to run game saying, they forgot or it's expired or my all-time favorite they are allergic to latex. When they come with that bullshit say we can go by the store and get lamb skin or say sorry I'm not on the pill.

Which brings me to when you say, you are not on the pill and they holla Oh baby, I will pull out, say you know men pre-ejaculate before they cum and this semen has some sperm in it as well. Pretty much letting them know, besides you not being a easy bitch, you not stupid one. That was the best hour lunch I ever had, and I'm sure it was for Kathy too. Not only did she learn a lot from me, but I was given a wake-up call by her. In the Navy I travelled to Iceland, Japan, Hong Kong, Korea, Guam, Singapore, Diego Garcia, and Bahrain. With all these places I never once felt defined by my skin color, now I will say in Bahrain they have a lot of men there that were sexist and had a women are beneath them type aura. Also most people there believed all blacks were from Africa and not America.

I can still recall the day when a white co-worker was talking with Charlean and I along with one or two other guys in the shop, he said he went to the Bahrainian Mall and two Iranian men spit at his feet and said white American trash. He said he felt anger and hurt all at the same time but did not react because it was their country and knew it would make the situation worst if he tried to defend himself. I sighed and went up to him and gave him a hug and when I pulled away I said, now you know how it feels to be a black man in U.S. there was a moment of silence and everyone started to laugh. I would never forget that day and I'm sure Charlean won't either but our co-worker that experience this stated it put things in perspective, of how it feels to be misjudged and misunderstood.

Here I was AZ2 Harminme Nicole Love back in America, my home state of North Carolina and I'm defined by the color of my skin. I was not only defined and misjudged by the condo complex I lived in with ALL WHITE neighbors but my mother I mean Regina who also treated me like I didn't belong there. Granted I did join the military to get away from my mother, but the second reason was I wasn't afraid to sacrifice my life for this town and the people in. There are thousands of people every day trying to bust their ass to be a part of this country, and I think about a conversation I had with an Indian man in Bahrain while staying at the Crowne Plaza. He at first like most people assumed I was from Africa.

I laughed and at first was not going to correct him, but told him the truth, which was I am from America. His face lit up like I just told him he won the lottery. He replied OH AMERICA THE GREATEST COUNTRY IN THE WORLD!!! He said he was trying to get to America, I asked why, he said its where dreams come true and people work, and have everything they need. The street are paved in gold and...I stopped him right there. I said I'm not sure where you are getting your information about America from but we have our struggles too as a country, not everyone works, because jobs are hard to come by at times, we have homeless people in America, children starving, the crime rate is high as hell, drugs, racism, hate crimes against the gay community AND OUR STREETS ARE NOT PAVED IN GOLD!!!

The look on his face I knew I was breaking his pro American heart, my subconscious was lingering, so after I said all that, I said but yeah there is plenty of opportunities in America and our Government does try to make sure the American people are taken care of; whether it be through unemployment compensation, disability benefits, welfare benefits, food stamps, Medicaid, housing, schooling, American does try to help those in need and those who CAN'T help themselves, yes American is the GREATEST COUNTRY in the world...he smiled and said YES SEE I TOLD YOU, looking down in the ground trying to not let him see the tears starting to surface, I said YES, YOU DID.

Ok...bringing my readers back now to the present. After giving Kathy some life lessons on men and sex I felt she should be able to make some smart adult decisions. Samuel and I were getting closer and I like the fact I was able to carry on adult and simulating conversations with him, unlike Devin which I have known majority of my life. Samuel, me, my cousin Candie, and her man went to a concert. I had original brought the tickets for Nicole, me, Devin and her man but since they were no longer in my life, I choice the next best thing. My cousin Candie and I weren't really close growing up, since my father is a Marine we traveled quite a bit and when I came back to North Carolina we really turned out to be two different people interested in different things.

My cousin Candie, was good for a laugh and always had I don't give what the fuck what people think about me demeanor. She always knows the gossip around town, and had a bluntness of telling how it is. Samuel after going out for about 3 months, asked me to marry him, I with no hesitation said yes. The news spread fast and my cousin Candie called to congratulate me and in one swift breath after congratulating me said "girl, you sure want some old man". I laughed and said yes because hopefully I won't have to teach him anything, especially on how to treat a woman. Samuel approached me about 3 weeks after asking me to marry him, wanted to move in with me. Though I had no hesitation with saying yes, to his proposal to marry me, I did however, for some reason hesitated saying yes to him moving in.

Samuel with a look of confusion on his face asked why I was hesitating. I told him, I was not sure if I was quite ready for that and what about your house. Samuel mentioned he would keep the house and just rent it out. I said to Samuel before I say yes, to this we need to go over what is to be expected while you're here. Samuel said you are my fiancé we are going to be husband and wife, yes I said but you are not my first fiancé and so there are things I expect. Samuel asked what my expectations were and I said 3 things: 1)if this is your home then you are to come home every night and not be gone days at a time, 2) I expect you to pay half of the cost to maintain this home, 3) never disrespect me. Samuel agreed to my conditions and he moved in the following week.

When Samuel first moved in the first week was good, he came home right after work or if he went to the store would call me to see if I needed anything. Week 2 with Samuel was pretty much the same and on the weekend after work he would run to the gas station to play some numbers and get a six pack of beer. Week 3 was almost the same as week 2 expect after work during the week Samuel would get a 6 pack of beer. By week 4 Samuel was buying and drinking a 6 pack every day of the week. I didn't say anything since Samuel was a hardworking man and drinking a six pack really didn't change him, he wasn't loud, violent, or aggressive just talkative but that was normal. It had been a month and it had come time for Samuel to pay half of the bills like we had agreed.

Samuel gave me a check for $750, I looked at him and said this is not half, half is $1500. Samuel said he will pay half but couldn't do half at the moment with him still having to pay the mortgage on his house, bills, and back child support. I told him that is not what we agreed to and if you knew you couldn't afford half and if I knew you couldn't afford half I would have never invited you to move in. Samuel begged me not to give up so easily on him and things will work on, remember husband and wife in the vows it states for richer and poorer. Part of me couldn't help but to think, I was being played somehow and Samuel was an opportunist. The other part of me wanted to believe I found my equal and things will get better soon.

Charlean called me and mentioned things had turned sour between her and her husband and they were in the process of separating. She mentioned she was looking at jobs on the east coast and had an interview with Department of Treasury. I told Charlean that my time in the Navy is coming to an end and I would likely be out in the next month or so. I asked Charlean what happened with her husband, she said "you were right Harminme, I told him I didn't want to have children, and he pretty much said that was it for our marriage". I told Charlean, I was truly sorry and that he wasn't the man God intended for her. She stated she purchased a townhouse and was facing some financial setbacks and I told her whatever she needs I will be there, I love you, Charlean said I love you too and we hung up.

It was almost the end of June and I was being processed out of the Navy, I prepared for this day since coming back to the U.S. but now that it was here it was a hard reality to accept. As things with my Navy career was coming to an end, at least I would have a future husband that could hopefully take care of me. Once out of the Navy I filed for unemployment and started searching for jobs right away, I figured with my military background and working on my bachelor's degree I would get a job in no time. Meanwhile, Samuel went from drinking a six pack of beer every day to a nine pack. I still did not address this noticeable pattern with him because again he wasn't a violent drunk.

One day after work Samuel came home and said he wants to sell his house. I asked him what happened to you fixing it up and renting it out. Samuel mentioned he did not want to be bother with tenants and maintenance and it was a home he shared with his ex-wife which he doesn't want the memories of, he wants to start over and erase the past. I put down my notebook and laptop and told Samuel that, I didn't think that would be a smart move, I mean suppose things go bad between us, where would you go. Samuel mentioned he was sure things between would not go bad and whatever money he gets from the sale of the house he would give me

$10,000 and we could use to buy our own home. Samuel seemed pretty sure about this so I didn't push it any further.

Samuel and I started renovating his house to put on the market, I helped financial as well even though I wasn't working and helped out wish things such as painting, removing tiles, cleaning, and yard work. While outside one day, Jerome had walked by he was heading to work and the way he looked at me I was thinking, I hope Samuel doesn't notice. Jerome had a way of looking at me that made me feel like I was wearing nothing. Samuel had got several offers once the house was on the market, he ended up going with the offer that was about $13000 below his asking price. Now that the house was sold, Samuel put me on a mission of finding him his dream truck which was also mine, he got a black dodge ram 1500.

I waited patiently for Samuel to give me the $10,000 he promised with the sale of the house, so at dinner one night I just came out and asked Samuel when he was planning on paying me the $10,000. Samuel replied that since he did not get what he wanted for the house that instead of giving me $10,000 he could give me $4000. I said, again Samuel this is not what we agreed to, but I'm not going to argue could you just make sure I have it in 3 days. Here we go again... strike two. I'm not sure what Samuel's end game was, but about two months after selling the house, he came to me with wanting to start his own business he mentioned he had been thinking about it for a while and now that he has the money it would be a good time to start it. Things were going smoothly until Samuel called me in a panic and said his account had been debited almost $30,000.

I wanted to sound like a concern future wife but part of me was like Oh well this is Karma bitch. Apparently the state took money out of Samuel's account for arrears in child support payments. Samuel went to an attorney and court to try and get his money back but things did not go in his favor. Samuel was mad as hell about the situation but there was no winning this. The job search for me was going slow, now I know what the senior Veterans in the VA hospital mean when they say "A hero's welcome" and they tell stories of how coming off active duty you feel like a stranger in your own land. People look at Veterans as damaged goods and can't get help from Veterans Affairs, family, friends, and no one will hire you.

Since, being separated from the military and moving back home, I have to admit even with being physically close to my family I was spiritually and emotionally distant from them. I would go months without a phone call from my sister or Regina and I hear their many shopping trips to Virginia and yet I never received a call being invited to go. Apart of me was a little jealous and hurt of my sister and Regina's relationship but I kept telling myself God gave me the mother I needed, not the mother I wanted to get me where and who I am today. With, the job search not going as planned I decided to look into taking a tax course so hopefully I could get a job doing taxes. This came about when I got my taxes done this year and handed all my receipts for the furniture I purchased for the condo because I read on the IRS website you can claim sales taxes off your purchases.

The lady at Liberty looked at me strange when I handed her my receipts like, why am I giving her this. I told her about the sales tax credit and she said no I can't do that. I smiled and said yes I can, she again said no you can't so I said you know what I am not going to sit here and argue with you on something I know I can do, and can you please get your boss. She got up and went into another room where I can see her through the glass talking to a man who I figured to be her boss, and I see him nodding his head saying yes, and heard the word she can do that. When the lady came back out she sat and smiled and said well, I learned something new today apparently you can claim sales tax. I smiled and said yes, I know this.

It took about 20 minutes for her to go through all the receipts I had and she gave me the total and I opened up the paper I had in my hand and stated Yeap that's what I got too. Since, she had pissed me off I didn't bother to inform her I had already calculated the receipts, figured this would teach her a lesson. When I left there I told myself I should look into doing taxes, because here this woman is working at Liberty for 15 plus years and don't know you can claim sales tax, there's no telling what else she may have missed on my tax return. I contact another tax franchise and was informed tax school will start the end of September. Samuel had came back to me about the subject of starting his own business. I figured he would had moved on from that seeing he was now $30,000 short.

He asked for my help which is another way of him asking me for some money. He asked if I would go half on the trailer needed to store his equipment, I told him that money is tight enough as it is, I do not have a job what makes you think I have money to give to you. Samuel said, this wasn't money for him but us and we could make a good living off this and be our own bosses. He stated this is our future and the investment will comeback 10 times fold. Against my better judgement I agreed to go half on the trailer and TRAILER ONLY!!! This cost me $1500. Samuel was stressing me out, while not having a job and going to school I noticed more and more about Samuel. There would be times when he would come home with his 9 pack of Natural light beer and I am in the Jacuzzi studying and he would come in and talk about himself and his day.

I would tell Samuel that I am studying and can we talk later, he would either act like a 2 year old with a tantrum and say, something like Oh come on I have no one to talk too. He would make another comment like a good wife always have time for her husband, or say okay I will let you study and then keep talking and not leave the bathroom. Another stress factor was the new neighbors that moved above us who were loud with heavy pounding the floor when they walk and their dog running overhead. I had got into it a few times with the man about his dog not being on a leash, even contacted the HOA and called the dog pound people on them.

One day the man who lived above us came and knocked on the door and started yelling at me about calling the pound and reporting him. I yelled back stating you need to follow the rules, and keep your dog on a leash, he fires back with well you should move I said why I need to moved I own my condo, he said, "black bitch" and I slammed the door in his face. I turned around looking at Samuel and said, did you just stand there and let that white man talk to me like that. Samuel said I thought that was between you and him. I told a deep breath and walked quickly to the bedroom, slammed and locked the door. I ran a hot bath looking at the water as tears ran down my face and said...strike three. I sat in the Jacuzzi prayed, really hard and I asked God to please remove this man from my life.

I couldn't help but to think if it had been Devin standing behind me that man, wouldn't of got three words out his mouth before Devin would of came to my defense. Here I was living with a man hardworking and smart but was a fucking coward, no courage to defend the woman he claims to love. As I sat there trying to figure out how I'm going to tell Samuel to leave I also had something to loss because now I would have to figure out how to make up the income I would be losing by letting him go. Truthfully I didn't care and figured God will get me through it somehow, for even with the sale of his house Samuel still was only paying $750 a month to live in a condo that costs $3000 a month to maintain.

I waited till the following week to inform Samuel the engagement was off and I wanted him to leave. He went through several emotional phases, he first tried to compromise by saying he could pay more towards the bills and could move into a house and not worry about neighbors above us. When I turned that down Samuel went into begging, saying I'm sorry I didn't defend you, I will cut back on drinking, and I won't complain about you going to bingo on Mondays. When that didn't work he tried to insult me by saying, what are you going to do without me, how are you going to pay all the bills, your unemployment is not going to last forever, and there not a harder working man in this town other than me. He became silent and I asked are you through now.

I told him when he find a place I would like to have a 3 week notice so I can be prepared. Also I informed Samuel after today he was free to fuck and date as he pleased. I called Charlean while in the Jacuzzi and told her about what happened between Samuel and I. She mentioned it was going to be hard but she's stated "you are smart and a fighter, this won't keep you down for long". Charlean mentioned she got a job offer with the Treasury in Arlington, VA and will be leaving heading to the east coast very soon and before she checks in she was planning on stopping by and visiting me. After calling off the engagement I was able to focus more on my studies.

While I wanted to get a job in the accounting field I noticed that in this area the jobs that were hiring were mostly healthcare related. So I did some research to see what job in the healthcare field I would like that dealt with numbers... medical billing and coding. Since I still had money for education with my GI bill I enrolled into AIU for an AA in Medical Billing and Coding. Luckily I was able to transfer a lot of my classes over from my Bachelor's degree so it didn't take long to get my AA in Medical Billing and Coding. I did volunteer work at the medical center and became good friends with a woman there named Shelly. She was an older woman and from time to time we had lunch together and went to her church or should I say churches. She would travel near and far looking for a church that she felt was a good fit for her.

Shelly was also an escape location for me to get away from Samuel, who just pissed me off just by walking through the door. There was one weekend I had a gathering at my home with family and friends and Samuel was rude and disrespectful. Though I didn't hear it for myself but my sister Danielle mentioned she was talking about relationships and how a good man is hard to find and Samuel called her a "desperate rider" indicating she was desperate to find a man. Danielle felt some kind of way about Samuel's comment and if there was a knife laying around he surely would have been cut... damn why didn't I have one on the counter. I knew if I really wanted to avoid seeing Samuel all day, every day I needed to find a job. I was thinking it's a shame when someone else runs you out your own home.

I went for a drive to Virginia to visit Chanel and we hung out, she mentioned she was likely to be discharge from the Navy. She stated with back to back pregnancies the weight wasn't coming off quick enough and she couldn't make weight or the run. Leaving from Chanel's I went to gas up and heard someone call out Mica, Mica, I turned around and it was Nickie. Nickie was one of the Air Traffic controllers I job shadowed while working in the air terminal in Iceland. I was surprise of all people to run into wow!! We exchanged contact information and made plans to meet that weekend. Nickie called Friday night we talked a bit catching up on life during and after the military. I told her about my past and current relationships and how I didn't expect life to be so stressful after the military.

Nickie mentioned she was a few months away from getting out but she already had a job set up at Norfolk international airport as an Air Traffic Controller there. She mentioned she was also married and had a baby girl. Nickie and I made plans and she drove down from VA to NC to pay me a visit. Unfortunately Samuel was home when Nickie arrived but he had just started drinking so hopefully he wouldn't show his ass. Samuel and Nickie had talked for a bit and I could tell he was starting to get too comfortable thinking if I don't rescue her now he will talk her to death. I told Samuel that Nickie and I had dinner plans, and quickly headed towards the door. Nickie and I walked to the restaurant since in the same area as the condos.

We sat in the restaurant talking, laughing, and drinking. Nickie mentioned Samuel seemed like a good man. I smiled and said yes, he has you and about 90 percent of this town convinced of that but believe me I had seen his demons. I told her I was saved by the fact that Samuel and I had lived together before announcing our vows in front of God, family, and friends because I got to see the REAL man that I would have ended up marrying. Not only did I not like what I saw but I saw how his demons tried to trick and lead me into a life where my happiness, hopes and dreams didn't matter and no longer would exist. I know with some religions that say it's a sin to live together before marriage but really I think it's the smart thing to do, so you would know the REAL person you are vowing to spend the rest of your life with.

Shelly called me one day while I was working on my classes, and she mentioned that a billing and coding position for the hospital's skilled nursing facility would be coming out and I should apply. It took about 5 days for the position to post but once it did I went on to the hospital's website and applied. I was contacted in 2 weeks for an interview and after 5 days was offered the position. I was excited and now hopefully I can manage financially working full time at the nursing center and part time doing taxes between December and April. After finishing my AA in Medical Billing and Coding, I enrolled at Colorado Technical University in the MBA program for Healthcare Management.

I started my position at the skilled nursing facility in November and I was fortunate that the previous biller was still around in the hospital to assist me. I was excited about my new job and I also realized something about myself which was I enjoyed the company of Senior Citizens. The residents in the nursing facillty life stories were entertaining and inspiring to me. I learned so much and the realization of growing old brought about concerns I never would have otherwise thought of at 30. Seeing one's own mind and body ending its life cycle I noticed how dying is like being born again... a baby, having someone who has to feed you, cloth you, wearing diapers, throwing fits because you can't get your way. From a seed to a flower, back to a seed again we grow, we flourish, we wilt, and we die.

Training with the previous biller seemed to have its challenges, I informed management that Ms. Diana seemed to be too busy to train me. My manager Frank had talked with Diana's manager about taking a week to train me on the billing for skilled nursing. The week with Diana I learned enough to get me going, but it seemed as though she avoided training me in depth, just covering the basis. Some of the questions I asked she replied oh don't worry about that or the insurance company doesn't cover it. Three weeks after the one on one training, I just felt like something was off, something was missing but I'm not sure what it was. I heard that Diana went to my manager saying she wasn't sure I was a good fit for the job. Frank called me into the office and we sat and talked and I told him about the training and how it seemed Diana was holding some things back.

Frank mentioned maybe the job wasn't for me, I didn't like how he was coming across, like I was incapable of doing this job. I would have lunch with Shelly from the other medical facility and we would talk about work and I told her about Diana. Shelly mentioned she really didn't know Diana so couldn't give me any advice on her character. Shelly mentioned to me if Diana wouldn't help you maybe someone else could. I thought for a minute and yes, that's true. Even though this was the only skilled nursing facility in a 60 miles radius, it wasn't the only nursing facility, so I reached out to other nursing homes asking to speak to their coding and billing person. This was an eye opener, matter of fact I wish I would have thought of it sooner and not months later sitting behind a desk waiting on one person.

I also contacted Medicare and Medicaid for training and questions about billing for skilled nursing homes. I visited their websites quite often to add to my resource and contacts. I was also working as a tax preparer so I was working from morning to night 4 to 5 days out of the week. Samuel was acting cordial of course it was to get things back on a relationship basis and to have sex. I still had sex with Samuel just out of convenience since he was the only dick in my bed and life at the moment. We went back to using condoms since with the new job I had to wait 90 days in order to qualify for healthcare benefits and my depo shot had passed the date of injection.

With me, having sex with Samuel he seemed to think there was still hope for us, but I reminded him on a weekly basis that he needs to make time to find somewhere else to stay. I guess he figured I would come back to him mentally since we were still involved physically but still when he walked through the door, I felt sick to my stomach and was like I can't stand this man. I also still prayed every night while taking a bath in my Jacuzzi, God please remove this man from my home. My healthcare benefits for the skilled nursing job had been in effect for about 3 weeks now and I made an appointment to get back on birth control though I wanted to get back on the depo shot I had been on it for 5 years and was told by the military doctor before discharge it was not good to be on the depo for a long time.

I looked into other options, I settled for the IUD which is placed inside you and can prevent pregnancy up to 3 to 5 years. There was also an option for a 10 year IUD which was great. It's not that I didn't want a child one day but being separated from the military, with an unstable job, a temporary job, and a man who is a functional alcoholic nothing was right with my life. During the appointment the nurse came in and asked me a few questions, she asked when the last time I had my period, I told her it's been about 5 years. I mentioned I was on the depo shot and did not have a cycle. She asked if I could be pregnant I said not likely but I can take a test. I took the pregnancy test and about 5 minutes later the nurse walks in and said CONGRADULATIONS YOU'RE PREGNANT!!!

I just stared at her and her big smile slowly erased from her face, she said I take it this is not happy news. I was thinking BITCH don't you see me here trying to get on birth control, how is hearing the news I am with child good news!! I replied can I have a moment...she closed the door behind her and I reached for my phone, and I had no idea who to call. I opened the phone and as tears hit the numbers I thought who do I reach out to in a crisis... I dialed a Marine... my father. I told him about the news that I was pregnant he asked is this a happy event, I said definitely no. He asked if Samuel knew, I said no, and he was the first one I called. My father asked what I was going to do I said I'm not sure, my father then said, you know Harminme if I could take the baby for you I would but I got so much going on my end. I told him thanks, I will figured this out.

I hung up the phone and called Samuel, he answered and I told him that I was at the doctor's office and the nurse just came in and told me I was pregnant. Without any hesitation, Samuel replied, "what you calling me for". I looked at the phone and hung up, that had to be the most pain and emptiness I have ever felt. So insensitive and I was carrying a seed from this man. I sat in that room thinking of all the pros and cons of this situation. My family, on my father's end I opine is in a loveless marriage, a mother who only will protect and serve the man in her life, a sister who is selfish, and the father of this seed...who takes more than what he gives. What kind of mother would I be...SELFLESS.

I called for the nurse and told her, I won't be having the baby and could I get information on a location for termination. She came in and mentioned the nearest location would be in Virginia. She also gave me a paper to take to social services to received WIC. That night back at home was like any other night I took a bath and again prayed to God to removal Samuel from my life. I also had a conversation with God about this pregnancy and I believe that everything happens for a reason. I also knew God knows my actions before I do and if I wasn't going to have this child, then I wasn't going to have this child. I called Nicki and told her about the doctor's visit and the comment Samuel made. She mentioned whatever I decided to do, she would be there for me.

Being at work took on a whole new stress level, but I decided I wasn't going to let this defeat me. I came into work early and stayed late to train myself on how to do this job. I noticed in the second week a trend with the patients' accounts, which explained the high outstanding balance with the skilled nursing facility. It was then I knew why Diana was trying to get rid of me. I will explain...when a patient checks into a nursing facility and say they have Medicare, Medicaid, and a third party insurance like Blue Cross Blue Shield, they have to be billed in ORDER. The first being

Medicare which cares the first twenty something days, second is the third party insurance for example BCBS, and the last to be billed is Medicaid.

Well apparently Ms. Diana was not billing in that ORDER. Ms. Diana would first bill Medicare and after the twenty something days let the patient account sit until day 69 when Medicaid allows patients coverage for skilled nursing facilities. Even if the resident of the nursing home had a third party insurer she never submitted form for payment which is why the skilled nursing balance was so high. I wasn't sure what to do with this discovery, if I took it to my boss would he believe me or assume I'm just trying to start trouble and making excuses. I figured it would be best to go with him with hard evidence to back my words up. I printed out copies of about 10 patients accounts where she stopped billing after Medicare and later pick up billing with Medicaid NEVER billing the third party insurer because Medicaid is ALWAYS billed last.

I called Mr. Frank and told him I need to speak with him and mentioned I could come down after lunch at 1:00. I went to Mr. Frank's office and I told him what I had discovered and laid out the accounts and showed him the trend in all 10 accounts. He sat back in his chair and for a few seconds just looked at the papers I had. Mr. Frank asked me if I had shared this information with anyone else. I said no Sir you are the first one I have shared this with. He got up and sat on the edge of the desk facing me and said "Harminme, you are not to relay this information to anyone, I will talk with Diana about this and you are to continue doing the job as if this did not happen". I said yes Sir, I understand.

When I left out his office, the first thing that came to my mind was these white people about to set a sister up. When I got back to my office, I went onto the Medicare and Medicaid website and wrote the fraud hotline. I took notes and wrote down dates and names and created a word document on the work computer and saved it. After work I called the fraud hotline and gave my information and was told I would receive a call back. The next day there was a different feel in the office and I knew Frank had spoken to Diana and now it was a matter of when they were going to make their move. The lady in the office that worked with me I caught on the phone giving Diana information about my job searches and I made it clear to her, not to be relaying information back to Diana or else she I would have a problem because I'm to the point now I won't hesitated to fight a bitch. I heard no more phone calls to Diana from her after that.

In dealing with the drama at work, I also still had not called to set up my appointment to terminate this pregnancy. I called during lunch on my cell phone and walked outside to make the call. They set me up for an appointment in 2 weeks which was the beginning of April. I barely looked or even spoke to Samuel after that phone call from the doctor's office. Some nights I just slept on the sofa, not wanting to be in the same bed with him. He came up to me one day while in the kitchen bluntly said are you going to give me some tonight. I looked at him thinking this mutherjumper here...is a piece of work. I said HELL NO!!! He replied you might as well you can't get any more pregnant and I can cum in you.

If there was ever a point in my life I felt a nervous breakdown coming, this was it. I went into the cabinet grab a wine glass and a bottle out the fridge and went to my place of peace...my Jacuzzi. This time before praying to God, I decided to share a conversation with my child... I apologized that I would not get the chance to meet you, and not having you is the best option. I'm not saying I wouldn't have been a good mother to you but more scared that I would be taking from you. The world is full of predators and dangers that I know if it came down to it would not think twice about taking a life of someone who would harm you. There are things that I have been through I bury deep.

I know the day the doctor will remove you from my body, you will still be in my heart and soul. I have no family for you...for this is no family for me. I love you...and give you...to GOD. I'm not sure why but my sister Danielle happened to call me, just to say hi, but I knew better abviously father must have either told her or hinted at something was going on with me. I told her I had news but she needs to promise me not to tell Regina. She promised not to say anything to Regina, and I told her I was pregnant but I wasn't going to have the baby. She asked did they give you a WIC form, I said yeah but I'm not going to use it. Danielle was like why not you get milk, eggs, cheese, and cereal.

I said because I'm not going to use something when the reason it was giving to me I know I'm not going to have. Charlean had beeped in on the other end and I told Danielle I would talk to her later. I clicked over to Charlean, she told me she was finally settled into work in Arlington and I told her about everything that was going on with me at the job and the pregnancy. Charlean with the quickness, said I will be down this weekend. The weekend came and Charlean was down. We sat on the patio and talked, we shared some laughs, and some tears. She mentioned her soon to be ex-husband had a baby on the way. I was like damn I guess whatever available uterus...Charlean laughed and said did you ever think life would be this fucked up after the military...I said, not even close.

Charlean and I both stated if we could turn back time, we both would do things differently, but really I feel no matter what path you take you, will always end up where and with who God has intended. It was three days before my "appointment" I received a phone call from Nicki and she asked for the clinic's address because she wanted to be there for me. I asked Samuel for half of the money for the termination, he asked when I was having it done. I told him in three days, and Nicki was going to meet me there for emotional support. I'm not sure why but Samuel wanted to go. I told him I didn't care he could do what he wanted. The day came and Samuel and I drove to Virginia.

As we were pulling up to the place there were like 10 protesters outside holding up signs of anti-abortion. I was thinking like I don't feel bad enough coming here. I for one believed in pro-choice. Samuel and I walked into the clinic and I filled out some paperwork. They called me to the back while Samuel stayed upfront. I was placed in a room with a bunch of girls/women who were all there to terminate their pregnancy. Listening to the different conversations taking place, I had a flashback of when I was in the Navy waiting on my flight to Iceland and stayed in the holding barracks where girls/women attached to the ship would get pregnant on purpose to avoid going out to sea. A matter of fact some of the girls/women in there were from the Navy getting an abortion because the ship had already took sail.

Other stories were from women with husbands and boyfriends who they weren't for sure was the father or not. One girl, white mentioned she was fucking around with 2 black guys and had a white boyfriend and since she let all of them cum in her at will she didn't know what color baby would go out. Another woman, whose husband was in the Navy was out on deployment and had been for 6 months and she was 2 months along. One thing about the women sharing their stories was that this was not their first time and there seem to be no guilt in what they were repeatedly doing. Though I was putting up a strong united front I felt sad and at the same time a sense of wonder of who and what I was about to erase. With the first black President running could I possible be killing the second or third or a doctor that finds a cure for AIDS, cancer, hepatitis.

The not knowing is what REALLY ran through my mind but at the same time I NEVER once felt as though I wasn't supposed to be here and felt the urge to leave...and this pregnancy wouldn't have come to term regardless. There are some things that are just started for something else to end. I got a text from Nicki who had arrived and was waiting in the sitting area with Samuel. My name was called and I went to the room I received an ultrasound, which I guess was to confirm if I was really pregnant then I went into another room with a doctor and another staff person. I laid down while they prepared everything. The doctor told me to relax and to count down from 20, I started to count down and the next thing I remembered was waking up in another room.

I looked at the time and almost 90 mins had past, which was like wow the last thing I remembered was stopping my countdown somewhere around 14. I slowly got up and a staff person was there to ask me questions to make sure I was thinking clearly. I walked out into the waiting area and Samuel got up and came to help. I checked out and Samuel helped me into the truck, the ride home was quiet for I didn't have anything to say to Samuel, at least nothing pleasant. I checked my phone and saw the text from Nicki that she had left and would call later to check on me. As I'm riding I think to myself how I felt nothing, I'm not sure what I was expecting after this but it was like my body and mind did not just go through what should have been a somewhat traumatizing event.

I guess part of me wanted to feel some type of physical pain, I guess in a way to punish myself and remind myself what I did was tragic. Now I see why some of the girls/women were there 3... 4 times because there was no trace of occurrence, no physical pain, and some no emotional breakdown, wondering did I just terminated a future part of me. Tears rolled down my face and as we crossed the North Carolina state line I told myself I have to erase and find a way to get away from this man who now forever has left an imprint on my soul. I wanted to take a hot bath but had to take showers for 2 weeks. Even in the shower I pressed my head against the tile and pray again God please remove this man from my life as tears and water ran down the drain.

That night I couldn't sleep, even though I was tired as hell Samuel, wouldn't leave the bed no matter what the situation. There would be times I would intentionally sleep on the couch to get away from him and he would just curl up next to me where I would pretty much just go to the bed since it was more room. Either way this man gave me no peace, when I needed or wanted it. Samuel was a selfish coward and I didn't care about making up his portion of the money he paid every month for the bills because there is NO PRICE FOR A PEACE OF MIND... Back to work on Monday I knew my time here was quickly approaching as well since I done caught on to Ms. Diana negligence and though North Carolina is not as bad as Mississippi I knew being a BLACK female with common sense, book sense, and I can read reports too...I went from the fall guy to a liability because I had proof, it wasn't me.

On Tuesday morning when I went into work, I wasn't there an hour before the hospital security came to my office. The Officer told me I had to clear out my personnel belongings and I was no longer an employee at this facility. I took a deep breath and said I understand, the Officer was on the radio with my soon to be ex-boss which I heard him say make sure she doesn't take any patient records. Like I'm that mutherfucking stupid to remove patient records, but I'm smart enough to have already emailed them to the Medicaid case worker. The Officer then escorted me out to the front of the building, now time for part 2.

I created a letter for the day I knew these bitches were going to fire me. This letter laid out what Diana was doing and NOT doing, how I informed my supervisor and what he told me NOT to do and to pretty much cover it up. I also included the addresses of the Board members in this letter and I stated I had been in contact with the Medicare and Medicaid fraud hotline and an investigation had been opened. I sent this letter to ALL the Board Members, the Pitt Memorial Hospital Director, Assistance Director with the facility I was just fired from falls under and to the Direct of the hospital and Chief financial Officer of the hospital that the skilled nursing facility was attached to. I didn't know if they would just view me as a black hostile female worker who just lost her job, but that was the reason why I stated objective evidence and NOT subjective evidence... all which can be proven.

I wasted no time filing for unemployment, for I knew a domino effect was about to happen and Samuel was next I'm sure. Samuel will either think I will NEED his ass now because I don't have a job and will beg him to stay or he will NOW leave wanting me to suffer and kick a bitch while she's down, either way I plan to be prepared. The following week on Friday Samuel came to me and mentioned he was going out of town for the weekend and wouldn't be back until Sunday night or Monday morning. I was like okay. In my mind I was thinking, and the games begin. Samuel was gone the weekend, and though I was happy he wasn't there I was also curious what he was up to. Maybe he found another woman...now he would be her problem.

Samuel came back Sunday night and when he did, he wanted to talk. He wanted us to work things out and get married like we planned. I told Samuel NO, that is not going to happen and I no longer loved him. Then he got ugly stating how was I expect to keep this condo and pay all the bills with no job, and what man in this town would be better financially for me than him, and I won't make it on my own. I smiled and laughed and said, Samuel I am no longer your woman, but I AM A WOMAN OF GOD and with him I have succeed before you, and trust and believe I will succeed after you. I grab my bottle of wine, a glass and filled the Jacuzzi to take a bath which after 2 weeks was want I needed to ease the stresses coming around every corner in my life.

As Samuel slept that night, I for one couldn't help but to wonder where the fuck did he go and who with. Obviously that shit didn't work out if he came back here begging for me to give him another chance. I needed to find out, I couldn't look through his phone since he had a code to open it which I didn't know. So I went through his pockets, wallet, and paperwork he had in the house, nothing. I sat on the coach thinking and I got the same feeling I had in Japan when I caught Chris with that white girl and to check his truck came to mind. I got the keys to Samuel's truck and went downstairs. I unlocked the door to the truck and on the passenger side was a stack of papers.

I picked the papers up and saw Samuel had signed a lease for a house over in the next county. The lease dated back almost 2 weeks ago. I was furious!! This son of a bitch was just going to leave me without warning, without notice. I took the elevator back up and went into the kitchen drawer and took out a piece of paper and pen and wrote down the address. I stormed to the master bedroom. I turned on the light and yelled Samuel's name, he woken out of his sleep in disarray, yelling what the hell!! I shouted you signed a lease, and threw the papers at him. He tried to play it off but I could tell, he wasn't expecting me to find out what he had done. He quickly turned the blame on me stating how I wanted him gone and he was doing just that. I said yes but you were to inform me ahead of time when found a place and when you were leaving.

Samuel mentioned he was thinking about canceling the lease that's why he made a final attempt to get us back together. I stared at him eyes burning red with tears, and my body wanting to attack, calmly I said I want you out of my condo and life in the next 24 hours for if you sleep one more night in my bed I can't promise your safety...and walked out. In the morning Samuel started packing his clothes and moving them to the house he had signed a lease for. He came to me later that afternoon, and said he moved out all his things and was heading to the house. I quickly said ok, he gave me my keys and I continued to work on my assignment. (Song: Strangers).

Here I was alone again for the second time, but I wasn't sad just disappointed. As I took my bath that night, I thanked God for finally removing Samuel from my home. There was a silence, a peace, a relief of owning myself and home once again. I was able to focus now on my third degree which I only had a few months left and my MBA in Healthcare Management would be completed. If it hadn't been for the many distractions from Samuel my GPA would have been higher but still I will finish the race. Now that there was no man in my life taking me on detours from my goals I set to put a plan in action to finish my degree and look for a good career.

I took different courses to make myself more profitable. I did a Peer Support Specialist class which I did to help myself as well as others cope with the misfortune and unexpected turns in life. I received a phone call for an open position in a Behavioral health agency for a peer support specialist in Elizabeth City, NC. The job position consist of a working in a team with 5 other members, which included a nurse, a psychiatric, and a social worker, and 2 qualified professionals called QRs. The first two weeks on the job was for the team to get to know one another and coming up with marketing strategies for us to get new clients, since this was a new agency in the area. One day while getting off work driving home, my car broke down.

I called my insurance company and had them tow "Dana" my car home. I took two days off to get Dana situated, I remember the very next day after this incident happened calling my sister Danielle for a ride into town. Now my sister literally stays not even 2 miles away from me in a trailer park. I made the phone call just knowing my sister Danielle would come to my rescue but instead, on the other end I heard, "I wasn't planning on coming out today" and followed by silence she hung up. I could not explain the hurt and loneliness I felt in that moment. I looked at my cell phone and tears filled my eyes. This was my sister, the one who would jump in the car in a heartbeat and drive to Virginia and go shopping with her mom, go to school and attend her son's PTA, drive all the way to Fredericksburg, VA to see our father, a sister I paid $1000 for on a bedroom set while I was stationed in Bahrain.

Though I was in my hometown surrounded by "family", there was little love and no support. In that selfish, careless moment, a hate and anger tore in me like a rip through an already weakened seam. It was then and there Danielle, my sister had EXPUNGED her name from my will. I didn't know who else to call, so I tried my cousin Candy. Candy mentioned she was at work but could pick me up after she gets off, and it was then Candy showed loyalty something my sister and mother had failed. I ended up having to get a rental car for about 2 weeks, the number 4 cylinder in Dana had broken which required taking apart the engine. Luckily she was still under warranty but barely the cylinder broke around 77,000 miles and the warranty expired at 80,000 though I do like the dodge brand I told myself never again will I purchase a dodge.

Okay back to work, things at the new agency was going slow, we would go out in the community to let people know who we were, what we had to offer, and where we were located. There was one team member who everyone seemed to have some type of conflict with...Mary. She was the psychiatrist on the team and frankly this chick had been in the field too long, for she needed to be on psychotic meds herself. While at work one day I received a phone call from my friend Shelly from the medical center, she mentioned that a job had posted on the hospital website for my old boss...Mr. Frank. She mentioned there are several stories going around one which included he was being fired, really transferred to South Carolina for a new job position.

Apparently the letters I had sent to the Pitt Memorial Hospital to the Board Members and Hospital Director, opened up a look inside the skilled nursing billing activities and saw I was on to something. Since, Mr. Frank did not disclose the information that I had stated to him, to cover themselves they are taking him out of the picture. I was so happy to receive that call I felt justice was finally being rendered but yet that bitch Diana was still there. I was relieved but at the same time knew once everything was over, it was likely going to mean the nursing facility shutting down and people losing their jobs and people's loved ones with no other nearby skilled nursing facility to go. The financial hole was so deep I knew the only way management was going to resolve it was to bring an end to it all.

Though Mr. Frank was being removed, his ass still wasn't fired. It's amazing how when white people fuck up they get transferred to a new position with the same or even better pay, but let a black fuck up we are fired, escorted out the mutherfucking building, and have to fight to received unemployment. NO, NO, NO I am not going to be bitter, everything happens for a reason and I know… GOD has a plan. This job I was currently working was just as unlawful and stressful as the nursing one. I was having a time with adjusting and trying to control the impulse to back hand a bitch, named Mary. At night when I soaked in my bath water thinking Harminme you spent almost 10 years in the Navy, didn't run or try to get out when 9-1-1 took place (like a lot of mutherjumpers did, I mean HELLO PEOPLE JOINING THE MILITARY MEANS THERE'S A POSSIBILITY YOUR ASS MAY HAVE TO GO TO WAR!!!) and take several anthrax shots…

Truth is I didn't fear death, hell sometimes I welcomed it, but I knew, ever since that night, Devin and I fell in the water and my soul left my body that we all go in our time and the way God means for us to go…I had a purpose. Because of how strong those winds were that night and not preparing my body to hold my breathe I knew FATE was real. "Yea, though I walk through the valley of the shadow of death, I will fear no evil, for though art with me, thy rod and thy staff they comfort me." Being a Veteran in this world I saw the shadow…in my light, I walked among family and civilians as they were evil, missing the comradery of the military. When I separated from the Navy it brought something out with me…and NO IT DID NOT COMFORT ME!!!

I was now on a whole new battle field with no Senior Chief, Master Chief, or Commanding Officer to take charge, I was…ALONE. As stubborn as I was though I wasn't about to let a civilian run me off, at least not until a backup plan was in place. I stuck it out for 7 months till tax season rolled back around where I went full time as a Tax Preparer. A new office had opened up in my hometown and like last tax season, this field I will say is worth knowing and being in. I got some interesting clients that waits around till tax time to put on a great performance. One guy who was a merchant marine and made 6 figures a year apparently was in tens of thousands of dollars in debt for back taxes for giving his pets social security numbers and claiming them as dependents on his return.

There was another client who walked in with a woman, giving me his information claiming head of house hold status with his three kids and towards the end of the interview when asked why the mother isn't claiming the children they both look at each other and she makes a comment what you know I don't work. I stopped typing and looked at the couple and asked, Sir, is this YOUR WIFE, he then put his head down for a few seconds and turns to the woman and yells what did I tell your ass in the car, let me do the talking. I smiled and stated to the man that lying on your tax return is against the law and if the IRS ever audits your return and finds any inconsistency you could be paying them back A LOT of money because INTEREST AIN'T NO JOKE.

He stated that yes the woman next to him was indeed his wife, I asked did you two live together the last 6 months out the year, the woman says hell we been together for 13 years. I said Sir, now that I know this information I cannot file you as head of household on your taxes when you are clearly still legally married. The man then says well her ass don't work can I claim her as a dependent. I smiled and said no Sir you can NEVER claim a spouse as a dependent, but buy claiming married filing joint will give you more benefits by reducing your tax liabilities and increasing your tax credits where you would get more money. The man with a big smile on his face said OK let's start over then.

I smiled and said ok Sir, but I'm going to need you and your wife to leave out the door and walk back in like we never had this conversation, we all laughed and I completed their tax return. Taxes was fun, the people were real, and the struggle was real in trying to get out of the IRS as much money as possible. I was no different really from a lot of my clients, expect I didn't necessary want to get more money out of the IRS just learn how to keep them from getting less of MINE. On lunch break one day I went downtown to pay a bill and across the street there was Jerome just staring at me. He just made me so uneasy like he was looking through my clothes and the fact he was still built and I hadn't had sex for over six months my body was responding in a way I didn't want. I quickly got in my car and drove off.

I went back to work and since it was a slow day me and the other worker Kira talked and I played spades on the computer missing my Diego

Garcia days. In the middle of talking about old boyfriends a blue car pulls up in front of our store. The car door opens and out steps Jerome. I said OH SHIT! Kira was like what's wrong, I said nothing, can you take this client when he comes in. When Jerome walks through the door Kira greets him and asked was he there to get his taxes done. He said, no, I'm here for her. I slowly push my chair from the desk and walk towards the front, where Jerome was standing, as I got closer he turns and opens the door and we head outside. With my arms folded across my chest I stood quietly and waited to see what he had to say.

He stated he had saw me earlier downtown, I said yes, and I saw you. Jerome stated he's been waiting for the right moment to approach me. When he heard Samuel and I were no longer engaged and had not heard of me seeing someone else, when he saw me downtown, he drove around town to see where I was at. I said ok, now that you found me, what. Jerome mentioned I had been on his mind off and on throughout the years and when he heard I was back in town, he sat back, watching and waiting for the opportunity to present itself. I asked what is it again that you want with me, he smiled and said, I want you. I smiled and said, NO!! I turned away and started to head back inside, Jerome puts his hand up against the door, where I am unable to open it and said, why not.

I replied, I'm not looking to get into another relationship and honestly I don't trust men, and I don't feel like wasting anymore of my time. Jerome, mentioned you know we have history together, I have known you for a long time. I am not looking to be your boyfriend, husband, or man just a friend to be there however and whenever you need me. Again as he looks at me though I am fully clothed I feel I am butt ass naked. He gives me his number and states he is always at Stop in Shop playing pool if I ever need him. I then gave him my contact number as well, Jerome then opens the door to the shop and I go inside. Kira smiling ear to ear, asked who that was. I mentioned an ex man trying to be a current. I had admit after Jerome pulled off, the memories of him and I resurfaced.

Though the shower head and Jacuzzi was satisfying my sexual cravings, there is still nothing like the REAL thing. Jerome still had that strong, bad boy attitude, along with a built body, that night while taking a bath I fantasized about us being together and wondered how sex with him would feel after all these years. Since Jerome now knew where I worked he drove by each and every day!!! He would send text messages asking how my day was going, and how I was on his mind. A week had passed I decided to give Jerome an invite to my condo. Before Jerome arrived I had opened up a bottle of wine and soaked in the Jacuzzi. When I got out I laid naked on the bed with the ceiling fan going which was something I always did, I called it air drying.

After air dying I put on my night gown, grabbed the left over wine in the bottle with the wine glass and headed to the living room to wait for Jerome to arrive. I was in the living room sitting on the coach watching t.v. and finishing the wine and in about 10 minutes there was a knock at the door. I got up and answered the door, Jerome had came in, kissed me on the cheek and waited to be invited into the living room. We sat on the couch and talked about old times back, when we I approached him about making Devin jealous. We laughed and joked but I mentioned that Devin and I did get back together briefly when I came home this time around but things did not work out. Jerome stated he was surprised to hear that because he knew how much Devin loved me.

Jerome mentioned, that back in the day he never said anything to me but him and Devin had a few words about me. I said really and you two didn't try to kill each other. Jerome stated it's funny you said that because the reason they had ended up face to face is because Devin had shot at him. I replied Oh My God, what!! Jerome mentioned during the time Devin and I were broken up and him and I were together that Devin saw him one day coming out of a mutually friend's house and Devin came out the back door and pointed a gun and pulled the trigger. Jerome mentioned he had a gun as well but did not return fire because he knew the shot was meant as a warning...but Jerome stated he knew where Devin hung out at and would make it a point to be at the spot to end this shit before something started that would have one of them in a body bag.

Jerome mentioned he saw Devin at the projects and called him out in front of his boys. I then asked Jerome was he by himself, he laughed and said yeah. Jerome said he didn't require back up because no matter how bad "D" thought he was and angry his blows may be thrown with emotions but my blows come with skills. As Jerome told me this story I was amazed at how far these two men had went because of me. Jerome mentioned he told Devin that he did not steal me away from him and that I still loved him even though I was physically with him, he told Devin my heart was still his. Jerome said now I'm a man and as a man I'm going to do what a man do...but I'm not keeping her from you. Jerome even mentioned he gave Devin some manly advice and from that day forward they been cool.

So I asked Jerome what is it that a man do...Jerome moves in to kiss me on my neck then slide down the shoulder strap on my gown exposing my breast he sucks my nipples and I grab his head. Moaning and breathing starting to deepen I reached for his tank top and pull it over his head. I go to unzip his pants and he stops me, I look at him in confusion and said why are you stopping me. Jerome states as he moves his hands up my thighs that he wants to please me first. I grabbed a pillow from the couch and laid it behind my head, Jerome grabs another pillow and places it under my lower back and ass lifting me up. Jerome then goes down and eats me out. He's down in that position for about 20 minutes and I'm wet and horny, wanting him to just put it in. I said please Jerome put it in...I want it now.

Jerome paused for a moment and said, don't call me Jerome, the people on the streets call me Jerome, I want you to call me by my name. I looked like okay isn't your name Jerome, he said no, my real name is Freddie. I laughed and said yeah ok sure, he said no for real my first name is Freddie, Jerome is my middle name, really so what is your last name he said Henderson. So your name, REAL name is Freddie Jerome Henderson. He replied yes. I said wow I've been knowing you for almost 15 years, had sex with you and about to have sex with you AGAIN and I'm just now getting your REAL name. So, why are you telling me this, Freddie replied because Jerome and Freddie are two different people and I want you to know me the REAL me which is Freddie.

Freddie stands up and unbutton his pants reaches in his pocket for the condom, which I then take out his hand open it up and put it on. He smiles, I say what are you smiling about he said that's my Harminme... takes control, makes it known what she wants and grabs it. Freddie slides his dick in me and starts thrusting, as we are having sex I'm thinking DAMN, he wasn't like this when I was 16. Then again it could be my focus wasn't on him but making Devin jealous with fucking him. Freddie had me in different positions enjoying the feeling of him from one position to the next. He asked did I cum I smile and with a brief laugh said, it is very HARD for me to cum and if that is what you are waiting on you will be here for days. I asked Freddie is that why he was holding back from cuming he said, yes and no. My body is just like yours stubborn and it takes a lot for me to cum to.

An hour and 45 minutes we moved from the couch to the floor to the couch to the foot stool to the floor again neither one of us reaching a climax, but the sex was INTENSE!!! I didn't like the fact I couldn't make him cum so I put forth a lot more effort to ensure I would make him cum for me whether he wanted to or not. The third time we had sex I was ready for him. After the first two times my body was able to pick up on what motion and rhythm that would likely bring him down. When he came over for the third night I had just got out the tub and was air drying on the bed. He called me to let me know he was downstairs, I mentioned the door was open and I was in the bedroom. I heard him come in closing and locking the door and he made his way back to the Master Bedroom.

Freddie stood in the doorway, seeing me laying naked on the bed, he smiled and said that pussy been on my mind all day. Freddie took off his boots, and came over to the bed grab my legs and pulled me towards him. He stated eating me out, which seemed to be his most favorite thing to do. I let him play down there for about 20 minutes then I grabbed and opened the condom and begged for him to put it in. He was being stubborn and would stop eating me and with his pants still on grind up against my pussy, kissing my neck and whisper in my ear who pussy is it I would turn to him and smile and say MINE!! He didn't like that response but it got him to finally give me what I wanted. Freddie took the condom out my hand and put it on.

Freddie started off like normal hard, fast, rough, wanting to hear me yell, hear me call his name. When he began grinding at steady and slow rhythm, that's when my alter ego kicked in and now operation mortal combat kicked in. I slid down lower spreading my legs even wider, now instead of running away from him like before, I was coming towards him...WIDE THE FUCK OPEN!!! I moved my hips in a back and forth motion changing his pace to what I wanted it to be. Once I got Jerome in the rhythm of my body, I pulled him closer to my breast, rubbing his back, whispering in his ear, do you like that...he responded yes baby, Oh that feels so good, don't stop. I then picked up the pace throwing it back harder, he shouts FUCK HARMINME what are you trying to do. While, picking up the rhythm I said, you will cum for me!!!

Freddie, went to huffing and puffing breathing hard and grunting and then the sweet words I longed to hear... Uh I'm coming!!! Jerome rolled over on his back trying to catch his breath, while he laid trying to recoup, I took off the condom. We went through this cycle three to four times a week for over a month it became a mind control on trying to get him to cum mentally I had to prepare and physically I had to be stern I activated the mortal combat pussy (MCP) and the words "finish him" played in my head then I gave him everything I HADJ I received a phone call from my cousin Candy, who was bored and wanted to know if I wanted to get together for drinks. Candy and I sat around talking and drinking and reminiscing about back in our younger days before bills and kids.

I mentioned to Candy, I actually ran into Jerome AKA Freddie and we were getting back familiar with one another. My cousin Candy stated she sees him all the time at Stop in Shop playing pool I'd don't think he ever goes home which I can't say I blame him, his wife is an alcoholic. In mid-range of the wine cooler to my mouth, I said to Candy... what did you just say, she looked at me and said, you didn't know Jerome was married, yeah and they have a child together a little boy. OH MY GOD!!! Are you fucking kidding me, to who and for how long, you know what fuck it, I'm about to get to the bottom of this. I called Jerome, I mean Freddie and ask him to meet me at my condo later on that night without hesitation he stated he would be over about 10, I told him make it 11 I'm chilling with my cousin Candy at the moment.

I tried to calm myself down before meeting with Freddie, I took a hot bath just to sort out in my head the news I just heard and why in the hell in this small ass town this information did not surface during week 1 hell day 1. I mean I've been having sex with Freddie for almost two months and just now finding out his ass is married with children. I get out of the Jacuzzi and air dry like normal, I put on my night gown and go to the living room taking my wine glass and bottle to finish up. I had a buzz going which kept me low key. I heard the knock at the door, I opened the door Freddie gives me a kiss and we go to the couch. I'm not sure how but Freddie could read me and knew something was off.

He asked baby what's wrong, I said Freddie is there something you need to tell me. Freddie with a look of confusion on his face sits quietly for a minute and was like no, not that I am aware of. I said REALLY are you sure...Freddie again with a look of confusion says no Harminme what is it baby, what's wrong. I calmly asked, are you are married? Freddie laughed he said, I throughout you knew I was married, I replied HELL NO!! Do you think I go around sleeping with married men, plus there has been some nights that you have stayed over, also you don't have a wedding ring on. Freddie said please Harminme, don't be mad, but this is a small town and I assume your family had told you or you already knew. No, and I'm feeling so stupid right now and betrayed.

Freddie told me he was married, and they shared a son together, he stated he married her because she was pregnant with his son he wanted to do the right thing at the time and marry her. He stated how he grow up without a father and not knowing the man that help created him has put a burden on him even as a grown man. He wanted to be a better father and be there to see his son grow up and know who he was. He mentioned his wife had gotten worse throughout the years, she was a drinker when they met but he didn't realize until they got married she was a full blown alcoholic. Freddie mentioned he stopped drinking because he didn't like the person he was when was drinking and two drunks in the house raising his son.

His story got to me, and as I'm listening to him I'm thinking what else don't I know about this man who I have known half my life like I didn't know about Devin. So, I asked Freddie what else about you that I should know. Freddie began to share that this was his third wife, his first wife was a white woman and they were together while he was in the military and she took off with his money, the second wife died of an overdose for she was strung out real bad on crack and cocaine. I looked at him and said, with the cycle you had with wives did you ever think marriage is not for you. Freddie laughed and said, I just prayed the next woman would be better than the last. Then I asked how many children do you have.

Freddie paused for a minute and said I'm not 100 percent sure but it could be at least 8 out there in the world that belong to me. I put my head down and closed my eyes hoping when I opened them this was a bad dream and I was alone in my condo and I did not meet Freddie two months ago. Freddie goes in to touch me and I quickly pull away. He says Harminme don't do this, I need you, if I knew that you were coming back home I would of made you my wife, I looked up and said, not likely. Freddie stated that you are the only good woman I've ever had in my life. I looked at Freddie and said I need some time to think about things. Freddie stated he understood, and gave me a kiss on the cheek and left out.

I went to work the next day thinking about the night before and what I was going to do about Freddie. I wanted to get my mind off things so I put more focus in my work and studies. Freddie called me two days after our meeting but I didn't pick up, I could see his blue car drive by, hoping he wouldn't stop. Even though a part of me wished he did. The whole week I went without contacting Freddie, which was hard since physically I was craving him, my body in heat. Saturday after work I went over to my sister's place where my cousin Candy, my Aunt Sandy, and Regina were drinking. We talked and joked which was what I needed to take my mind off Freddie at least for a little while. I got home a little after midnight I took a bath and laid on the bed.

I wasn't down for 5 minutes and I could hear a car outside underneath the condo, not thinking much of it figured to be one of my neighbors. Then I hear a knock at MY door. I looked through the peek hole and saw it was Freddie. I backed away from the door but he had already heard me approaching so he knew I saw him. He shouted from behind the door Harminme if you don't open up this door I will bang on it all night long waking your neighbors. This mutherjumper knew I did not like drawing attention especially from my neighbors having them categorizing me as being "ghetto" or "LOUD". I unlocked and swung the door open saying what the fuck...and before I could finish he grabbed me, kiss me and said I'm not leaving you.

I was sooooo turned on I wanted him and while he had me against the wall, I started unbuttoning his pants and we shuffled to the bedroom, while undressing each other. The sex with Freddie was always intense and long he definitely wasn't a one minute man. Needless to say things were still on with Freddie and I, even with him having a wife. That night he stayed over, I was thinking to myself if I was his wife I would have been thinking right now where the fuck is my husband. Freddie woke up the next morning, he gave me a kiss on the cheek and left out. I stayed close to home that day, I only went out to get groceries and worked on school assignments. Freddie called throughout the day to check in and see what I was doing. At work on Monday things was business as normal. At the end of the work week Freddie came to my job and when he stepped out the car he stood outside for a moment and smoked a cigarette.

Smoking was a habit I didn't like but tolerated, Freddie didn't drink alcohol anymore so I didn't give him too much lip about it expect during sex when I could tell it was fucking with his breathing. During sex when I started to hear him huff and puff, I would look into his eyes and smile and say Awwww, them cigarettes busting your ass, do you want to take a break. Then he would fuck me even harder for teasing him, which is what I wanted. He would come in the shop when there was no one there or one or two people. When he entered he walked to the back where my desk was and gave me a kiss calling me his babygirl. Freddie sat down across from me and with the look on his face I knew something was bothering him.

I asked him what's wrong, he smiled and said you can read me well. He mentioned something has been lingering on his mind since we hooked back up. I replied and that is, Freddie said, I want to leave, I said leave what, Freddie said my home... my wife. I sat back in my chair and crossed my arms, and before I could reply Freddie said "I'm not saying I'm leaving her for you but that I want to leave for me". I unfolded my arms and said good for you, and I am here when you need me. Freddie gave me a kiss and left out. Freddie hadn't been gone but a few hours before I saw him rushing back, he stood to the door and called my name, Harminme, I need to see you outside. I went outside to meet Freddie and I'm not sure of how he said it or even if he asked verses told me, the only thing I knew was he was moving in with me.

I know my alter ego was like HELL NO!!! But I caved in. Here I was again, for a third time living with a man who I felt loved me and would do right by me. I went back to work in a daze thinking what happened was all a dream, but I knew it wasn't because "SHE" my alter ego was lecturing me about making yet another decision with what my heart and body wanted and not using my mind. I was sure though things would work out and be different with Freddie because he was older, so I figured that he had his time playing and sleeping around, and he knew me, just as long as Devin so he knows I'm a good woman. My inner voice said you'll see Harminme MEN ARE ALL THE SAME, THERE IS NO LOYALTY!!! I disagree, fine my inner voice said but If I am right and when Freddie fucks up and breaks your heart we are doing things MY WAY here on out.

Being confident in Freddie and I, I agreed to do things HER way if Freddie betrayed me. When I got home that night, Freddie was there waiting on me. We sat on the couch and I took a deep breath and told Freddie that I understand that he is going through a transition and that he can stay here and we could share a bed together or not but I'm not looking for a commitment from you and you and I both could be involved with other people. Freddie stop me and said that is not what I want, I just want you and no one else. I had my share of pussy and as you get older realized it's not as important as love. I was happy to hear him say that, but I also figured if I gave him sexually freedom I found my back door from being obligated to my alter ego's terms.

I told him what I expected and what his financial responsibilities would for staying here. Freddie agreed to the amount due each month. I also mentioned that I will not tolerate him being gone days at a time and come back like it's nothing, I didn't take it from Devin and I won't take it from any man living under my roof. Freddie agreed and said he would not disrespect me like that. Home life was good, Freddie and I both worked and I would cook occasionally since Freddie really wasn't a big eater. When Freddie came home we had sex and some nights for hours. When Freddie first moved in we had sex every night for 12 days straight and on night 13 he threw in the towel and said he was tired.

That was something I did out due with the men in my life was out sex them, they couldn't keep up or couldn't out last me. Tax season was coming to an end and my Aunts and I had gotten jobs working at the beach cleaning houses. It was a weekend job and during the week I studied and looked for a full time position on line. Nicki called me one day asking what I was doing for the upcoming weekend, I told her I was cleaning houses at the beach but my night was free. She mentioned a friend of hers was having a party and wanted to know if I was interested in going. I told her sure I would be there. It just so happened after I hung up with Nickie my sister Danielle had called. She asked what I was doing I mentioned I just hung up with Nickie and I'm going to Virginia Beach this weekend to a party.

My sister replied Oh really, that sounds like fun, and sound like a lot of alcohol, and fun. I knew from the roundabout conversation she wanted to go, so I asked, Danielle do you want to come with me this weekend to the party. She said Oh my God really are you sure, okay. I called my Aunts to let them know I would be taking Sunday off which they were relieved since they needed a break from walking up and down the stairs. Saturday afternoon, Danielle and I headed to Nickie's house in Virginia Beach. I introduced my sister to Nickie and gave her a brief history of how we met which pretty much just told her she is an old Navy buddy. We started the evening off drinking at Nickie's house and listening to music.

Nickie, made a phone call to a friend, whose house we were headed to next. When we arrived at this friend's house, there were others there eating, drinking, and carrying on. I said hi to everyone then headed to the kitchen where I started nibbling on the variety of food items. My sister Danielle on the other hand headed straight to the alcohol. She said with excitement OH MY GOD Harminme, they have Patron!!! DAMN they got all the good alcohol!!! She reminded me of a child on Christmas Day, not knowing which present to open first. I laughed and kept nibbling away and I too took a glass of alcoholic beverage. After about an hour at

Nickie's friend house me, Danielle and 4 other girls piled into the cars and head to the club.

On the drive to the club Nickie is driving and I go into an Awww moment thinking this chick was sober in Iceland and drove into a building here her ass is buzzed and is staying in between the lines...I'm so PROUD OF HER J When we arrived we were scanned by security outside and again when we walked in. We all headed first to the bar for a shot of Patron, my sister had two shots hers and mines because I was through drinking for the night at least Patron. We got a table and did some people watching and watched people dance. A song came on I liked so I headed to the dance floor, Nickie and two of her friends followed behind. The other two girls stayed at the table with my sister, who had the look like she just got a free alcohol pass from AA.

We danced up something, because the D.J. was playing jams back to back we, had a ball. Nickie asked, "does your sister dance"? I had a look of confusion and replied, I don't know. Nickie walks off the dance floor and heads to the table where my sister Danielle is sitting and I am watching from afar and seeing her trying to get my sister to come dance, it was funny. I don't know how she did it but next thing I knew Danielle was coming to the dance floor. This was the first time I've ever seen my sister dance and to be honest she reminded me of a stripper on a pool dancing for a purpose...She danced to about 3 songs before she slowly walked off the dance floor. My sister being a heavy set girl I figured she would tire out quickly.

She went to sit down at the bar since the table we were at was occupied by others. I stayed on the dance floor for a minute and watched Danielle and Nickie at the bar. When I saw my sister ask the bar tender for water instead of another alcoholic beverage it was then I became a bit concerned. When I saw Danielle slowly get up from the bar and Nickie and the crew all got up with her, helping her stand up right I walked quickly off the dance floor to her. When I approached her, I asked was she alright she stated yes, she just needed to go to the bathroom. There was Nickie on one side and another girl on the other I walked behind them watching and praying she was okay. I turned my head away for a second and when I turned back around Danielle was on the floor.

Danielle was laughing and trying to get back up, I on the other hand damn near went into shock. I stood still looking around just knowing Ashton was about to pop out yelling you been PUNKED!! No Ashton... No white boy... No camera...SHIT!!! With my head down in Shame, I went to help my drunk sister to her feet. As we're walking my sister to the bathroom one of the security people states, she's got to be able to walk on her own to stay in the club, if not she has to leave, those are the rules. Already pissed off I looked at the security guard and said she is fine. The security guard said okay again she needs to walk out the bath room on her own. We all went into the bathroom with Danielle talking to her through the stall, asking her if she was okay.

I was staring in the bathroom mirror, praying to God asking him, to please let my sister be alright and be able to walk her ass out of this bathroom on her own two feet. When Danielle finally came out the bathroom stall she first went to the sink to wash her hands and put cold water on her face. I looked at her thinking to myself this BITCH supposed to be the "professional drinker" in the family. As the crew and I prepared to leave the bathroom there were two girls in front and Nickie, I and the rest in back of Danielle as we left out the bathroom. Danielle walked out the bathroom and with each step my heart felt like it had skipped a beat, it had to be under 10 steps before she went down again. The security guard just waiting, shouted AND SHE'S OUT!!!

We got her to her feet again and we were escorted out the club. While outside we talked amongst ourselves deciding what we were going to do. While talking Danielle is sitting on the curb outside the club flirting with the security guard outside, whispering and curling her finger saying hey you come here, you're cute, do you have got a girlfriend. Then she says even if you had a girlfriend you'll still try to holla, you men ain't SHIT!!! All could say was Oh my God, I told the guard please forgive her, she's drunk, he just laughed and said no worries I've heard worst. We then take Danielle to the car and put her in the back seat. We are outside of the car still talking about what we were going to do.

Majority ruled to stay at the club and leave Danielle in the car and we will take turns checking on her. My sister was like NO, NO I know you not going to leave me here, I'm fine. I looked at her with an evil look and said NO THE HELL YOU'RE NOT!!! She leaned slowly back in the backseat hearing the pisstivity in my voice. I agreed with the group to ahead and finish up our night at the club and just keep watch. I told the rest of the girls to go ahead and I would be in shortly just wanted to sit in the car a minute with my sister. Nickie sat with me, we talked about Iceland, life after the Navy and our future plans. My sister in less than 5 minutes while we were in the car fell asleep. I made sure all the doors was locked but for the first time that night could not get back in the party mood.

I walked back outside to the car where my sister laid in the backseat knocked out and I called Freddie. I told him about the whole night and how my sister is not the professional drinker she made herself out to be. Freddie always made time to talk and listen to me which was something I valued in him as a man. He made me feel like I was top priority no matter what he was doing. I knew Freddie had his side hustle which kept him busy morning to very late at night, and he would talk mad shit, and be so disrespectful in his tone but when he got on the phone with me Jerome turned into Freddie which loved him some Harminme. I hung up with Freddie and told him love you and see you tomorrow.

The ladies were heading to the cars about 5 minutes after I got off the phone. Nickie, Danielle, and I headed to Nickie's house to turn in. Morning came and Danielle and I said our goodbyes to Nickie, my sister especially and kept apologizing for last night. Nickie stated "girl as long as you had fun" my sister with a big smile said yeah girl I did. I just looked at them both like Mmmmm, the drive back home to North Carolina for the most part was quiet since Danielle feel asleep 30 minutes into the ride. I dropped Danielle off and headed home, Freddie was at his usually place Stop in Shop playing pool. I ran my bath water ready to wash the cigarette, weed, cigar smell and alcohol off me.

While running my bath water I received a phone call from Shelly, she was telling me about a new church she went to and informed me about her mother's health taking a turn for the worst. I expressed my sympathy, she mentioned her brother had actually stepped in to help with their mother's health which limits her from her normal daily life activities. I stated I didn't know you had a brother, Shelly mentioned they really are not close so she doesn't talk about him too much. She mentioned he was into music and writes his own songs, then Shelly shouted Oh my God, maybe he can hook you up with the guy he records with and you can get back in the studio and record your songs. I mentioned yeah that's sound like a plan. We hung up and I went to soaking in my bath.

She sent me a text about 15 minutes later of the name and phone number of the studio guy her brother used for his music. When I got out the tub I called the number and spoke to the studio guy, and come to find out he has a studio in Elizabeth City which was conveniently close. We made arrangements to meet next weekend and lay down a few tracks and so he could get a feel of my music style. After I hung up with the studio guy, Freddie called, when I answered, the voice on the other end wasn't Freddie but a voice of a female. She asked, is this Harminme, I hesitantly said yes...and this is, she said her name was Shaquanda and she was with Freddie. I then said okay, did he want you to call me for something. She said no, matter of fact Freddie doesn't even know I'm calling.

So, I stated, then why are you calling me. She said she wanted to know who and what was my relationship was to Freddie, it was then a smirk came on my face. I said, maybe you should ask Freddie who I am. She said, she did asked and he said you two were friends and he was staying with you till he found his own place. I replied well, if that is what Freddie told you than I would go with that. Shaquanda mentioned she felt there was something more, between Freddie and I, so I asked why she thought that. She stated because Freddie is arrogant and ruthless when he talks to people on the phone giving orders, giving commands, but when he is on the phone with you...there is a change... something different.

She said Freddie speaks to you in a calming, softer tone which he doesn't even talk that way with his wife. When I asked him about you, he goes off saying let it go. She said her and Freddie were sleeping together and she has feelings for him and what's to know the truth. I took a deep breath and replied sweetie I'm sorry but I don't get involve with Freddie's life outside these walls and Freddie's girls are not my concern. I said, now if you don't mind I have school work to do. Shaquanda said okay, sorry for disturbing you, I said no problem I understand and hung up. I was expecting a call back right away from Freddie but instead 30 minutes later Freddie walks through the door.

Freddie says hi and I say hi back. He walks to the kitchen and pours himself a drink, not looking up at him, he asked, did you get a phone call from my phone, I said yes. I'm sure he was waiting for a big interrogation, but I kept typing away on my computer. Freddie asked what did she say to you, it was then I exhaled and replied, what do you think she said to me Freddie. He said I don't know...well Freddie this young lady wanted to know the nature of our relationship since she claims you and her are in a relationship and fucking. It was then Freddie went to his defense, he said the girl was helping him move some things around, and she was also being used as a diversion having his wife think it was her he was involved with avoiding a trail back to me.

He stated she had gotten attached to him, and she wants more from him then the working relationship that they have. He mentioned she was not use to men being involved and nice to her like he was and not require any sexual favors. She said she had heard him on the phone with me several times and noticed how I talk to you which is in a calm tone and respectfully since every other call I make I'm cussing a bitch out. So, she got curious or really nosey and wanted to know who you were. I stood up and went to the kitchen grabbed a bottle of wine and pour another glass. I stood in front of Freddie and said, didn't I tell you in the beginning that you and I could just be bed mates, where you and I can fuck other people just so we know condoms stay on and I don't get any drama.

Freddie stated Harminme, I love you and want ONLY you. I have had more pussy than one man should have in a lifetime, and being in my 50s I'm looking for that woman I can build with, grow old with, and for the first time be in love with. I would do whatever to keep you protected and have a life that is drama free. I believed Freddie, not because I wanted to but needed to since he was the last straw, the last man I plan to love. If this relationship failed there would be no full recover and my alto ego will rule here on out. Freddie takes me by the waist and kiss me, we had sex starting in the kitchen into the living room. Sex with Freddie was "mean" we fucked each other like we had a point to prove, and it was proven.

The weekend came and I headed to Elizabeth City to record. The studio was easy to find, when I arrived there was an intercom at the door, I rung the bell and the voice on the other end asked who I was I said Harminme. The door unlocked and I walked down the hallway to recording studio on the right. When I opened the door, I was in shock and so was he. We had seen each other before, when I was involved with Devin, he had been to the condo discussing "business". We stared at one another for a moment and I reintroduced myself and so did he. He stated his name, which he called himself "Confetti" but government name was Williams. He first had me sit down on the couch and tell him about my music and my writing style.

I mentioned my music comes from life experiences, mostly my own as well as others. He then asked how does the music come to me, I stated it is at random, I could be driving, cooking, watching tv and a melody comes to my head or I start singing some words till eventually a song is written. I mentioned there have been times that some songs come to me in my dreams, and I only remember bits and pieces when I awake but it's enough for me to build on. He asked if I ever recorded in the studios before, I told him my cousin Larry has a studio out of his home and we also recorded at Elizabeth City State University but I was around 15 years old at the time.

Williams with excitement said hold up Larry from Windsor go by Big L, I said yes, he said that's who got me into music he was and still is my mentor. I smile and said wow, what a small world. That was the "ice breaker" with us and we carried on like high school buddies from then on out. He asked what song or songs I wanted to work on. I mentioned I wanted to record my song titled "And Still I Rise". I sung it to him so he could catch the melody and told him what else I wanted to add. Since, this was pretty much a song about fighting for what is right, and dealing with discrimination and racism I wanted to have the speech by Dr. Martin Luther King Jr. in the song and what part of the speech I wanted. It took us about 2 hours to lay down the tracks for the song and I was VERY pleased with his work.

After I finished we talked a little more he asked what happened between Devin and I. I mentioned post prison Devin wasn't the same men I fell in love with and this Devin still wanted to hang out late at night, be away days at a time not call and run the streets with his boys. I for one wasn't going to put up with that behavior, so I let him go. Confetti asked if I write lyrics to beats; I told him, it was something I never did before, but I can give it a try. He hands me a disc which he said had two beats, music he created and wanted to see what I could come up with, I stated so this is like a homework project for me. He laughed and said, yes but there's no failing grade.

We made an appointment to meet back in two weeks, he mentioned he would have the speech for my song by then and we could finish "And Still I Rise". I stopped by Stop in Shop to see Freddie he was in the back playing pool, when he saw me he just smiled he met me half way and we went outside. We stood outside and I told him about my studio session, he stated he knew him and he used to live here. Freddie said matter fact he knows me too, next time you go there ask him if he knows Jerome. I leave Freddie and head home, I prepare dinner and log on to class. I did about an hour of class work and then I put the CD I got from Williams in my computer. The first beat was fast, R&B, dance type beat with Janet's verse from her song "Let's wait awhile". The second beat put me in the mind of my high school days, first crush, and first love.

So I pulled out some paper and got to work. I at least wanted to have something to present to Williams so, I played both songs back to back until one made the pen write. A call came in from Freddie who was just checking up on me and asked what I was doing. He mentioned he would be home early tonight and to not fall asleep and he will put me to sleep when he got home. I said yes, Freddie, I will be awake. After I hung up with Freddie it was the first song that took on its identity, and the song "Flames" was written. **(Song: Flames).** It took me about 20 minutes to write Flames, and I could not wait until Williams heard it. As for the second song on the CD the emotions and feelings were there but not taking me anywhere.

Two weeks later I was back at the studio with Williams, we greeted each other and he played the speech I asked for by Martin Luther King Jr. and I pointed what section I wanted to include in the song. He asked if I came up with anything for the music he created I stated yeah for one, but the other is a bit of a challenge for me but I don't like to force music I let each song be born when it wants to be born. But the first beat you created I came up with Flames. When I sung it to him, I could tell he was very pleased with what I came up with. He asked what inspired me on this track I said the man in my life, matter of fact you may know him. Williams asked his name I said he goes by several names, I call him Freddie but people on the streets call him Jerome Rome.

His face was a look of surprise and he mentioned you're Rome's girl I smiled and said NO, I'm Freddie's girl. He laughed and said, yeah I know Jerome AKA Freddie; he still be at Stop in Shop playing pool and talking shit. I smiled and yes this is true. Williams asked me what were my plans for my music, I told him to be honest I would like to write for a music label one day, I personally don't want to be a singer because I don't like my voice, but I do LOVE writing it's a release for me. I wouldn't even mind having my own label one day. Williams mentioned that was a dream/goal of his too, to have his own label, his own brand. He asked if I had any other songs I wanted to record, I mentioned not at the moment since I am still in the middle of writing them.

I did mentioned I would continue to work on the other track he made and will give him a call as soon as something comes to mind. Before heading home, I stopped at the gas station to get some gas, when I got out the car, I heard a man call my name. I turned around and saw it was Devin. I was caught off guard and for a moment lost for words. He asked how I was, and what I had been up to these days. I stated I was fine and working as usual. He stated "it's good to see you", I said thanks and went inside the store. My heart was racing and all the emotions I figured were long gone and buried for Devin had suddenly resurfaced. Then it came, the song to Williams other beat...My first love. **(Song: My First Love).**

On the drive home, I received a phone call from Freddie, he called to ask how things were going at the studio and if I mentioned him to

Williams. I stated yes, I did and yes he knows you. I told Freddie our session was actually done and I was heading back as we speak. Freddie said okay, you know where I'm at, I stated yes I do. When I pulled up to the condo Freddie's car was in the car port. Before I got out, I sat in the car for about 10 minutes. I took a piece of paper and pen and replayed the CD William had created and started writing the chorus and first verse to My First Love. I took the elevator and when I walked in I saw Freddie wasn't in the living room or dining room, and in the kitchen was a vase with flowers and a card that said I love you.

I walk to the master bedroom and Freddie had rose pedals laid out on the bed, I was in amazement since Freddie wasn't really the romantic type. I heard the shower running, and I ran my hands across the bed full of red rose petals and smiled. I started to get undressed and went into the bathroom, opened the shower door and Freddie and I started kissing and I with my hands started stroking his dick. He said you like my surprise I smiled and said very much, Freddie turns off the water and we lay wet and naked on a bed full of rose petals. He begins with his usual pleasure of eating me out, which I enjoy but he tends to stay down there for so long but I just be wanting to feel him inside me. I laid back and let him enjoy his meal which was me.

It had to have been almost 15 minutes into his meal, and I begged him to come up and put his dick inside me, but he didn't. Another 5 minutes goes by and I begged Freddie again, baby please fuck me, but he didn't. Another 5 minutes goes by and I said please Freddie put it in, but he didn't. It had been over 30 minutes of him having oral sex and I just kept begging for him to put his dick in me. Then I stopped begging and laid my head back, my breathing had gotten faster, and deeper, I kept moaning Freddie, Freddie, please!!! I felt funny...I felt strange... like something was happening, something I was mentally trying to ignore, physically trying to control. My pleasure in that moments turned into FEAR...

I then moaned Freddie, stop, but he didn't. I took my hands and pressed down on his shoulders and again I moaned Freddie, please stop, but he didn't. Tears were coming from my eyes, and I yelled Freddie DAMNIT STOP, but he didn't. I took both hands and pressed down on his head, moving up the bed away from him but this mutherjumper was locked on like a Pitbull in a dog fight. My mind could no longer ignore what my body was trying to control, I started feeling my body starting to convulse...shake..., I then started to yell Freddie STOP, PLEASE, I CAN'T...hanging halfway off the bed Freddie without missing a beat wraps his arms underneath me and pulls me down bringing me back towards him. Since, I could no longer fight him or my body I just yelled and cussed till he finally stopped.

Freddie stood at the edge of the bed and I curled up in a fetal position. Trying to regain control of what felt like a seizure, I was mentally trying to talk myself down. I yelled to Freddie, WHY DIDN'T YOU STOP!!! He said, it was time, my body learned to surrender, and he wasn't going to stop till it did. I couldn't even reply to that comment, because...shit I didn't know how. I just grabbed the blanket holding it tightly hoping and praying to God, I would soon stop shaking. Freddie, then takes the blanket and pulls me down toward him and I'm like Oh Lord please let his ass be tired, NOT AGAIN!!! He gives me a kiss and slaps me on my ass and says I love you, I replied Mmmm.

As he is heading to the bathroom, he calls me, he said...Harminme, and I didn't answer and he calls me again, Harminme..., I said yes Freddie, he said look at me, I slowly lifted myself up and looked at him. He said next time... don't stop me, I replied Mmmm and laid my head back down. As he is in the bathroom, I'm thinking this mutherjumper done got cocky now, shit it took years for him to make my body surrender, one little victory, but it won't happen again. Then I think, FUCK, is that what an orgasm feels like. Who the hell wants to feel like their having a fucking seizure during sex and not have control over their body movements and mind? I for one DO NOT LIKE TO LOOSE CONTROL. But now that I know what it feels like when it's coming on I just have to find a way to stop it.

For the next two days Freddie and I did not have sex, and wasn't because he didn't want to but I didn't. My mind was still fucked up from having convulsions beyond my control. On the third night I felt I was ready for Mr. Freddie and I to have sex again, this time I took the lead and started sucking his dick, which is something Freddie in the past would stop me from doing and when I asked why he would say, he really didn't enjoy it as much since he had it done so much in the past. I didn't agree with him even though it was something I did enjoy. After giving him head for about 15 minutes he moves up, taking me down and he goes to eating me out, it had to be only 10 minutes and I felt that shit coming on again, I shifted my hips to reposition his tongue, his mouth, his head slightly to avoid IT.

Within seconds he was back at it again, and again I slightly moved my hips to reposition him. He stopped and looked up at me and said, "I know what you're doing". I replied sorry what are you talking about, then, I just laughed. He went back down again and in minutes I felt IT coming on again, I'm thinking shit, how is he doing that, how the fuck does he know. I shift my hips slightly again, this time he comes up and sticks his dick in me. I whisper in his ear, yes Freddie, this is what I want. So we are having sex and he whispers to me, Harminme throw it back, so I move my hips up towards him thrusting and holding his back pulling him closer into me. I hear him moan louder and louder, asking is this my pussy, and I would say...no it's mine, then he would push up in me harder, asking me again, is this my pussy, and again, I would say no it's mine.

He then goes to the foot of the bed and pulls me down towards him and sticks his dick back in me. About 10 minutes into it, I start to feel IT again, and I go to move my hips and Freddie grabs the side of my hip with his hand and I'm thinking OH FUCK!! He picks up his pace, moving faster I move my hands, up against his chest trying to put some space in between us, he grabs my hands and holds them down. I start to play mind games with him then, moaning to him baby, cum for me, I know you want to. He says to me I'll cum when you come, then I started to feel my legs tremor, and I started to run up to the head of the bed, and Freddie is not letting up, I see there is no escaping him, so I go to begging and pleading with him, moaning Freddie, please don't.

Then he asks, is this my pussy, I smile and then I started crying, trying with all my strength to get him off of me, but he's too strong. Then he asks me again, Harminme, is this my pussy, I didn't reply, then he says don't fight Harminme, surrender to me. I yelled out OH MY GOD, PLEASE FREDDIE BABY PLEASE DON'T, he grunts and asks again is this my pussy, you are mine, I yelled YES FREDDIE IT'S YOUR PUSSY, IT'S YOUR PUSSY. My body once again goes into a seizure like state but since this time I knew what it was I was experiencing I was better prepared, and was able to recover more quickly. As Freddie gets off the bed he kiss me on the forehead, and then kiss me on my ass.

Freddie goes into the bathroom and starts the shower, I'm lying in bed in a fetal position again, thinking, this man just became a serious problem for me. Not only does he know how to give me an orgasm on command but can do it both orally and sexually. This mutherjumper is DANGEROUS!! I don't like to be defeated but at the same time, I will admit defeat...The following week I received a phone call from my placement agency for a job position in Moyock and they wanted to start the next week. I was excited, since I am somewhat of a workaholic and just doing school work all day was long and tedious. I informed Freddie of the news and he was happy to hear I was happy. I love the fact when it came to Freddie he was there to talk when I needed him.

At my new job I was a purchasing agent, which consisted of ordering parts and supplies for government and private companies and tracking their movements. I liked it because it reminded me of the Navy and made feel a sense of importance, purpose. That night I fell asleep and Freddie was still out doing business, when he came home he took a shower, which had woke me and when he got out I had a towel in my hand ready to dry him off. This night we laid in bed talking, he asked about my time in the Navy and the places I traveled and the things that I did. Not that I wasn't intrigued that he was interested in my military career, but I did ask what brought this on. Freddie mentioned he noticed that some nights I have what seems to be a nightmare and I talked in my sleep.

I asked him what is it I be saying, he stated he couldn't make it out, but I kept repeating no and stop a lot. I said wow, well I can't recall any of the nightmares, I'm sure it's nothing. Freddie stated, "Harminme, you know I was in the military too and saw and experienced some things, and maybe you need to talk to someone, maybe go the Hampton VAMC and just see if it will help". Since, I wanted this conversation to end quickly, I told him I would look into it tomorrow. I was impressed and now cautious of how much he physically and mentally noticed. We kissed goodnight and he held me in his arms till I fell asleep.

The next day, I did call the VA medical center in Hampton and made an appointment. On my appointment day, since it was my first time there since I was discharged from the Navy, I had to do a complete check in and be assigned a primary care provider and was set up for all kinds of labs and procedures. While waiting in the waiting area, I saw hundreds of Veterans, and most with bags and cases of medications. I'm thinking I do not want to be one of them. I found out during my visit that as an OEF/OIF Veteran I was actually entitled to 5 years of free healthcare from the VA after discharge. I'm thinking to myself this shit would have been nice to know 3 years ago.

I was set up for a mental health examination where I talked with a Psychiatrist. During my mental health exam, she asked about my military career and if I was in combat or experienced any kind of trauma. I said no Ma'am I enjoyed my time in the Navy. She asked about my transition since leaving the Navy, which I'm not going to lie I mentioned it was and still is an adjustment. She asked what issues did I have, I mentioned honestly I just don't like how civilians do things, they lack order, discipline, mission, and self-pride. I stated these were things that were embedded in me through the Navy and since I got out I don't seem to have a place with anyone or anything anymore...I'm lost.

I isolate myself from the outside world, family, and have no friends but the one friend I do have is because we were stationed together in Bahrain and helped one another through a lot. I don't sleep well and easily get agitated and then there are days, I am numb and don't feel or care about anything and want to say fuck it and just give up. Apparently in that 30 minutes session I was considered to suffering from anxiety and depression. She also set me up for a screening for posttraumatic stress disorder (PTSD) and I heard and knew enough that I didn't want to have to carry that "LABEL" around, so during my appointment which was the same day, I just said NO to most of the answers, he said okay that was it, I'm thinking ok...next thing I know I'm picking up pills for mental and physical conditions.

I'm like this is how it all starts, being a druggie, being prescribed all these pills, that fix one problem and create another. I continued to go to the Hampton VAMC since I still had 2 years of free healthcare available. It was during my 2nd visit they explained to me that certain condition could be service connected and I could receive compensation. I mentioned yeah, I tried and was granted for back and knee with zero percent. My primary doctor mentioned you can also appeal, their decision if you're not happy with it. I was thinking it took them nearly 3 years to come back and tell me no on some things and then give me a zero on what they said yes on, no thank you, it's not worth the headache.

I have to admit, waiting in the waiting area, had its benefits. Listening to other Veterans and their claim process and experiences, I decided to appeal my claim. From leaving my VA appointment I headed to the Navy exchange at NAS Oceana, my old and last Command. While at the exchange I came across an old Navy buddy...Kisma. We shouted and hugged each other and sat at the food court in the Navy exchange, catching up on things since Japan. Kisma, mentioned she was dating a white Navy Officer and they were currently engaged. I was happy for her, because it seem like she was accomplishing her goal of an easy wife life. I asked her about Nathan, and she had a look on her face. I asked is something wrong, is he okay?

Kisma, mentioned Nathan had renewed his orders in Japan, and a few months after his orders were renew, he was sent back to the U.S. I asked did something happen, why they sent him back to the U.S. Kisma mentioned, they only reason a command sends a person back to the United States for something other than a felony crime...is for medical reasons... and you knew Nathan was gay and looking for love in all the wrong places. I said Oh shit!!! Damn Kisma for real, have you tried to contact him? Kisma mentioned she did try to locate him for a while but, either he never returned her emails, or phones calls. She mentioned she heard he took it pretty hard, and not sure what happened to him after that. I sat quiet for a moment, thinking damn maybe I should have said something THAT DAY.

Kisma and I exchanged numbers, but I knew the likeliness of me calling her were slim to none, since we had nothing really in common. Kisma was a high price, high maintenance, gold digger who wasn't looking for love but benefits and financial gain. On my drive back to North Carolina, I couldn't help but to think about Nathan and prayed to God, he would find a way to deal with it. I was thankful, when it came to my sex partners I had a practice of using condoms, and having them tested when our relationship went to the next level of not using condoms. Freddie and I for example were currently not using condoms since he wanted to be exclusive, so I did ask to see his most recent visit to VA medical center of all the medications and treatments he was receiving and when his last HIV test was performed and the results. Then here "she" comes my alter ego...D, saying "Yes Harminme he may have been clear then, maybe now, but what about later...are you really going to trust a MAN, this MAN, with your health, your life, your soul. Look at the track record no one has ever passed the finish line." Though my alter ego was pestilence, thinking and seeing the worst in others I felt was always looking out for my best interest, protecting me from harm.

I planned to keep my promise if Freddie failed, then I would let her take over in my relationships there on out. Which, D did not believe in LOVE, since she claimed there is only unrequited love and NO MAN can be trusted, father, uncle, brother, nor husband, was capable of AUTHENTIC LOVE. I on the other hand believed in love and real love could conquer all. But it didn't matter now since Freddie was the last and final round. Once home I couldn't stop thinking about Nathan, and how one decision in one moment can change the course and path we were once on. When Freddie came home, I told him about my friend I ran into at the Navy exchange and Nathan. I felt the need to ask him again about his decision to be exclusive and he again said he wanted no one else just me.

Another work week had come and I received a call from Charlean. I stepped outside to have our conversation and she mentioned she had news. I'm figuring a new job or promotion but instead he she said... I'm married. I didn't say anything for a few seconds, since this came as a bit of a shock seeing how Charlean claimed she would NEVER get married again. Charlean, calls my name saying Harminme are you there...I said yes Charlean I am here. Though Charlean was the only one D and I together approved of, D was as protective of Charlean as she was of me. It was then D took over the conversation. She asked Charlean when did she get married, and you haven't known this man long, do you even love him.

Charlean with despair in her voice, said, I wanted you of all people my closest friend, to be happy for me and give me your blessing. You are my best friend and nothing will come between us. D, faded out. I came back with, I'm sorry Charlean, and this was not expected is all. I just want what's best for you and if you're happy then I am happy for you. I'm sorry about going off on you earlier. Really I was lying to her because even though I did not know this man, I knew he could never make Charlean completely happy nor would he be able to keep her satisfied, unequivocal he will fail. I loved Charlean, I always felt in her was an extension of me.

I went back to work, but was unable to concentrate thinking about the phone call earlier with Charlean. I spoke with my supervisor and asked to leave early. I usually take the highway to go straight home but for some reason felt the need to drive through town. I drove by a hotel in town and just so happen to look, and there was Freddie's car. I pulled into the driveway next to the hotel and sat there for a minute repeating to myself, no that's not his car, no that's wasn't his car. I backed up and pull into the hotel parking area and yes it was Freddie's car. My breathing started to increase and my hands shaking, I picked up my cell phone and called Freddie. He picks up and says hey baby, what you doing.

I said I'm fine sweetie, where you at, Freddie said he was at work. I said okay, then can you explain to me why your car is at this hotel. Freddie then says are you not at work, I said no, I got off early, wasn't feeling well. Now back to what I asked, you, why is your car at this hotel. Freddie, said it's not what you think, I am taking care of business. I said really then what room are you in, Freddie stated again baby I am at work. I said really, Freddie mentioned if you don't believe me come out to my job. I drove to Freddie's job and he came out, he got in the car and I asked him why are you here and your car at a hotel.

Freddie gave me a story about Shaquanda staying with her grandfather who is disabled. Their lights and water got turned off and he put her and her child up in a hotel for a few nights and while she is there she is handling business for him. I replied I'm sorry to hear that, and that was really kind of you. I think I should stop by and see how she is holding up, what room is she in. There was a hesitation and I said what Freddie, is there a problem. He said no, not at all, I'll call her and tell her you are stopping by. I arrived to the hotel and knocked on the door. Shaquanda opened the door, and I stepped in. On the bed was a little girl, I took to be her daughter. I reintroduced myself and she mentioned yes, you were the one I talked to on the phone that day.

I told her that Freddie had told me about her situation and I just wanted to stop by and offer any help that I could. She mentioned Jerome was taking care of everything and their lights and water should be back on soon. I said you have a pretty little girl, Shaquanda thanked me. D at that moment emerged...she said, "Freddie, I mean Jerome has a kind heart and is a giving person, which is what I LOVE about him." Shaquanda then asked, are you two together... D said "well, things between us have excelled and YES, we are together NOW!!" Shaquanda indicated Jerome thinks highly of me and she could tell he cares about me a lot. I wasn't sure why D wanted to share this information with this girl, but had a strange feeling a trap was just set...for Freddie by D.

When Freddie got home later on that night, I asked how Shaquanda and her little girl was doing. Freddie mentioned they were fine, and they were getting help from Social Services with the lights and water. I asked where her grandfather was at through all this and Freddie mentioned at the nursing home, I replied the nursing home where you work he replied yes. I played it off, because I knew D was waiting for Freddie to fuck up, so I asked no further questions. We went to bed that night and like most nights started to have sex. This night was a little different because D wanted to play. Freddie started with oral sex, which he had a well appetite for. He came up to go inside of me, and with D at the wheel knew this was going to be a BATTLE!!!

D was more of an aggressive lover, she liked to talk shit, and give orders and my body responded differently. A few moments inside of me and Freddie noticed too. Freddie started grunting, as my hips moved up in slow motion against his body, my legs opened wider letting him in deeper. Freddie stops moving D asks, what's wrong baby, can't take it and smiles. Freddie didn't reply, he started moving again this time he takes one hand and holds the headboard. He starts off slow, going deeper, he picks up his speed and hits "the spot" and he knew. I'm thinking OH SHIT, and D yells FUCK!!! I knew this was not going as planned. D did not let up, matter of fact since "she" was much stronger minded, and was able to mentally coerce the orgasm.

Grabbing Freddie on the back of his neck lowering him into me, drowning him causing less friction. D moans Oh Jerome fuck me...he grunts, my hips move faster and harder. His breathing increases, with an outburst he says FUCK HARM IN ME OH MY GOD BABY I'M ABOUT TO CUM, he says don't stop and in that D mentally says "FINISH HIM" and in seconds Freddie cum. He rolls over on his back head turned to the side looking at the wall. I resurface and with a BIG smile on my face, look at Freddie and kiss him on the cheek. Trying to slow down his breathing, he says baby can you get me some water, I said sure. The next day at work was a struggle, I was physically and mentally tired. But I had a smile on my face the whole day.

Freddie called at least twice to check on me, and I mentioned I was doing fine. He mentioned he was dragging and been replaying last night all day. Well I'm glad I could leave an impression, Freddie replied, yes you did. Though I shouldn't be jealous of my alter ego because she was still me, I felt sexually the men I was with favored her in the bedroom more. But often she didn't waste her time and efforts but apparently she had SOMETHING to prove even though she didn't like Freddie. To come to think of it she didn't like or love any man I had in my life. My thoughts were broken from a phone call, I looked at my cell and it was a call from Nickie. I said hey girl what's up, Nickie mentioned her friend was throwing an engagement party next weekend and wanted to know if my sister and I would attend.

I laughed, and said you mean the sister, that got us kicked out the club, had to carry out the club, talking shit to the security guard and left in the car while we rotated shifts checking on her. Nickie laughing on the other end, was like yes my girl Danielle. I said I'll think about it but don't be surprised if I show up by myself. I decided to wait 3 days before saying anything to my sister about the party next weekend. I wanted to do a face to face conversation since, shit was serious, and I DID NOT want the same occurrences that happened the first time to happen again. When I arrived at my sister's home, I sat on the couch and the first thing I said is we need to have a serious talk.

My sister sat down on the other couch and waited for me to speak. I started off by recalling the first event at the club that took place, and how embarrassed I was, and how handling one's alcohol intake is important. I could tell from the look on her face I was losing her and was likely thinking is this BITCH giving me an after school special. So, I quickly got to the point, and mentioned Nickie had called me earlier in the week and a friend of hers is having an engagement party and she stated she would like for US meaning you and I to go. A BIG smile came on her face since my sister was very fond of Nickie because Nickie has such as outgoing personality. I told Danielle I would considered taking her BUT we need to go over some rules. It was then I had her attention back.

I told her BEFORE she starts drinking she needs to eat, and while she is drinking to nibble. My sister then replied OH MY GOD, is that why you went straight for the food when we arrived at the house. I replied yes, because I knew to delay or prevent me from getting drunk off my ass I had to intake food so the food would absorb most of the alcohol. Danielle said that was smart, I replied yes, you are talking to a SAILOR...and in the terms of "A Drunken Sailor" we are known for fucking up a bar, whether that be fights or drinking. You need not to reach your an elevation so you need to just stop drinking, UNDERRSTOOD, Danielle replied... understood.

Danielle and I though we were sisters we was not CLOSE sisters. Growing up, I always felt Regina favored her more than me, since I was pretty much a "problem child" for her. There have been times I have forced my opinion to her especially when it came to my nephew. Though my sister was a loving and caring mother to A'nyyon I felt she was raising him to be selfish, anti-social, and most of all weak. I would often times say to her, A'nyyon will soon enough be a man, and unlike a female he can't get pregnant and live off "the system" the majority of his life, society is going require him to work. She would make fun of it saying he will live at home with her forever. Then I would say, Danielle, you are overweight which comes with a lot of health issues, what happens when you die.

I said on top of that, you have NO freaking job or employment history that will take care of YOU, when you are too old to make a living and maintain. Do you know it takes 40 quarters which is 10 years for one to qualify to receive Social Security benefits, you don't even have a year of work history. Then Danielle would come back and say she has two years of work history and she would get a little something from Social Security because they sent her a statement showing what she would get. I reply... is it enough to get by...she is silent. I stated A'nyyon needs to learn how to be considerate, how to talk to people, and most of all, not be a push over.

Then we breakout into an argument and she replies "Harminme, you don't even have kids so how you going to tell me how to raise mine." My response was I've been out here in the REAL world outside and this small ass town, and there are predators in all forms, and you need to have a conversation with your son about life, so he is not a victim, and you and I of all people know how that feels. I got up to leave and told her I would pick her up next Saturday at 1800, sorry 6pm. On the drive home, I was thinking, I don't even know why I waste my breath, but I see the potential in Danielle especially when I hooked her up with a job doing taxes, which is a trade that is NEVER going away. She is capable... and that what makes me MAD!!

Next Saturday came, Danielle and I headed to Nickie's place in Virginia Beach. We stayed at Nickie's place for about 45 minutes while she finished getting ready and we headed out. We pulled up in front of a white house with like 10 cars parked out front. We entered the house and saw about 12 women spread out from the kitchen to living room area. There was food and music and of course alcohol. Danielle and I were mingling and drinking, having a good time. Some of the women were Veterans or currently in the Military so I felt...at home. We had an interesting conversation about benefits and how being a Veteran could get you access to resources that not only benefit the Veteran but their family as well.

As I am listening to the conversations I'm thinking more and more about my claim which the VA has been sitting on for over 3 years now and seems as though Winston-Salem office does not seem to care about my physical or mental pain. There was a knock at the door and two men came in, one of the women took the two men upstairs. A bit concern, but it was none of my business, so I went back to the conversation. About 15 minutes later there was another knock at the door, another male. This male did not go upstairs with the other two, he actually joined us for the party. He went into the kitchen and started drinking, one of the women went up him and she introduced him, his was name Jamal.

It was clearly obvious, this guy was gay from the hand movements, to him saying GIRLFRIEND, and his conversations about men... He for whatever reason decided to share the story of how he knew he was or how he became gay. He started, it was my math teacher...I'm like DAMN what is up with these SCHOOL TEACHERS!!! The lady that went upstairs came back down and had announced for all the ladies to come to the living room area. So we all gathered in the living room area, and the woman that took the two men upstairs made an interesting announcement. She said that we were to be entertained tonight, and there are no rules to how far we can go. From there she pressed play on the CD player, with the music loud and we all waiting calmly in the living room and down the stairs came the two men, OH MY GOD, their strippers. All the ladies started screaming with excitement and I was still in shock saying Oh my God!!!

The two men started dancing and moving about the crowd, they started taking off their outfits and rubbing baby oil all over their bodies. We were all having fun, and some of the women very engaged with the entertainment. Jamal was all over the place or should I say wherever a stripper was. Then one of the men headed back upstairs and we were left with one stripper dancing. Then something happened that took me by surprise, the stripper exposed his dick. I'm like Oh My GOD, is that legal, is that allowed. I was sitting next to my sister Danielle, and it had no effect on her. I said, is that normal, she said is what normal, him exposing his business like that. My sister laughed and said, "Yes, I take it this is your first stripper". Yes I said, it is.

I have been to several female strip clubs and they were topless, but never a male strip club and never knew they exposed their dick for all to see. Some ladies at the party was stroking and touching his dick like a new adult toy they just got out the store. I'm thinking Ewww you don't know where his dick been at. I look at my sister and say is that sanitized, because some women were kissing his dick and one white girl at the party was looking like, this bitch about to give him some head, she acted like she been dick deprived. The male stripper made his way to where my sister and I were sister and a course my sister touch his dick with no problem when he came to me I sat back in the couch and said I'm good.

Then out of nowhere, came Jamal who got in between me and the other girl I was sitting next to, and in that moment I had to catch myself, because I gave him a look, I hadn't given anyone since Chris tried to put his dick in my ass, and I turned around and said ARE YOU LOST, I have some background in air traffic controlling and can direct you back to where you NEED TO BE. Chris got the message, a sister wasn't trying to explore any new ventures. My sister Danielle called my name because she knew I was aggravated with Jamal, I got up and headed to the bathroom. I took out my cell phone and called Freddie to calm me down. Freddie answer the phone and asked if I was enjoying myself, I mentioned I was until, the gay guy at the party started to cock block.

I told Freddie about the entertainment that was taking place, and about the ONE gay guy at the party. I said Damn, don't he got a dick to play with. Freddie laughed but he could tell how upset I was. He mentioned not to let him ruin the night and not to worry because I had my very own dick to play with at home. Granted that comment brought a smile to my face, we talked a few more minutes and I hung up. As I walked out the bathroom, I saw Jamal once again between two other women trying to get himself a closer view. I could tell the stripper was getting annoyed with Jamal, I was thinking of acting out as a News Reporter and asking him, Sir, how does it feel as a straight male stripper to be "VIEWED" by a gay male.

The rest of the night was somewhat enjoyable, the stripper took one of the ladies and picked her up with his face right in her private area. The party was winding down, Nickie, Danielle and I was saying our goodbyes. We headed back to Nickie's place which the plan was to stay overnight like last time, but D wanted to head back home. D told Nickie something had come up and we would be heading back to North Carolina tonight. Danielle said goodbye and we headed back. When I arrived home it was almost 3 in the morning, and Freddie wasn't home, I started to take a bath and go to bed but instead D suggested we take a ride into town to see if we would see Freddie. I drove around town and did not see Freddie's car, part of me was relieved since D figured he was doing something or someone.

I went back home and took my bath and went to bed. My cell phone ranged around 7am and it was Freddie, he mentioned he needed me to pick him up because his car broke down. He told me where to pick him up at and he would meet me at the end of the street. I picked Freddie up at the end of the road near the cemetery, and though my first instinct was to make a u turn and drive back to the condo, D wanted to drive down the road I picked Freddie up from. As I turned down the road I saw his car parked in a yard in a house right across the street from Wayne's house. As we were driving back, D asked Freddie why he didn't come home last night. Freddie mentioned his car broke down and knew Danielle and I were staying overnight at Nickie's and so he just waited till morning, when he figured I was heading back.

D didn't expect such a clever answer, and didn't dig any further, but she say to me, "Harminme pay attention to this day, and take note". I rolled down the windows and D said to Freddie wherever you were last night, you stink really bad, Freddie mentioned really, I said yeah when you get home, you need to shower cause you making me nausea. When Freddie and I got home, he took a shower. When he got out I asked him did he know what was wrong with his car he mentioned a buddy of his was supposed to come by and check it out. A few weeks passed and all was well with the world no drama, then I get a phone call again from Shaquanda. She mentioned she was looking for Freddie, and he wasn't picking up his phone.

I told Shaquanda that Freddie left out a few hours and if he calls I will let him know she was looking for him. I mentioned to her for future reference unless it is a matter of life and death DON'T just causally call my phone looking for Freddie because, I'm sure he wouldn't like it. When I hung up the phone, I couldn't help but to feel like there something left unsaid. Freddie called me about an hour later to check in on me and I mentioned Shaquanda called, he asked why is she calling you. I said I have no idea but told her for future reference not to do it again since I'm sure you would not approve. It was Halloween, and I asked Freddie was he planning on taking his son out to trick or treat. Freddie mentioned he did not celebrate Halloween because it represented the Devil.

I laughed and said are you serious, he mentioned yes kids dressing up as ghosts, witches, and demons asking strangers for candy, is the Devil's work. I stated there are other things kids dress up as like their superheroes, princesses, and Barbie and they are not evil. Freddie mentioned he was going out to see his son, I said okay and I will prepare dinner. I was cooking pickle herrings with onions and potatoes. I received a phone call from my sister Danielle, she asked where I was, and I mentioned I was at the condo cooking dinner. She mentioned that her and Candy were downtown trick or treating with the kids and she saw Freddie downtown trick or treating with Shaquanda and her little girl.

I said what did you just say, Danielle said I took a picture with my cell phone and I'm sending it to you now. I hung up the phone and opened the incoming text Danielle had sent. The picture was dark and hard to make out but my sister had no reason to lie. I turned off the stove and headed downstairs and got into the car and headed downtown. On the drive I'm trying to control my breathing and thinking to myself, there has to be a good reason, don't overreact. I got downtown and saw Freddie sitting in his car by himself, I drove in front of his vehicle and blocked him in. I could tell by the look on his face, he was nervous. I got out of my car and went and sat on the passenger side of his car.

With a smile on my face, I said Freddie, what you doing here. Freddie mentioned he was just watching the kids in their costume trick or treating. Really, because the conversation we had earlier you stated Halloween represents the Devil and you did not celebrate this holiday. So I ask you again Freddie, what are you doing here, he mentioned he was just passing through and stopped for a moment and was about to head to Stop in Shop and play pool. I said good, then I'll come with you. I said just let me move my car out the way. Freddie asked why I was moving my car, I said because I'm riding with you. Freddie smiled and said girl you are something else, I said yes, and you have no idea.

While I was moving the car D came to surface, so when I got back in the car with Freddie, D was now controlling matters. D mentioned the cell phone was dying and asked Freddie for his, I knew what she was doing. By having control of Freddie' cell phone she could see what phone calls and text would be coming in. Just as she expected several phone calls and texts came in from Shaquanda asking where are you, and to call me back. When we got to Stop in Shop I told Freddie that Shaquanda had called him several times and she wanted him to call her back and let her know, you're alright. Freddie stated he would call her later. As Freddie was playing pool, I got a phone call from my sister Danielle, I walked outside to take the call and the first words out her mouth was "GIRL YOU ARE CRAZY"!!!

Danielle mentioned her and Candy saw everything from when I pulled up and blocked Freddie in to when we left out. Danielle mentioned her and Candy saw Shaquanda and her little girl waiting and looking for Freddie, she couldn't believe he just left them like that. D still in control told Danielle that she and Freddie were at Stop in Shop and just waiting to see what the rest of the night had in store. I'll call you later with the details, and D hung up. D walked back into the store, and told Freddie that she wanted him to come home and eat dinner. Freddie mentioned he really wasn't hunger, D said Freddie, I want you to come home and eat dinner!! Freddie said okay Harminme I will come home.

Freddie took me back downtown to get my car, and he mentioned he would met me at the condo, D told Freddie he had exactly 45 minutes or else. Freddie with an unsettled laughed mentioned he would be there in 30. When I arrived at the condo, D had called Shaquanda. She picked up the phone and D said, Shaquanda this is Harminme, I am going to ask you some questions and all I want from you is an answer. First question, were you and Freddie trick or treating with your daughter earlier today downtown, Shaquanda said yes. Second question, Freddie's car broke down near the cemetery a few weeks ago, was it your house his car was parked, Shaquanda said yes. Third question, the day I came to you in the hotel room and informed you Freddie and I were together, were you fucking him then, Shaquanda said yes.

Fourth question, did he use a condom, Shaquanda said NO. Fifth and final question are you and Freddie still fucking, Shaquanda said yes. My rage would had got the best of me but since D was holding me (Harminme) back I stayed tame. I will make this quick Shaquanda because I am sure Freddie will be calling you soon, she responded that he was actually calling her now. D said very well then, woman to woman tell me this; in the hotel that day when I mentioned Freddie and I were now involved, now together why not say something then. Shaquanda mentioned she wanted to but Freddie, had threaten her and made it clear if she had said anything about them being together, she would regret it in so many ways.

Shaquanda stated Freddie, was in LOVE with me and made it clear to her, he would not lose me or leave me. It was then tears started to fall, the pain and disappointment was not D's but mine. D mentioned to Shaquanda when she returned Freddie's call not to mention a word of this conversation, she agreed. Before we hung up I (Harminme) had a question for Shaquanda, I asked, why is it that you fear him. Shaquanda response was "I have known Jerome for years, and Jerome has no heart, no soul, no love for anyone, and no conscience. "But YOU, have a way of reaching Jerome. I have known no woman not even his wife to have a hold on him, like you. I figured if Freddie was capable of loving you, maybe I could get Jerome to love me."

I said goodnight, and hung up the phone. Part of me empathized with her wanting love in some way...anyway. About 20 minutes later I heard Freddie pull up underneath the condo. I was in the kitchen when Freddie walked in, he came in and gave me a kiss. I told him, to have a seat and we need to talk. Freddie knew by my tone, it was not good. I asked, Freddie, do I not please you, Freddie reaches for my hand said yes baby, you please me very much. I asked, then why did you lie to me, Freddie said lie to you about what. I said you can stop the act, I know you were downtown with Shaquanda and her little girl. Freddie response was he was driving downtown and saw the kids in their costume and was just watching. So Freddie did you see Shaquanda, Freddie replied no.

Really, so the picture I got in my cell phone of you, her, and her daughter is a fake I guess. Freddie replied what picture, who sent you a picture. So I ask you once more, did you not see Shaquanda downtown, Freddie again replied no. D was really getting pissed now, this mutherjumper has been caught on camera and he still will not confess. Freddie I know you are lying to me and you have been lying to me for quite some time. For example, whose yard did your car breakdown in a few weeks ago Freddie, replied he didn't know it was just where his car stalled at. Really so Shaquanda don't live there, Freddie, then changes his mood and tone with me. Shouting WHAT IS IT HARMINME, you trying to find a reason to leave me, is that what it is!!!

D came out...you muthafucker, really, you going to play mind games with me. How about we give Shaquanda a call, and ask her, matter fact I'll call. D opened up the phone to dial the number and Freddie grab me by my wrist and the phone fell out my hand. Then D went off, you MEN are stupid and heartless, you cheat on me with some a girl who didn't finish high school, don't even have custody of all her kids, barely got a job which I found by the way you hooked her up with, this BITCH ain't even half of the woman I am and the smell on you from her house, he pussy is passed expired. I FUCKING HATE YOU!!! I WANT YOU GONE!!! The look in his eyes, as if I stabbed him in his heart, he steps back and in a swift moment grabs me by my waist.

I turned my head, not sure what he was going to do next, he whispers in my ear, "I fucking love you, I will always love you"!! Then he lets me go. He walks to the door and just stands for moment, he reaches in his pocket and take out the key to the condo and sets it on the end table. He said, I will be back in a few days for my things and leaves out. It felt like the ground had fell from underneath me, I was lost, I was confused I gave everything once more and AGAIN, I am left all alone, with no answers, no reasons, no explanations as to why. It was a week later when Freddie came back for his things. When I opened the door I didn't speak or even look at him.

When he finished loading everything into his car, he came back up and asked if he could explain what had happen. I said go ahead, Freddie admitted, he was downtown with Shaquanda and her daughter. He mentioned, he did have sex with her, but it wasn't like a regular thing. He claimed, she has threaten to go to his wife about where he was and who he was with, and to prove there was nothing to threaten him with, he fucked her. Freddie claimed he didn't want to bring any drama my way with his wife...I laughed and said, so are you telling me you fucked this girl to shut her up and avoid us being found out. Freddie said yes, I said do you know how ridiculous that shit sounds. Freddie stated "I know but it's the truth".

I said then why not tell me that, you fucked this girl, with no condom, I have no idea what this bitch has and you come home and lay down with me like the shit didn't happened. I told you in the very beginning you could of slept with other women, and you I could still have sex, but with condoms. You risked my life for a piece of ass. Freddie mentioned she was clean, I said Oh REALLY because the last time I checked your name didn't have MD on the end of it and her taking a bath doesn't make her clean. You know my mother always said black went with everything, I see now that's not just for clothes... I could feel the tears starting to roll down my face, there was a moment of silence and Freddie, said "please Harminme, don't cry, I can't take seeing you cry". I replied then leave. Freddie heads towards the door, and before he walks out, he says "I love you, and you are my heart". **(Song: Like everyone, but no one else). (Song: This is the way). (Song: Coattail).**

My alter ego D was right, LOVE IS OVERRATED, and UNREQUITED LOVE is what I have received all my life, from mother, to sister, family, and MEN. I can't do it anymore, I WON'T do it anymore I now exonerate myself. The curse of love has been broken, when love has burned you over and over and all that is left behind is ash, there is no raising up. From this day forward, MEN are no more to me than a means of physical relief and for entertainment purposes only. My name is NOT DOROTHY...BUT I HAVE BEEN WITH THE MEN OF OZ.

Devin the scarecrow with no brain, Samuel the lion, with no courage, and Freddie, the TIN MAN, the muthafucker with no heart!!! I am a true believer that GOD places people in your life for a season, a reason, or a lifetime and I know with these men I have had a lifetime of pain, and lifetime of lessons.

I came back home, thinking this was the safest place to be, because my family was here and of the familiar surroundings. I see now this town has NOTHING to offer me; I have no value and no future here. I need to get away, to go somewhere I can start over, and I can be THE OTHER ME. The best of me is not gone, but is heavily guarded...to those who read my story, you now know 95% percent of my life. My FIRST LOVE...WAS NOT A MAN, BUT MUSIC. To bleed my soul on paper, crying tears from love, sorrow, and pain. To sit back and tell you some of the things I been through changed me for the better is only part of the answer. Really, there are dark places, and burdens I face alone, so I don't repeat the mistakes that were once made. Harminme is laid to rest, buried under a past with no forgiveness. I am not the person I want to be, I am now the person within me, D is now the JUDGE, the JURY, and the EXECUTIONER and what she seeks...RETRIBUTION.

Covered by his job and clothes he wears
Hidden identity for those who stare
Eats at our table and where he sleeps at night
Secret desires by no man, which is right
Touches me in places that should go unseen
Emotions of confusion of is it me
Raped from his desires and hunger of lust
Wounded a mother's and daughter's trust
Empty from the innocence and trust he stole
Lost in confusion of my mother's oppose
Calling you out in public for all to see
Hoping you realize you can't silence me!!

Tomica Rankins Song: Child Molester
Created: 2004 to 2015
Approx. run time: 3 mins 27 sec

Verse I: Treated you like family, treated you like a friend, an outsider I had let in, home no longer a safe place, it was now where you slept and ate. I'm calling you out loud and clear, wanting the whole world to hear, the kind of man you truly are, no you'll never get far____.

Chorus: You're a child molester and yes I'm telling the world, you're a child molester (yes you are). You're a child molester and yes I'm telling the world, you're a child molester (yes you are).

Verse II: My mother thought I wasn't telling the truth, saying what a grown man, want from you, torn to pieces and filled with hate, cause a mother and daughter bond you did break. Truly alone and trapped inside, of a home with a man I despise, sorry mother for hurting you, but I told you the truth_____.

Chorus x 2

TOMICA RANKINS SONG: **HELLO TO TOMORROW...**
WRITTEN ON: **06 MARCH 1993**
RUN TIME APPROX: **4:14**

Verse I: There comes a time where we all must follow a road, the memories we carry inside will follow where ever we go.

Chorus: Hello to tomorrow, goodbye to yesterday hello to tomorrow for yesterday has slipped away.

Verse II: The dreams we all look for is knocking at our door, but we seem to slip and fall then some how we lose it all.

Chorus:

Verse III: Now I give to you a piece a mind and words worth listening to hold on and be strong cause no one said life was hard.

Chorus X2:

Tomica Rankins Song: My First Love
Written on: March 25, 2010
Run time Approx.: 4mins 23 secs

Verse I: Saw you the other day, and to my surprise, feelings I thought that were gone, came to rise. After all this time you still got a, hold on me and I can't control the way I feel. My hands go to shaking, my heart starts racing and I know you to me_____ will always be baby.

Chorus: My, my first love, coming off you is like coming off a drug. You will always be baby my, my first love no one could do what you have done.

Verse II: Reminisce about the past, like Bonnie and Clyde, quick to come to my defense, when someone stepped out of line. Baby made it known that I was number one even if another chick had you, your heart I had taken my soul you had embraced and I knew_____ that you will always be baby.

Chorus

Verse III: Part of me wish things could be different but I know it's for the best. The Navy had turned into a woman that won't put up with no mess. The streets it had taken, taken the heart that I once held in the palm of my hand, and though I had to let you go the pain still rips through my soul I don't understand_____ you will always be baby.

Chorus x 2

Tomica Rankins Song: I thank you for being a friend
Written on: May 28, 2016
Approx. run time: 3:39

Chorus: I thank you for being a friend, NO, that's not the way and how the story goes, best believe it for sure. NO, that's not the way and how the story ends____, you were never a friend.

Verse I: The lies, I believed you when you looked me in my eyes time after time. A friend_____, I stood by you through the thick and thin from the heartaches of men. Soothe your fears____, held you in my arms helped dry your tears, my love was real_____.

Chorus

Verse II: The pain____ stood by you when others turned away. I figured change a fool_____ I played the victim and the survivor too, but I never got through to you. Time, supposed to heal all wounds but that's a lie____ these cuts opened wide.

Chorus x 2

T omica Rankins Song: Bad Boy
Written: 2007-May 2016
Approx. run time: 4 mins 10 secs

Verse I: I knew it come a day, you'd come around my way, I didn't want to see your smile, your face_____. Why you'd feel the need to come and see me, why couldn't you just let me be, alone_____. Oh

Chorus: Bad Boy, why you knocking at my door, what you come here for, bad boy. Bad Boy, why you knocking at my door, what you come here for, bad boy____.

Verse II: Save your breath, I already have someone else, no need to apologize, for yourself____. We said our goodbyes, no need to recapture the whys, just so you can leave me here to cry____. Oh

Sing Chorus

Verse III: I still love you, yes part of me will always do, but the love we have won't strong enough to pull us through_____, I gave you my life, hoping one day I would be your wife but the time apart brought death to once gave life_____. Oh

Sing Chorus x 2

Currently available for purchase and listening on ITunes, Amazon, YouTube

TOMICA RANKINS SONG: **CRUSH**
WRITTEN ON: **27 JULY 2003**
RUN TIME: **4:47**

Verse I: Baby when we first met I admitted, I didn't want commitment didn't want a boyfriend, just looking for someone to get me through those lonely nights, a man with the right touch a man with the right size. But you had so much more to offer, pretending not to notice sticking to the terms and now that I realize I want to be with you I may of lost that chance for what I did to you. (But I just want to know).

Chorus: This is more than a crush, crush, crush, crush; baby between us, us, us. This is more than a crush, crush, crush, crush; baby between us, us, us. This is more than a crush.

Verse II: Tell me are you out to hurt me trying to pay me back for sleeping with whats a name behind your back. Don't I get credit honey for telling you, I want to start over and baby with you, a man without a stressful past tell what can I do, to win your heart to gain your trust. What can I do baby for there to be an us. (Just ask and I will do).

Chorus:

BREAK: What can I do to make it right I won't go without putting up a fight if you want me I'll stay want me to leave I'll go away but this is what I have to say, Yeah this is more than a crush for me yeah baby can't you see, yeah I won't waste your time no I won't telling you no lies.

INSTRUMENTAL CHORUS X .5

T
omica Rankins' song: **Strangers**
Written on: **November 15, 2009**
Approx. run time: **4 mins 58 secs**

Verse I: You don't know me and you never will; I don't know you_____.
When we walk on by, when we see each other in public, don't wave, don't
say hi_____, let's pretend to be.

Chorus: Strangers, strangers_____, you and me baby. Strangers,
strangers_____ let's pretend to be, strangers, strangers_____ you
and me baby, strangers, strangers_____.

Verse II: The games you tried to play, I seen that shit all before, so think
you got away_____. The best thing I did for you was to let you go, if
you stayed no telling what I'd do behind these closed doors.

Chorus

Verse III: Such a good man is people would say, but I knew you won't quite
that way_____. Words you would say and bring me down harden my
heart to the point I didn't want you around. You see now that you need
me and you know that you were wrong what's the saying don't miss a good
thing, till____ it's gone_____.

Chorus

Breakdown: *Let's pretend to not know each other's name, not know where
we stay, in the middle of the night call me asking is it alright if you can come
over, over cause I'll just give you the cold shoulder and Mr. Flame is on the
way to take the spot that you once laid_____.*

Instrumental Chorus first half

Tomica Rankins Song: Flames
Written on: February 20, 2010
Approx. Run time: 4mins 23 sec

Verse I: Your love, warms me when it's cold outside; melt me when I look in your eyes, my heart beats fast, my body it cries baby, love me tonight. Feelings, emotions that I can't compare, never even knew they were there, I love you more than words can say. (Something I think that you should know, but any way).

Chorus: Your love, your has got my body in flames, and baby it's no hard to explain, the way that you making me feel I never felt nothing this real.

Verse II: Holding you, I never ever want to let go, when you leave my body turns cold, not having you here I feel so empty inside. No one, can come along and take your place, or bring you to shame, cause baby I know the game, I'm here to stay.

Chorus x 2

Rap: Your love hu, baby boy, got me on fire, flames are burning with every desire, when it's cold outside, hu, you bring the heat, got my body temperature at its peak. Want me drink some water, want me eat some ice, put a spell on me baby, yeah, I'll be your wife, I better clam it down, before I bring the rain but not even mother nature can kill this flame.

Chorus x 2

T
omica Rankins Song: **Like everyone, but no one else**
Written on: January 11, 2016
Approx. run time: 4 mins 55 sec

Verse I: Maybe it's not you, but me, that needs to have a reason why to leave. You're like a habit, when you make love, like a sweet bottle wine I must drink up. Got me seeing what you want me to see, so I don't run away, I won't leave. Got me thinking we have a chance, to live out this lie, but I can't cause…

Chorus: You're like everyone, but no one else, you got me hypnotize I can't help myself. You're like everyone, but no one else, you got me in a trance I can't free myself.

Verse II: Got me locked up in these chains that lets wander freely till I try to escape. Pulls me back in, in front of you, so you can talk me out of freeing you. You're like every man I've had before, good at being bad wanting more. There's no pleasing you, there's no pleasing me, a permanent sign on my heart no vacancy.

Chorus

Break: Let me breathe_____let me breathe_____ let me breath_____ let me breath.

Chorus 1.5

Tomica Rankins song: This the way my love is
Written on: July 16, 2013
Run time approx.: 3 mins 40 secs

Verse I: This the way, this the way, this the way my love is. Can't sleep at night_____ wondering, who's by my side_____ comforting, holding me _____ like you use to do, feeling pain_____ since I left you.

Chorus: This the way_____ this the way, this the way, this the way my love is. Open up your heart, open up your heart and you know it's real. This is the way _____ this the way, this way, this the way my love is. Open up your heart, open up your heart and you know it's real.

Verse II: You cry your tears_____ I cry no more, your dead inside_____ my life is restored. Calling me_____ but I won't pick up, thinking_____ if you had enough.

Sing Chorus

Breakdown: Wait, you cheated on me did you think I was going to be around waiting on the side line when I wore the crown. I mean really the girl you cheated with ain't no prize; no education, a bunch of kids, no job to provide. You men trip me out, always downsizing with a bitch but it's cool because when I leave you gonna feel it.

Sing Chorus x 2

Tomica Rankins Song: And Still I Rise
Written On: September 5, 2009
Approx. Run time: 4 min 57 secs

Intro: This song is anyone that's ever been hurt whether it be by someone you love a friend, family, boyfriend or someone at the job and you know you were doing right and they were doing wrong, pray on it, for in the end you will be the one to rise.

Chorus: And still I rise above the sky, And still I rise above the lies, And still I rise along with the truth, And still I rise above you.

Verse I: Try to take me down but my knees they aren't weak, try to silence my voice but now I speak, try to make me disappear but my presence won't go, try to trick me yes but I did know.

(Sing Chorus)

Verse II: No pain, no glory if I am defeated it won't be I didn't fight not because I didn't seek it. My justice, my story it will live on, forever in the words of this song.

(Sing Chorus)

Verse III: I have hope because I know in my heart; God put me here to finish what one had start. Don't miss replace me by the color of my skin what you fear ain't on the outside but what is within.

(Sing Chorus X 2)

"I have a dream that one day this nation will rise up and live out the true meaning of its creed: "We hold these truths to be self-evident, that all men are created equal." "One day live in a nation where they will not be judged by the color of their skin but by the content of their character". Martin Luther King Jr.

Currently available for purchase and listening on ITunes, Amazon, YouTube

TOMICA RANKINS SONG: **BABY OUR LOVE**
WRITTEN ON: **04 SEPTEMBER 1993**
RUN TIME APRROX: **3:53**

Verse I: Baby I know that you like me (go mica) and you want to be a part of my world (go mica) well baby I got to tell you that I'm someone else's girl (go mica) now what goes around comes around don't give up baby you'll be found I feel our love was meant to be (go mica) so hold on baby you will see.

Chorus: Baby our love will come around, baby our love will be found, baby our love is worth a try baby our love I hope will never die.

Verse II: At night I dream of you (yes I do) and all the things I know will interest you, and when morning comes around your still deep inside of me, your apart of me.

Chorus X2:

RAP: Devin, Devin that's his name and let me tell you it's a real damn shame to let a man like this go to waste with a body of steal good hair and good face and yes it should be a crime for a man like this to not be mine, but hey if we were really meant to be God will bring us together in perfect harmony. (And our love)…

Chorus X2:

Tomica Rankins Song: Coat Tail
Written on: August 1, 2015
Approx. run time: 4 mins 38 sec

Verse I: Boy_____ why you mistreated me, when I gave you all you want and need, took you out the hood from a wife who won't no good. Such a shame, a man your age still playing games, can't learn to appreciate, when I took you across the border to a condo on the water oh, won't get me twice, friends with benefits that the line, don't try to cross it with some lie, saying baby I have change when your ass is still the same.

Chorus: Boy, get up off my coat, tail_____ I saved you once and oh well, I won't be saving that ass again, cause best believe that I won't win that's just how it is.

Verse II: Don't be mad, can't blame no one else that your sad, can't say I wasn't handling that, cause I took care of home, and in the bed held my own. No challenge to me, a girl with no job and no degree, a girl who isn't half of me, so need to compete, when the winner clearly me.

Chorus x 2

Rap:

Boy what were you thinking cheating on me, when I'm the one with the master degree, Hun I'm school you, you obviously miss class thinking you can run around cheating on my ass, boy here's your passport sending you back home, cause I'm a real woman that hold down the throne, call you when I need you in the middle of the night for that sexually healing to get me right.

Chorus

Tomica Rankins Song: A Good Man
Written on: May 18, 2004
Approx. run time: 4 mins 07 sec

Chorus: I take nothing less than a good man someone who's real and who understands and only needs one woman, that's the man that I want. I take nothing less than a good man someone who's real and understands and only needs one woman that's the man that I want.

Verse I: Trying to hide from me a cell number a girl named Beverly boy I wasn't born yesterday I can tell when I'm being played. I've been with men older smarter then you so you need to come up with something new because that shit that you're doing I can see right pass just like looking through a piece of glass.

Chorus:

Verse II: After two days of all of this shit you get a new cell phone cause your old ones not working, but it was working just fine two days ago when I heard you on the phone with that HO. Life is full of lessons and now I see your just another lesson God had for me. My momma always said the Lord works in mysteries ways I didn't know what she meant until that day.

Chorus X3:

Tomica Rankins Song: Here we go again
Written: 1996 to 2016
Approx. run time: 2 mins 58 secs

Verse I: Here we go again, here we go again, being more than just friends, here we go again. Why you stressing me (why you stress me), want to know where I be. Here we go again, always at my job (always at my job) want to know when I get off. Here we go again, hu.

Chorus: Here we go again, here we go again, being more than just friends. Hu. Here we go again____. Here we go again, here we go again, being more than just friends. Hu. Here we go again.

Verse II: What don't you get, what don't u get, I just want the, the dick. Here we go again. There's no relationship, no relationship, so you can get off this bullshit. Here we go again.

Chorus

Verse II: Wanna be in my life, be in my life just know I ain't no wife, are you feeling me. Don't be clocking me, don't clocking me cause you're on borrowed time baby.

Chorus

TOMICA RANKINS SONG: **FISTFIGHT**
WRITTEN ON: **31 MARCH 1992**
RUN TIME APROX: **5:12**

Verse I: My man said he loved me and that he'd always treat me right, but he did me wrong when we got into a fist fight so I kicked him out the house now he's sitting up in jail it'll be about 10 years before he sees bail he came at me with his words and his fist that'll be the last time a man hits me.

Chorus: Fistfight, fistfight to hit a woman don't make it right, it right, no, fistfight please understand hitting a woman don't make a man.

Verse II: Sometimes I feel that I'm the one to blame what is the wrong that I do to cause this pain that I'm going through. I gave me best the best that anyone could give. I gave good love the kind of love any man would feel.

Chorus:

Verse III: Ladies if you're out there and you can hear me and you're tired of being beat on and cheated on sing with me, sing with me, sing with me. Said I'm not gonna take no shit said I'm not having it I can do bad by myself I don't need no man's help and if your unable to bring to the table what I'm capable then you need to move on your not the one no, no, no, no.

Instrumental Break

Final Chorus: Fistfight, fistfight to hit a woman don't make it right it don't make it right to get into a fistfight, fistfight, fistfight please understand ladies if you hear me take a stand.

T omica Rankins Song: Easy Come, Easy go
Created in 2003 to 2015
Approx. run time: 3 mins 55 sec

Verse I: You let me slip away into another man's arms, cause I won't gonna waste my time for you to make up your mind, you wanted me on the sideline for a raining day, or just to have someone to come to when your other girl went away, let me tell ya, I'm ____ no fool____, I can make it without you. I took all I can take, listen, when I say_____.

Chorus: Easy come, easy go, another girl, another ho, and now that you want to come back sorry but it's not like that. Easy come, easy go, another girl another ho, and now you want to come back to me sorry baby you're not for me.

Verse II: Out running the streets, with no care in the world, sitting home thinking, I'm your only girl. Player go play_____ and you can watch me walk away, don't come back when she's gone cause I won't be hanging on_____.

Sing Chorus

Break: Just go away, just leave my space____ I'm gone, move on_____ no lonely night (no more lonely nights) save your goodbyes leave me, I'm free.

TOMICA RANKINS SONG: **SO COLD**
WRITTEN ON: **27 AUGUST 2003**
RUN TIME APPROX: **5:37**

Verse I: Boy I'm tired of playing silly games (bounce to this) I'm tired of all the childish masquerades about you baby, baby yes I am if you can't be the man that I need in my life, then baby I suggest you stop wasting my time and move on baby leave me alone.

Chorus X2: And you wonder why I treat you so damn cold so, so cold so, so cold, it's because you turned my heart into a stone O yes you have baby yes you have.

Verse II: Gave you everything you want and need and you still had the audacity to cheat on me (say what) with a girl in fact who wasn't all that. Love had me blind and I could not see, the signs that were standing in front of me just walking by see love had me on high.

Chorus X2:

Break: We fight to unite and this is what we do you treat me so cold that I'm singing the blues O baby (say what) O baby (one more gin) we fight to unite and this is what we do you treat me so cold that I'm singing the blues O baby (say what) O baby (girl you tripping) and you wonder why I treat you so cold (treat you so cold) the shit you put me through I would think you would know why O baby (say what) why I go I go crazy. (Bring the chorus back around).

Chorus X2:

T omica Rankins Song: Figures
Written On: May 5, 2007
Approx. Run Time: 3 mins 35 sec

Verse I: Don't be fooled by my license plate ain't sayin I'm a gold digger but I get paid. I put in my time and I pay my dues so don't think for one second that I need you. This young lady yes I roll alone when I want you in my bed I'll give you a phone call to let you know when to stop by but don't get too comfortable I want you gone by sun rise.

Chorus: No I don't care about your figures cause I don't need no nigga to work for me to get what I want I gets mine on my own. No I don't care about your figures cause I don't need no nigga to work for me to get what I want I gets mine on my own.

Verse II: If you got kids and a wife at home your best bet is to leave me alone. Don't want no drama and don't want no stress if you're carrying baggage I ain't checking you in. Don't be trying to get all up in my face best believe you have been replaced talking about you can give me what I want and need I don't see how when you have three mouths to feed.

Sing Chorus (original)

Change in chorus 2: No, I don't care about yours, cause I don't need another, to work, to work, to work_____. No I don't care about yours, cause I don't need another, to work, to work, to work_____. No I don't care, I don't care about yours, cause I got mines, to work for me to get what I want cause I get mines on my own. No I don't care, I don't care about yours, cause I get mines, to work for me to get what I want, I get mines on my own.

T omica Rankins Song: Don't Hate on Me
   Written on: April 29, 2010
   Approx. Run Time: 3 mins 10 sec

Verse I: Won't speak that's fine, it won't ruin my day matter fact I'll say hi (hey girl) to your ass anyway. Cut your eyes at me trying to ignore but wanna see what it is about Harminme that got your ass going crazy.

Chorus: Girl, don't hate on me, cause you want to be me. Don't hate on me, cause you want to be me, baby don't hate on me.

Verse II: Let me school your ass, you obviously miss the class, where I don't give a fuck about you being um mad, better watch your suit or else he might get a substitute an upgrade to me, make his ass do a real salute.

Sing Chorus

Break down:

Hate on player, hate on player, hate on, on, on. Hate on player, hate on player hate on, on, on.

Sing chorus

What cha going do, don't get in my face, cause I'm going pull my rank, what cha going do, don't get in my face, you better step down to your grade, grade.

Here I sit with the feel of the morning breeze, beginning day, beginning life, things I have yet to see. Innocence is just a moment we lose along the way, not knowing when we awake, challenges we are to face. Will I be a victim, hide inside my soul, giving power, giving life to a predator's heart turned cold. Will I be a fighter, speak, take action on those who prey, on the innocence, on hope, God's one human race. Losing time, walking paths, where's my puzzle piece, trying to figure out where I fit, what's the missing key. Water be still, here comes the rain to cause an awful flooder, anchor down, I stay ground, in these troubled waters...

Printed in the United States
By Bookmasters